D1551320

William Langland Revisited

Twayne's English Authors Series

George Economou, Editor

University of Oklahoma

TEAS 537

OPENING INITIAL OF *PIERS PLOWMAN,* WITH IMAGE OF DREAMER-
NARRATOR, OXFORD, CORPUS CHRISTI COLLEGE, MS 201, FOL. 1R
(BEGINNING OF THE B VERSION).

The Archives, Corpus Christi College.

William Langland Revisited

Joseph S. Wittig

University of North Carolina at Chapel Hill

Twayne Publishers
An Imprint of Simon & Schuster Macmillan
New York

Prentice Hall International
London • Mexico City • New Delhi • Singapore • Sydney • Toronto

Twayne's English Authors Series No. 537

William Langland Revisited
Joseph S. Wittig

Twayne Publishers
An Imprint of Simon & Schuster Macmillan
1633 Broadway
New York, NY 10019

Library of Congress Cataloging-in-Publication Data
Wittig, Joseph S.
    William Langland revisited / Joseph S. Wittig
        p. cm. — (Twayne's English authors series ; TEAS 537)
    Includes bibliographical references (p.   ) and index.
    ISBN 0-8057-7038-0 (alk. paper)
    1. Langland, William, 1330?–1400? Piers the Plowman.   I. Title.
II. Series.
PR2015.W53 1997
821'.1—dc21   97-9385
                                                                                                CIP

The paper used in this publication meets the minimum requirements of American National Standard for Information Sciences—Permanence of Paper for Printed Library Materials. ANSI Z39.48-1984. ∞ ™

10 9 8 7 6 5 4 3 2

Printed in the United States of America

Contents

Preface

William Langland's *Piers Plowman* ranks, with the works of Chaucer and the *Gawain* poet, among the most engaging to emerge from that extraordinary flowering of Middle English literature in the second half of the fourteenth century. But unlike Chaucer or the author of *Gawain*, who often strike us as being at least "Renaissance" if not nearly modern, Langland is unmistakably medieval: his subject matter, his techniques of developing and exploring it, and the verse in which he expresses it are very much those of his age. Yet despite the relative difficulty of his language, despite his immersion in a Christianity whose traditions are increasingly unfamiliar to many readers, his poem still captivates and fascinates.

Piers Plowman has had an enthusiastic audience from the time it was written. Its first readers probably did not admire the poem, at least not consciously, for literary or aesthetic reasons; they were more likely attracted to it because it castigated society's corrupt and powerful while championing the underdog and celebrating long-cherished ideals. But it had to have been obvious, from the very beginning, and had to have been part of the reason for the poem's success, that it accomplished this castigation and celebration with an enormous, driving energy, with startlingly vivid and concrete detail, and in a language powerfully wrought.

Unlike most other authors treated in this series, Langland apparently devoted his entire writing life to creating and revising this single masterpiece. *Piers Plowman* is a challenge to the modern reader not only because of its medieval subject matter and techniques of representation; the poem's structural complexities more closely resemble those of Dante than anything else in the English of its period. The challenge for this book is to introduce such a rich and complex text to the serious reader who is not a specialist in the Middle Ages. It should go without saying that a book of this scope cannot conceivably exhaust a major work of literature. One might indeed ask whether such a book can provide even an adequate introduction, and in response to that question, I offer an analogy.

Several summers ago, I had the pleasure of visiting York, England, and its magnificent minster (cathedral) for the first time. It is an enormous and complex structure. Successive layers go back through time: contemporary restorations and nineteenth-century glass in a thirteenth-to fifteenth-century Gothic cathedral, overlaid on a Norman one, all the way back to a Roman military fort on the lowest known level. The minster is, of course, massive and deliberate on the largest scale: basic cruciform design, central and side towers, three elaborate entrances, side chapels, a famous chapter house attached. But competing with these grand features for one's attention are endless, painstakingly crafted details: reliefs and gargoyles outside; inside, tiny stone figures, wood carvings, elaborate capitals, and designs in the windows, on the vaults, and on the ceilings.

On the first day of my visit, I joined a tour led by a woman who had been associated with the cathedral for several decades. As we began, she warned us that she could not show us everything, that despite her love for the building and long familiarity with it, she did not know everything. The tour she led would perforce be *her* tour, reflecting her experience, her knowledge, and her interests. She urged us to explore further on our own and indeed to take another tour with another guide: we would see the same church in a very different way. I took her advice, and she was right.

There is no need to labor the analogy between York Minster and *Piers Plowman*. As we will see, the latter also has its layers, its archeology. It has its major structural units, and it teems with careful and deliberate detail. We cannot conceivably pause over every feature. But more to the point, despite my long and enthusiastic relationship with the poem, I can give you only my tour, one necessarily conditioned by my own experiences, interests, and understanding. If this book is successful, you will come away with a working, overall sense of the poem, an appreciation for its craft, and some familiarity with its milieu. You will want to revisit *Piers* often on your own, and you will feel encouraged to come back with other guides.

Meanwhile, you deserve to know something about the guide proposing to lead you now. We could approach *Piers Plowman* in many ways. We could, for example, regard it "from the outside" as an artifact produced by a distant culture whose values and attitudes we wished to challenge. We might identify and characterize that culture's constructs (e.g., of "authority," of "value," of "gender") and then examine the poem as a vehicle perpetuating them, or as an arena in which the author, however unconsciously, wrestled against them. Such approaches would certainly be legitimate and potentially quite interesting, but I have not taken them here.

I have attempted rather to approach Langland's poem "from the inside" or "on its own terms." That is, I believe that we can legitimately, and empathetically, reimagine a great deal of the poem's Christian culture, of what its author wanted to convey, and of how the poem might have affected its original audience. As artifact, the poem is surely tied inextricably to, and produced by, its cultural context, and I do not regard it as merely an aesthetic object. But it also came from an individual author, reflecting that author's particular concerns as well as his enormous poetic skill and imaginative energy. In this book, I hope to convey my understanding of the poem's situation in its culture, of its shape as a literary creation, and of Langland's extraordinary poetic achievement.

Acknowledgments

I would like to express my general but very real indebtedness to Stephen J. Laut, S.J., who introduced me to this fascinating poem, to R. E. Kaske, with whom I first learned to study it seriously, and to George Kane, under whose collegial eye I learned to pay more adequate attention to every word.

I thank the College of Arts and Sciences of the University of North Carolina at Chapel Hill for released time in the Fall of 1995, and the University for a W. R. Kenan, Jr. leave in the Spring of 1996; together they afforded me the opportunity to complete this book.

I owe much to the generosity of friends who read this book in manuscript: John A. Alford, Gail and Hoyt Duggan, Thomas D. Hill, and George Kane. They offered welcome encouragement, informed corrections, and many helpful suggestions. The book benefited enormously from their advice, and I bear responsibility for such inadequacies as remain.

I especially thank my wife, Ellen, who patiently bore with me during the writing, read successive drafts, helped improve clarity and style, and assisted with the details that inevitably occupy the final stages of any such project.

Chronology

c. 1387–1388   Langland dies, C text of *Piers* circulates.

c. 1390   Gower's *Confessio Amantis*.

c. 1390–1400   Chaucer's *Canterbury Tales*.

1393–1401   *Pierce the Ploughman's Creed* (first known work in the "Piers Plowman tradition").

Chapter One

"Here Is Will": Introducing Langland

"You busy yourself with verse-making," one of the authority figures in *Piers Plowman* scolds the poem's narrator, "when you could be reciting your Psalter / and praying for those who give you food."[1] This accusation and the narrator's rejoinder offer a tantalizing glimpse of conflicting attitudes toward poetry. Who wrote this poem, and what do we know about him?

The only solid piece of external evidence (that is, evidence outside the text of the poem itself) identifying the author of *Piers Plowman* occurs in a note appended to one copy of it:

> Be it remembered that Eustace de Rokayle [was] the father of William of Langland; this Eustace was of good family [*generosus*] and lived in Shipton under Wychwood, a tenant of the Lord Despenser in the county of Oxford. The aforesaid William wrote the book which is called Piers Plowman.[2]

Because this note occurs alongside other accurate information about the Despensers, and because scholars have been able to confirm the connection between the Despenser family and the de Rokayles, they see no reason to doubt the note's assertion that William Langland wrote the poem. The information fits well enough with what readers have long understood as a playful self-naming by the poet:

> I haue lyued in *londe*, quod I, my name is *Longe Wille*. (B 15.152)

Such other scraps of information as have turned up either tend to confirm William Langland as author or fail convincingly to refute the ascription. Why was his name "Langland" and not "de Rokayle"? We do not honestly know, because naming conventions were less rigidly set in those days; one plausible suggestion is that the surname was connected, for whatever reason, with a long piece of arable farmland, "the long

1

land(s)," a common English field name.[3] What sort of person was he, in what kind of household did he grow up, who were his friends and associates, what did he do for a living, and when exactly did he write? The only answers we can find to those, the really interesting, questions must come from internal evidence, that is, from the text of the poem itself. Or rather, from the texts of the poem, for there are more than one.

Versions and Dates

Piers Plowman, written in the days before printing, comes down to us in handwritten manuscript copies, some 50 of which survive; three early (1550) printings, not based on any of the surviving manuscripts, supplement the evidence they provide.[4] As generations of readers and scholars discovered and compared the manuscripts, they encountered marked differences between them that cried out for explanation. Were many of the copies horribly garbled? Were there multiple poems by multiple authors? Or had one author written the poem and then revised it multiple times? By the 1870s, Walter W. Skeat, one of the heroes of *Piers* scholarship, had established what is fundamentally still agreed upon today: Langland wrote *Piers Plowman* and then revised it twice; the three versions (an original and two revisions) have been dubbed (drably but clearly) the A, B, and C versions. (Critics often use "text" instead of "version," as in "the B text," or simply refer to the version by letter, as in "*Piers Plowman* B.") As the letters suggest, scholars believe that A is the earliest form of the poem, which was subsequently revised to the B text, which in turn was revised to C.[5] Perhaps the best way to visualize the whole process is to think of *Piers Plowman* as an ongoing project that was released for "publication" (that is, which the poet allowed to be copied by others) at three different stages. He finished the stage we call A and then continued to work on the poem. Later he "published" B and again continued to revise. Finally (and apparently after Langland's death) the C version was published. In effect, as Ralph Hanna aptly comments, the work was "always in progress and always one" (Hanna, 10), and I will speak of the versions as making up a single poem.

When were the versions written? Certainly before the earliest surviving copies of them, which date from about 1400. But scholars, by looking for clear references in the texts to datable historical events, have tried to narrow the time of composition further. For example, A must have been completed after the events it refers to. And if one can logically say the poet stopped working on the A version before he began work on B, then one can go a step further. If the latest datable reference in A points to the year 1370, and if the earliest datable reference after 1370, in something added in the B version, points to 1375, then we might postulate that some time between 1370 and 1375 Langland "finished" the A version and "began" B.[6] That is, he allowed copies of the A stage of the poem to be made while turning his attention to revision. As one might imagine, vigorous debate has arisen over identifying datable references, but on the basis of such evidence, it now seems that Langland allowed the A text to be copied some time between 1370 and 1375, the B text between 1377 and 1380, and the C text between 1380 and 1388.[7] So William Langland seems to have composed the work by which we know him, and so to have flourished, circa 1365 to 1388.

Circulation and Audience

We can learn something further about the poem, and by implication about the poet, from its circulation. First, *Piers Plowman* was known throughout England within a generation of its composition. This is highly unusual; only three other pieces of Middle English verse come down to us in more copies.[8] John Burrow, examining what we can know about these copies (who owned them, who bequeathed them in wills, what other works occur in manuscripts containing *Piers*), argued that the poem was read by two rather different types of readers, the lower clergy and the newly literate laity, and that these readers collected the poem along with other nonliterary works of piety and instruction.[9] Anne Middleton, reviewing the same evidence, countered that one should not exaggerate the differences between types of readers, and that the poem's audience had indeed regarded it as "literature."[10] We need not dwell on the question of classes of readers: *Piers* was not a court poem aimed at the highest society, nor one collected in academic circles; it appealed to what we might call the middle class, both clerical and lay; the lower classes, however much featured in the poem, were illiterate and could not read it (even had they been able to afford to have a copy made). In order to address the second question, the poem's original status as literature, we need first to consider its form.

Piers is written not in rhyming verse (as were Chaucer's works) but in the alliterative long line found in *Gawain*. Anyone who has tackled *Gawain* in the original Middle English knows that it was composed in the dialect of the Northwest Midlands, very different in appearance from the London dialect of Chaucer that underlies our Modern English.

Moreover, alliterative poems typically employ a specialized vocabulary, most notably synonyms for common words (*man,* for instance, might appear as *mon* or as *renk, segge,* or *tulk*). Thus alliterative works appeared in a language both dialectally and stylistically specialized; poems using it apparently were not easily understood outside the West Midlands area and did not circulate widely. It is possible that Langland himself came from the West Midlands: the Malvern Hills that provide the setting for the poem's opening episodes are found there. And because, based on dialectal evidence, it appears that the C version was often copied by scribes from that region, it has been suggested Langland was living and writing there toward the end of his life (Hanna, 17). So if he was from the area around Malvern, he could have had firsthand experience of the alliterative revival (the movement that produced several dozen alliterative poems in the West and North during the late fourteenth century), have learned the verse form, and have been acquainted with the kinds of poetry it produced.

But although he used the long alliterative line, Langland did not use the dialect, or the specialized language, typical of the alliterative revival. Rather, copies of the A and B versions of *Piers* suggest that he employed the dialect of London, and he avoided nearly all the difficult diction of a poem such as *Gawain*. This fact led Burrow to argue that Langland had deliberately shaped his poem to reach a national audience. Maybe. It seems clear that Langland was not writing in the West Midlands for a local audience; perhaps he was writing elsewhere, for instance in London, for a more general public.[11]

And this brings us back to the "literary" status of *Piers*. At stake are not the poem's inherent qualities (which Burrow most certainly recognizes). The question concerns, rather, how the poet conceived the work, and how its original audience might have apprehended it: was it chiefly utilitarian (pious, didactic) or something more playful, more aesthetic? Given the poem's frequently serious, and sometimes challenging, subject matter, the question is worth entertaining. Middleton argued that Langland had recognized, in one of the typical genres of the alliterative tradition, a kind of poetry that he could adapt to his purpose and that his audience could recognize and respond to: the *chanson d'aventure* (Middleton, 114–19). This kind of poem typically featured a protagonist who, wandering outdoors, encounters some vision or other portentous experience that unfolds in a nonliteral world; the poem reports the fictive encounter. Middleton's point is that seeing *Piers* as a recognizable kind of *poem* suggests that its readers might well have regarded it as a literary (as opposed to merely a pious or didactic) experience, and this argument fits admirably with the inherent qualities of the work. The kind of aesthetic experience, the sort of "play," involved we will consider later; we will also return to the matter of genre. What should be emphasized here is that Langland saw himself as a poet, one who aimed at reaching a general, nonaristocratic public and succeeded in appealing to a national audience.

Langland's Persona

External evidence can give us the poet's name; examining datable references in the poem can allow us to reach intelligent estimates of when he wrote; considering the extant copies and the verse form can suggest something about the poet's intended public and actual audience. What else can be inferred from the text of his work? The poem, after all, is recounted by an "I"; to what extent is "I" William Langland?

Besides having characteristics of the kind of poem called *chanson d'aventure*, *Piers* also obviously uses the conventions of the "dream vision," in which the poet says he fell asleep, dreamed, and, having awakened, now reports his experience. Fictional representation of self is a necessary feature of such poems, because the poets represent themselves as having experienced events that are in fact impossible.[12] Certainly, part of the rationale for such a vision lay in suggesting that the poem *might* derive from some source beyond the poet's controlling ego, that some higher power might be expressing itself, and so both Chaucer and Langland remind their audiences of the possibility that dreams can convey such "truth."[13] But this convention really functioned not to assert the "reality" of the dream but to shift the spotlight away from the author to what the author said, and what the author said drew its force from its inherent qualities, from its recognizable authority (derived, for example, from Scripture or tradition), or from its universality. The dream was a fiction, and consequently its "I" could be equally fictive; the author could at any time exploit this opportunity for positioning himself before his immediate public, which, in many if not most cases, consisted of a coterie who knew him.[14] We will not, therefore, call the "I" of the poem "Langland" or "the poet"; we will instead call him "the dreamer" when he is represented as asleep and dreaming and "the speaker" before, between, and after the dreams.

Given the inherent fictionality of speaker and dreamer, can we safely ascribe anything Langland's persona says about "me" to William Langland himself? When dream-vision poets named themselves, they conventionally used their real names, and so we are not surprised to find the dreamer called "Will" at several points, and (as mentioned earlier) Langland hinted at his full name once.[15] This tends to confirm, without really adding to, the ascription of authorship in the Dublin manuscript. The speaker twice says, in what we recognize as a combination of fact and fiction, that he wrote what he "dreamed" (B 19.1, 481), and the passage quoted at the head of this chapter represents him as needing to defend time spent writing poetry. So, to some extent, the "I" mirrors William the poet. How much further can one go?

For example, the dreamer says he led a dissolute life, pursuing lust and greed for 45 years (B 11.47), and a character (Ymaginatif) apparently representing an aspect of the dreamer's mental powers says he has accompanied the dreamer for the same length of time (B 12.3); does this recount the poet's actual experience or tell us his age? The speaker mentions a wife Kit and a daughter Calote (B 18.426); later the dreamer speaks of himself as aging and, to his wife's disappointment, impotent (B 20.192–98). Was Langland married? Or is all of this part of the speaker-dreamer's fictive self-representation?

The most celebrated "autobiographical" passage of *Piers* occurs in the last version (C 5.1–108). E. Talbot Donaldson, in a humane and engaging essay, argued vigorously that this passage was indeed autobiography: why else would Langland have written it?[16] Donaldson fleshed out an informative historical context for the sort of person the passage seems to portray: a married cleric in minor orders who says prayers for the deceased and the living in exchange for his livelihood. But one cannot conclude that this portrait depicts the real Langland. For one thing, a great deal more is going on in the passage (including criticism that all classes of society fail to fulfill their roles, and preparation for a "confession" scene to follow). For another, a combination of motives arguably guided Langland to represent himself as such a lower-middling "professional."

Langland certainly intended his persona to engage the audience's sympathy and to influence its reactions to his poem. It targets the human will, the human power of choosing and loving. *Liberum arbitrium* (free will) plays a crucial role in the dynamic Langland explores; a *fre liberal wille*, as he describes it in his punning fashion ("a free/generous and selfless/free will"), lies at the heart of his concerns (B 15.150). And at the point where the poem begins to focus on the inner life of the persona, on that persona's responses to what he sees and hears, he is spoken of in a way that obviously puns upon Langland's "William," the persona's "Will," and human volition: "Here is Will," a character named Thought says, introducing the dreamer to a character named Wit, "Here is Will who would like to know, if Wit could teach him . . ." (B 8.129). The pairing of Wit and Will, of knowing and choosing, was a commonplace, and within the context of the poem as a whole, the punning identification is inescapable.[17]

Donaldson had asked, if not autobiography, then what? George Kane answered by calling attention to the kinds of interaction one should expect between dream-vision poet, his persona, and his audience. Given the inherently fictive nature of this mask, the audience would naturally find engaging the relationship between the created "reality" of the persona and the historical actuality of the poet, responding to the poet's implicit challenge: "How much of this is true of me?" (Kane, *Fallacy*, 15). We must also keep an additional dimension in mind. When the poet wants his readers to identify with the persona, to sympathize with the persona's reactions and find in them a model for their own, the poet implicitly poses another question: "How much of this is true of *you?*" Without inventing a persona utterly divorced from his actual experiences, therefore, the poet has reason for representing not only what he has personally lived through but also what he can empathetically imagine, a persona who, distinctive but not simply individual, invites recognition by his audience as "anyone of us." Finally, when a poet engages in satire and social criticism, as Langland constantly does, he also faces the challenge of situating his persona, with respect to both target and audience, so as to render the satiric voice effective. Just as Chaucer creates the naive pilgrim through whose viewpoint the satire of the "General Prologue" innocently passes to us, so Langland must have been concerned to create a persona whose point of view would maximize the satire's effect for his audience. Kane suggested that, over the three versions of the poem, we can see Langland discover more fully and confidently the fictive "reality" of his intermediary (Kane, *Authorship*, 60 – 65); we see, at the same time, his growing exploitation of Will, critic of his world as well as mirror and model for the audience's response.

Langland the Person

Assuming these complex motives underlying the poet's self-presentation, in the absence of any confirming external evidence, we can never do more than hypothesize about the extent to which the persona reveals the

real poet. But we can certainly infer something of the poet's personality
from the qualities of his text. Donaldson found that personality, among
other things, "curiously provocative and attractive . . . self-consciously
picturesque, ironical and realistic, tactless and inquisitive, playful yet
savagely sincere" (Donaldson, *C Text*, 199). Although every reader will
arrive at his or her own characterization, I think Donaldson's suggests a
representative range of impressions. And we can infer more.

Langland was clearly a moralist—that is, he was a person passionately interested in human behavior, its motivations, its manifestations in
society, and its implication for humanity's ultimate success and failure.
He was a poet—someone who chose to express his feelings and convictions, not by writing treatises or preaching sermons in church or on the
street corners, but by casting them into formal verse, expressing them in
vivid and arresting images, and discovering for them larger and dynamically interactive shapes that could intrigue, illuminate, and stir. He was
an intellectual—someone who took pleasure in using his mind, in
appropriating concepts and constructs into his imaginative activity. He
defends knowledge but does not champion scholarship for its own sake;
on the contrary, he cautions that human greed and weakness easily pervert knowledge. Unlike the scholars of his day, he wrote in English, and
in English verse. Unlike most writers of English religious instruction, he
did not merely versify information.[18] Unlike the English mystics, he did
not write intensely introspective treatises focused on the individual
soul's relationship with God.

He had certainly received more than a rudimentary education. Not
only is he literate in English, but he knows Latin, then the basic language of "grammar school," well. He quotes only a little French in his
poem, but given his Latin and general education he probably, like other
educated people of even modest professional standing, could use French
at least passably. His familiarity with Scripture is intimate and extends
to knowledge of standard notes and commentaries on it (exegesis). He
quotes in Latin schoolroom authors (e.g., Cato), proverbs, and legal
maxims. He is thoroughly conversant with the teachings of Christian
theology, which he discusses familiarly and with confidence; he may well
have read in patristic authors such as Augustine. He knows the central
traditions of Western philosophy and the names, at least, of its origina-
tors (e.g., Aristotle, Plato)—although the knowledge the poem evinces
could well be secondhand.[19] He was not, in my judgment, a professional
university philosopher or theologian; he does not write like a "master" (a
licensed professor) of philosophy, theology, or law, and if he had ever

studied logic or theology in university, he succeeded wonderfully in keeping technical ideas and jargon out of his poem.[20]

Was he a "cleric," a priest or someone in minor orders, a member of a religious order or community? Any answer must be hypothetical, but I think the odds favor that he was. Although an attentive and devout layperson, especially one with education and leisure, could have gained Langland's familiarity with, indeed intimate knowledge of, scripture, liturgy, and basic theology, such knowledge seems more likely to be found in one whose daily routine included praying the Divine Office, attending Mass, and reading thoughtfully. His learning, although it does not strike me as that of a university academic, nevertheless suggests regular access to the scriptures, scriptural commentaries, and patristic and devotional collections, the sort of library one would more likely find in a religious establishment (e.g., in a cathedral school or attached to the residence of an ecclesiastical official) than in any but the largest lay establishments.

Where did he live? We can join internal with external evidence to answer hypothetically. As noted earlier, the Malvern Hills in the poem, together with the many copies of the C version made in that region, point to a connection between the Malvern area and the poet's life: he may have been born and reared there, and/or have had kin there whom he visited, and/or have gone there for the last years of his life.[21] London (its royal and legal courts, its ceremonies, its denizens) appears more prominently in the poem, and Langland seems to know the city intimately. He may have learned so much about it secondhand, but the more plausible inference is that he lived there at least part of the time, and London would have provided the most likely center from which his work could have achieved the circulation it came to enjoy.

The "C autobiography" (C 5.1–108) portrays the poem's persona as a character on the very lowest fringes of the educated, professional class, living with wife and daughter in a hut on London's Cornhill, subsisting on handouts from benefactors. We cannot, as we have seen, assume this picture to be literally true of Langland. Then how might he have lived? I have suggested that he was probably a cleric. It seems unlikely that he was a friar, for he attacks them all mercilessly. He could conceivably have been a monk;[22] John Lydgate, that most prolific poet of the early fifteenth century, who traveled widely and consorted with royalty, demonstrates that medieval reality did not confine Benedictine monks to the cloister or preclude their writing verse. Langland certainly could have been a priest, either parish clergy or attached to one of the many establishments of a secular cathedral. Or one might visualize him as a lesser member of the *familia* (household) of some ecclesiastical official or lay magnate. A younger son of a good family might easily have been educated in grammar school and cathedral school anywhere in England (quite possibly receiving the tonsure and minor orders in the process) and then have become attached, even in a quite modest capacity, to such a household (assisting, for example, with secretarial or accounting or teaching duties). Whether he was lay or cleric, if he had connections with any considerable secular or religious *familia*, he could expect to spend time in that household's London establishment.

If he lived in the London of Chaucer and Gower, did he know them or they him? This question is intriguing because it invites another approach to the question about how the real Langland fitted into his world. Fourteenth-century London was, by our standards, little more than a large town, and the notion that a poet of Langland's brilliance, and timeliness, could have escaped notice seems untenable.[23] Is it conceivable that Langland, Chaucer, and Gower moved in the same circles? In describing that city as the locus of cultural and intellectual activity in the later fourteenth century, William Courtenay writes:

> As academic achievement became less crucial as a means of career advancement in late medieval England, the cultivation of extra-university contacts and attachment to households of *familiares* became even more important. It was in such settings that university scholars met poets, musicians, artists, and architects. And it was as secretaries and envoys abroad or in the halls and chambers of London that both scholars and literary figures came into contact with Italian humanism. (Courtenay, 378)

We recognize instantly the milieu of Chaucer and Gower; we do not recognize that of *Piers Plowman*. There are banquets and great houses in Langland's poem, but he does not celebrate "brilliant society." His is not the world of scholars, poets, musicians, artists, and architects; it is the world of academic frauds and social climbers, tale-tellers, fiddlers and tumblers, loafers and earnest toilers. Chaucer and Gower both had court connections and court patronage, and their immediate public was the top level of the professional class, the elite. The world Chaucer and Gower portray is sometimes that of royalty, often that of dukes and duchesses, knights and ladies, and they write about that world intimately and comfortably. Langland had no lofty patronage that we know of, wrote for a more general public (as his choice of verse form seems to imply), and gives through his persona the impression of having occupied a much lower rung on the social ladder. He writes about kings and knights, popes and bishops, but from the viewpoint of their subjects, not from that of their close associates.

But when it comes to placing the real Langland in his real world, how helpful are these impressions? Langland embraces a larger segment of society and concentrates less on the elite than do his two contemporaries. But more significant is the fact that his tone and perspective are uncompromisingly otherworldly, oriented toward what he perceived as significant realities transcending this life on earth. Chaucer and Gower certainly shared Langland's acceptance of those realities, but they do not fix on them so single-mindedly. More people probably focused, then as now, on this world rather than on the next; but class or rank does not necessarily determine such focus. Therefore, although Langland's focus sets him apart from his two illustrious contemporaries, his tone and moral perspective really tell us very little about his actual place in society.

Given Langland's perspective, what place does poetry hold for him? In the lines spoken by Ymaginatif and quoted at the beginning of this chapter, we saw the dreamer chided for his writing:

You busy yourself with verse-making when you could be reciting your
   Psalter
And praying for those who give you food; for there are plenty of books
To tell people what Dowel is, Dobet and Dobest too,
And preachers, many a pair of friars, to demonstrate it. (B 12.16 –19)

Chaucer, in his "Retractions," appears to renounce fiction and verse, to call into question all that does not conduce directly to "virtue," to give way to the plain prose of the *Parson's Tale*, which conveys the crucial and unambiguously significant "truth." Critics heatedly debate just what this retraction finally means; but it raises the same kind of questions Langland himself allows Ymaginatif to raise.

One response we may be inclined to offer on behalf of both poets is that they were supremely good at what they did. They must have derived enormous personal satisfaction from their achievements: how could they *not* have written poetry? I think that expresses at least part of an answer. Practically speaking, Chaucer's writing also seems to have contributed to his personal advancement, to his winning admiration and patronage. We have no evidence that suggests this in the case of Langland. But there is a more fundamental answer, one that I offer for Langland but that I believe has implications for Chaucer as well.

Ymaginatif said there were "preachers, many a pair of friars, to demonstrate" what behaving well involves (B 12.19). Throughout *Piers Plowman,* friars appear, singly, in pairs, and in flocks, without ever demonstrating anything of the kind; they spout words contradicted by the lives they lead. This constituted a particularly cruel failure, because the church hoped the friars might be effective especially with ordinary Christians, stirring them to good lives, to love of God and neighbor. Langland seems to have found in poetry a vehicle he thought could "demonstrate," could reach and stir and animate, could transmit his passionately felt convictions, could energize and enliven. Prose statements of plain "truth" may enter the intellect efficiently enough, but they are unlikely to stir the spirit, excite desire, or move the will. Poetry can do these things, can metaphorically speaking make the word flesh. However much he must have loved "making" for its own sake, Langland must have hoped it capable of making his audience love.

Last Preliminaries

Before turning our full attention to the poem, we must consider a few last preliminaries, beginning with its title. "Piers Plowman," as we shall see, is the name of a central, if somewhat mysterious, character who appears at crucial points in Langland's narrative. His name is the one most frequently given the poem in the early copies where, at beginning or end, it is called "the book of" or "the dialog of" or "the vision about Piers Plowman," or sometimes simply "Piers Plowman."[24] The longest, and most accurate, title found in several manuscripts is "the vision of William concerning Piers Plowman"; William is the name of the poet, Will of the speaker-dreamer, and he dreams *about* Piers.

The Poem: Versions and Divisions

Earlier in this chapter we considered the three stages, or versions, of the poem, A, B, and C; a critic begins citation of the poem with the version letters unless context makes clear which version is meant. Each version of the poem is further divided into sections or chapters. The first, in any of the versions, is now always called "The Prologue" (abbreviated Pr). In keeping with the terminology of the manuscripts, subsequent sections are referred to as *passus,* a Latin word that originally meant "step" or "pace" and came to be used in the sense of "passage" or "section." (It is a word whose plural is the same as its singular.) The A version of *Piers* consists of prologue and 11 passus,[25] B of prologue and 20 passus, C of prologue and 22 passus. (C is actually somewhat shorter than B; C has more passus because it breaks several of the longer sections of B into smaller units.)

Focusing on the B Version

Although the poem exists in multiple versions, in quoting and citing thus far I have referred almost exclusively to the B version. A is incomplete in the sense that at the time Langland allowed it to be published, he had written only about half of what he was to put in B and C. Although it is the latest version, C has struck many readers as somewhat less poetic than B, having occasionally sacrificed imagery for clarity; other readers would strongly contest that judgment, pointing to vivid sections and images added in C. Be that as it may, my chief reason for choosing to focus on B is that Langland did not live to complete the C revision. This book, then, will speak primarily of the B version, and all references are to B unless A or C is specified.

Citation, Quotation, Bibliography

I cite and quote the text from the edition by George Kane and E. Talbot Donaldson; line references will thus correspond exactly to those in Donaldson's translation.[26] Those using Schmidt's student edition may sometimes need to look back or forward a few lines to locate the passage referred to.[27] Anyone seriously studying a passage of the poem will want to consult as well other editions that contain useful annotation and commentary.[28] The bibliography at the end of this book offers a list of criticism and other useful tools, including bibliographies that cover the poem exhaustively. I have not thought it appropriate to make this a survey of *Piers* scholarship; in what follows, secondary sources are cited selectively and with the idea that interested students will pursue further references contained in those sources.

Finally, a word about quotation. I would prefer always to quote Langland in the original Middle English but have concluded I should not, in an introductory book, because the poem's syntax and vocabulary can be difficult. Giving both original and translation in every instance would require more space than is available. I have therefore adopted the following procedures. Where the actual language of the original is especially crucial I quote the Middle English and provide glosses. Where I have wanted the reader to get an accurate sense of an extended passage, I paraphrase. Otherwise I translate into Modern English. I hope that the reader will have a text of the original poem at hand and will consult it regularly.

Chapter Two

"Do Well and Do Evil, Where They Both Dwell": An Overview

Despite the excitement one feels when reading *Piers Plowman,* despite the fact that its energy and vitality carry one along from detail to detail and from scene to scene, one easily gets lost in this poem. Readers frequently find themselves groping for a sense of direction and development, for a general plan and overall strategy. As R. E. Kaske remarked, "One of the things that make *Piers Plowman* an unusually difficult poem is the fact that it seems organized so many different ways at once."[1] We will go on to explore some of those ways and indeed will emphasize the kinds of organization peculiar to the poem. But we should look first at its most obvious formal structure, outline its main narrative incidents, and consider a context within which to approach its overall theme and purpose.

Formal Structure

The poem's basic structure comprises a brief introduction followed by a series of eight dreams. There are waking interludes, two markedly longer than the others, between successive dreams, and a scant half-line conclusion following the last dream. Two of the dreams, the third and the fifth, enclose a dream-within-a-dream. (The rubrics *Visio* and *Vita* used in the outline will be explained in the following section.)

The Series of Dreams

(References are to Kane and Donaldson.)

> *Visio*
>> Introduction: Prologue 1–10
>
> Dream 1: Pr.11–5.2
>> Interlude 1: 5.3–8

Dream 2: 5.9 –7.145

    Interlude 2: 7.145 –8.66

Vita

Dream 3: 8.67–12.297

    First dream-within-dream: 11.5 – 406

    Interlude 3: 13.1–21

Dream 4: 13.22–14.355

    Interlude 4: 14.335 –15.11

Dream 5: 15.12–17.356

    Second dream-within-dream: 16.19 –166

    Interlude 5: 18.1– 6

Dream 6: 18.7– 425

    Interlude 6: 18.425 –19.5

Dream 7: 19.5 – 480

    Interlude 7: 19.481–20.52

Dream 8: 20.52–386

    Conclusion: 20.386

Rubrics: *Visio* and *Vita*

Giving this list of dreams, however, is like saying that the poem consists of a series of boxes without saying what the boxes contain; unfortunately the poet has not neatly labeled the dream boxes for us. The manuscripts do have some subtitles, or rubrics, that seem to have come not from the poet but from various readers and scribes. The rubrics typically call the first two dreams the *Visio* (vision) and the remainder of the poem the *Vita* (life). Moreover, in many manuscripts, rubrics further employ the poem's terms *dowel*, *dobet*, and *dobest*[2] to subdivide the *Vita* (comprising dreams 3 through 8) into a *Vita de Dowel*, a *Vita de Dobet*, and a *Vita de Dobest*. Because discussions of the poem often employ the terms *Visio* (prologue through passus 7) and *Vita* (passus 8 to the end), I have included these terms in the list of dreams, but I have not used the subdivisions of the *Vita*.[3]

Describing the poem as a *Visio* followed by a *Vita* still does little to explain it. The next step is to outline briefly the major narrative episodes that make up the poem and, to some extent, correspond to the dream structure. (In what follows, I have summarized only the two longest interludes.)

Narrative Episodes

Visio: Dream 1

The speaker falls asleep and dreams he sees a "fair field" poised between the bright, lofty castle of Truth and the low, dark fortress of False; filling the field between the two are all sorts of people, most pursuing their own selfish ends while society staggers along chaotically. *Prologue.*

A commanding figure, whose name turns out to be Lady Holy Church, appears and, in response to the dreamer's questions, explains to him Truth and False, forcefully articulating in the process some fundamental Christian perspectives. *Passus 1.*

Having asked to be shown more about False, the dreamer sees Lady Meed (lucre), who is about to "marry" False; but should this wedding be permitted?[4] She is brought before the king and questioned in the presence of Conscience and Reason. As the king and justice struggle against bribery and greed, the outcome remains uncertain: will the people cooperate with Conscience and Reason? *Passus 2–4.*

Visio: Dream 2

Reason, and then Repentance, address the people, and in response, the Seven Deadly Sins confess. However, after a brief, abortive effort, the people act no differently than they did before, apparently incapable of proceeding on the "way" to Truth. The character Piers Plowman enters to tell them the way, but it seems daunting. *Passus 5.*

Promising to guide the people on the "pilgrimage" to Truth, Piers sets about his immediate task of producing food as he tries to lead them through an agricultural season tilling a half acre. In the process, he encounters loafers and ruffians as well as helpers, hunger as well as harvest. As was the case after Meed's trial and the sins' confession, so here the future of the community remains uncertain. *Passus 6.*

In the face of these frustrated, or at least suspended, attempts by human society to perform as it should, "Truth" offers struggling humanity a "pardon," but it amounts simply to "do well and [consequently] have well." Piers and a priest debate its meaning and value, and Piers decides that from now on he will be less solicitous about his body's livelihood and more so about his soul's. The argument between the priest and Piers wakes the dreamer. *Passus 7.1–145.*

The longest waking interlude follows, passus 7.145–8.66, in which the speaker muses about dreams, pardons, and the idea of "do well." Setting out to find Dowel (the speaker has made a verb into an abstract noun), he meets and argues with two friars, who cannot explain Dowel to his satisfaction; he rests, sleeps, and dreams again.

Vita: Dream 3

As the quest for Dowel continues, the dreamer, explicitly identified as "will" (the power of choosing) (8.129), encounters a series of characters representing aspects of "intellect" (the power of knowing). The action here comprises a series of taut, often highly charged, dialogues as Will meets Thought (intellectual activity in general), Wit (natural intelligence), Study (its systematic application or misapplication), Clergy (its product, learning, and in particular theological learning), Scripture (the primary "data" addressed by this learning), and, following the inner dream, Ymaginatif (a character who represents something like knowledge personally and pertinently applied to oneself). The discussions range around what and how knowledge contributes to Dowel. *Passus 8–12.*

First Inner Dream

Scripture derides the dreamer for knowing a lot about everything except himself. In response, the dreamer falls into a dream-within-a-dream. First, he visualizes himself following Fortune and indulging his lust and greed in a world of sensual delights until he has squandered his life, faces old age and death, and becomes frightened about his own spiritual fate. Next, a famous Roman emperor, Trajan, abruptly appears to champion the importance of behaving well, challenging the expectation that one can count on being "saved" simply because one is a Christian. Finally, the dreamer, taking another look at the world, now seen as wonderful and orderly except for human behavior, suddenly and with shame recognizes himself as a weak and errant human. From this inner dream he emerges to face Ymaginatif. *Passus 11.5–406.*

Vita: Dream 4

The dreamer, invited to dine at the palace of Conscience, sits with Patience at a small side table eating "plain fare" while, seated at the main table beside Clergy, a Doctor of Theology gorges on "fancy food." The dreamer, barely restrained by Patience, prompts the doctor to define Dowel; what he offers seems self-serving. Clergy, invited to offer his definition, reports that a certain Piers Plowman values all "science" except love as worth no more than a crust of bread; they must wait for Piers to demonstrate Dowel for them. Patience also defines Dowel as love but ends with a riddle. Then Patience, Conscience, and the dreamer leave and come upon "Haukyn, the active man," who thinks of himself as the honest worker but who, on closer inspection, is wretchedly beset with all the seven deadly sins. The encounter with Conscience and Patience leaves Haukyn weeping tears of frustration and remorse, and his wailing wakes the dreamer. *Passus 13–14.*

Vita: Dream 5
Falling asleep once more, the dreamer sees a character named Anima (speaking for the redeemed soul), who utters a long speech—a tirade, really—directed chiefly against the clergy, from simple parson to prelate, for failing to teach Christians by example how to live in love and "charity." Along the way, Anima says that Piers Plowman alone (here associated with Christ) can take, or give, the true measure of charity. When the dreamer asks for a better description of charity, Anima pictures it as the fruit of a tree cared for by Piers Plowman. Hearing that name again, the dreamer falls joyfully into the second inner dream.

Second Inner Dream
Piers shows the dreamer the garden in which the tree grows, supported by the three "props" of the Trinity; when Will prompts Piers to pick an "apple," fruit falls from the tree and a hustling devil makes off with it. Piers chases the devil with the "prop" of God the Son, and suddenly we see Christ becoming flesh in Mary, growing up to make whole the sick and the outcast, and being handed over to "joust" with death on the cross. *Passus 16.19–166.*

The dreamer, waking from this inner dream with tears in his eyes, searches all over for Piers Plowman, the guardian of charity. On a "mid-Lenten Sunday" he encounters Abraham, then Moses, and finally the Good Samaritan, who are associated, respectively, with faith, hope, and charity.[5] A series of bustling conversations, conducted while the participants hasten after Piers toward Jerusalem, considers the relationship of these three virtues to Father, Son, and Holy Spirit. *Passus 15–17.*

Vita: Dream 6
Having fallen asleep again, on Palm Sunday the dreamer experiences a striking, often lyrical, recreation of the Redemption. He sees riding into

Jerusalem a young knight, ready to be dubbed, who resembles the Samaritan and also Piers Plowman; Faith tells the dreamer that the knight is Jesus, who, wearing Piers's coat of arms, will joust against the devil to win back Piers's fruit. Christ's trial and crucifixion are quickly recounted, and the focus shifts to the aftermath, the harrowing of hell, the confrontation between Christ and Death over the souls of the just in Satan's dungeon. The bells of Easter morning wake the dreamer. *Passus 18.*

Vita: Dream 7

In church on Easter morning, the speaker falls asleep during mass. In a conversation that recounts the Resurrection, Conscience dwells soberingly on "Christ the Conqueror," who will judge humanity and its response to the Redemption. Then the dreamer sees more of salvation history in review: the Ascension, Pentecost, and the "planting" of the early church by Piers/Peter, who "sows" the cardinal virtues.[6] Piers builds a "barn" into which to gather his harvest; then, as Pride and his allies mass against Piers's enterprise, the barn becomes a fortress, "Unity Holy Church," within which Christians gather. But as the dream ends, members at all levels of the community begin to reject the cardinal virtues, and the condition of society threatens to resemble that portrayed in the early dreams of the *Visio. Passus 19.*

In the last, and second longest, interlude a problematic character named Need confronts the speaker. Need's argument that anyone has the right simply to appropriate what he "needs" seems to threaten virtue and community. *Passus 19.481–20.52.*

Vita: Dream 8

The tyrant Antichrist comes to ravage Pier's "crop" of Truth and besiege Christendom; most flock to Antichrist's banner. Conscience urges Christians to take refuge within Unity. But only "fools" comply; the rest pursue lust and greed as if there were no hereafter. Conscience, needing "doctors" for the "wounded" within Unity, admits friars, who betray him. Despairing of Unity's ability to withstand the siege and unable any longer to find Piers Plowman within, Conscience prepares to go in search of him, crying out for "grace"—and with that the dreamer awakes. *Passus 20.52–386.*

Such an outline of the poem's major narrative episodes may be useful, but it remains obviously unsatisfactory. Synopsis, especially in the recapitulation of the later dreams, compels the use of bare, shorthand abstractions and ruthless simplification. Luckily, anyone who plunges into the text will find so much happening in these episodes, so much vigor and inventiveness in language, style, and detail, that the experience of the poem quickly transcends bald generalization. The text, moreover, constantly stimulates the reader to discover connections between scenes and motifs.

Second, however "objective" such a summary may appear, it nevertheless constitutes an act of interpretation. Readers of *Piers Plowman*, faced with its cornucopia of characters, events, and ideas, have not always agreed about which are more central, and which are more peripheral, to the poem's main thrust. Moreover, the poem so fertilely associates images and ideas and densely intermingles them with its narrative elements that highlighting those narrative elements can seriously misrepresent the whole. In the foregoing summary I have had to select what I take to be the poem's most significant events and the terms in which to represent them. The summary thus has omitted much and has paid little attention to the portrayal of the speaker/dreamer or to the intervals between dreams. And this leads to a third consideration.

Even though the summary is highly interpretative, it falls short of satisfying because it does not interpret enough: It may suggest, but it does not make explicit, an overall narrative purpose or even some recognizable abstract scheme to which the episodes correspond. It tells us some of the things the poem is about without telling us, coherently, "what the poem is about." Let me propose an answer to that general question.

Central Themes and Purpose

I would argue, first of all, that *Piers Plowman* is a profoundly moral poem. Morality can be made intolerably dull, and there are banal and trite Middle English moral poems. But what bores is not morality itself; some of the most gripping fictions we encounter concern how people do and should behave. We are bored, rather, by trite and unnuanced pronunciamentos about morality that plod down all too predictable pathways. Langland, obsessed with morality, is anything but banal, unnuanced, or predictable. Indeed much of the brilliance of his achievement arises from the way he manages to startle, surprise, and provoke even when we think we know where he is ultimately headed.

I would argue, next, that in *Piers Plowman* the poet intends to address an audience he wishes to reform, that he creates a masterful rhetorical appeal calculated to move that audience and to change it. But this takes place within a context of fourteenth-century attitudes and beliefs that may no longer be familiar and that consequently require discussion. And so the remainder of this chapter endeavors to establish a context within which to understand *Piers Plowman*, the matrix that provided its central themes and direction; we will subsequently return to the rhetorical and poetic strategies that the poem deploys.

Society and Sin

Langland portrays his society as nearly dysfunctional: the poor are oppressed; the rich and powerful are arrogant, irresponsible, and self-seeking; the common man is all too often greedy or lazy; and the ministers of church and state fail to perform their essential functions. A writer who felt this way today would very likely find fault with "the system," with "the establishment," with the form of society's institutional and economic organization. Langland, it is now generally acknowledged, was orthodox in his attitudes toward the institutions of his world. For instance, he apparently distanced himself from the Peasants' Revolt that fleetingly challenged the existing political hierarchy.[7] Although he shared their disgust at corruption, there is no evidence he shared the opinions of John Wyclif and the Lollards, who heretically challenged church doctrine and hierarchy.[8] Langland's views on the economy were conventional: when he visualized its ideal, he did so in terms of a traditional agrarian system that was rapidly changing beyond recognition.[9] Langland directs his criticism not at "the system" but at the behavior of the individuals who inhabit it.

A modern social critic, even one inclined to see individual behavior as the root of society's woes, might look for explanations for failure in an abusive or oppressive environment or in some physical malfunction (a chemical imbalance or a defective gene). Langland's reactions, and those of his world, were quite different. For him, the problem with society and its individual members lay in the voluntary behavior of individual human agents: they failed to behave well; they did not choose "the good." The more power an individual had in the secular or ecclesiastical hierarchy, the more influence his or her actions might exert, and Langland expressed great concern with individuals who set a good (or bad) example; but it is the cumulative effect of individual wrong choices that, for him, disrupts and endangers society at large.

Unless one's intellect was defective, so that one was "simpleminded" (because of an accident or a birth defect, for example), one pretty much knew the good that one should choose; the problem was making that right choice. When Adam and Eve fell from grace in the Garden of Eden, they, and all humanity after them, lost control of the passions by reason. That is, before the Fall, humanity existed in a state of original justice, a state of internal harmony in which the rational powers serenely controlled human appetites; after the Fall, those powers were subject to massive assaults by the passions, those susceptibilities to the fierce desires of the flesh (gluttony and lust), the irascible appetites (anger, envy), and even disordered reason itself (pride). Indeed, the seven deadly sins came to represent the fundamental inclinations to disordered choice, human nature's hankerings for alluring false goods. Thus, according to the fundamental outlook of Langland's world, fallen human nature is weak, is inclined to sin, sins frequently, and must therefore struggle constantly to amend its behavior.

The consequences of sin for the individual human being we will take up in a moment. But we should first note that throughout the poem Langland emphasizes the horrible consequences of sin for the collective human community, for sin consists of behaviors that, through selfishness, greed, laziness, idleness, and self-directed nonlove of neighbor in general, deprive others of what they desperately need, whether that be food and clothing for the body or effective priestly ministry for the soul. Rampant sin devastates kingdom and village, universal church and local parish.

Thus sin is an offense against society; but it is also, of course, an offense against God. The human being, composed of body and soul, mortal flesh and immortal spirit, has by its very nature a specific destiny: the body will die, and the soul will live on to be judged by God and, thereafter, to spend the rest of eternity either blissfully with God in heaven or with Satan in hell's torments. Realizing this nature, human beings should choose the true goods natural to them, not false ones as if this world were their heaven: sin is an offense against the nature of things and nature's author. Therefore behavior has the gravest, most permanent consequences for each individual human agent. And although Langland is very much concerned with the reformation of human society on earth, the gravest condemnation he can lodge against the human community is its failure to foster the lasting good of each immortal soul.

For Langland, therefore, as he confronted the fundamental problems of human behavior in his world, these were the bleak facts: humans are weak and inclined to sin; sin, choosing false goods or pursuing good things selfishly and for the wrong reasons, maims society; and each individual soul is in danger of failing to achieve its destiny of union with God for all eternity, being instead lost forever. Taken alone, this outlook would be utterly dismal and terrifying. But God, having condemned humanity because of the Fall, redeemed it when Christ came to die on the cross and win forgiveness for humanity; the Redemption stands over against the Fall, grace (God's "free gift") over against sin and human weakness. So it might seem that Redemption and grace solved the world's problems, but in fact the Christian dispensation generates another set of issues that, given his concerns, Langland necessarily confronted.

Redemption and Grace

If Christ has redeemed humanity, is everyone who believes in Christ the Redeemer therefore saved? Does the grace of God somehow compensate for human sin? Does grace do this in such a way that people need not be concerned about their individual day-to-day behavior, no matter how selfish and hurtful it might be? Can Christians count on some sort of predestination or on being individually exempted at the last minute? Many readers will recognize in these questions issues that have animated theological debate throughout the Christian era. Although they had basically been answered for Langland's world, the issues were potentially complex and the answers subject to subtle, sometimes wishful, distortions. A moment's thought will show that for Langland, addressing human behavior in the Christian community, these questions were crucial: the wrong answers, or the wrong emphases on the right answers, could in effect remove all practical motivation for individuals to change the way they act, consequently eliminating all stimulus for change and improvement. Langland clearly believed that individuals who settle for the wrong answers, along with the societies they made up, were doomed. The relationships between Redemption and grace are therefore central to the poem's thematic and rhetorical thrust, and without ever producing an abstract treatise, Langland dramatizes them continually. Sketching the basic terms in which he addresses grace requires some modestly technical theology, but one cannot hope to comprehend *Piers Plowman* without considering it.

Baptism and Sanctifying Grace

As mentioned earlier, *grace* was a general term for God's "free gift";[10] grace is not owed to humanity but results from God's love and generosity, the culmination of which had been seen in Christ's self-immolation on the cross. Such gifts are spiritual and therefore invisible; they some-how help people choose and do the right things, providing encourage-ment and strength so that people might avoid sin, practice virtue, and love neighbor and God. One particular kind of grace had come to be regarded as more permanent and abiding, a kind of spiritual condition that was the distinguishing mark of any soul fit for heaven: *sanctifying* grace, the gift that renders the soul holy, pleasing to God. Having cre-ated Adam and Eve and placed them in Eden, God had generously bestowed this gift of sanctifying grace upon them; by Original Sin they, and through them all their descendants, cast this gift away. Without it they were unfit for heaven, and because they had chosen to disobey God and follow Satan, they belonged to Satan and were worthy of damnation.

The sacrament[11] of baptism takes away the guilt inherited from Adam and Eve's Original Sin and restores sanctifying grace to the soul, and Christian theology held that one who died "in the state of grace" (possessing this sanctifying gift in one's soul) went to heaven. Does this mean that all baptized Christians are saved? Alas, one is ordinarily bap-tized as an infant and then has the rest of one's life to live; inclined as humans are to sin, there is every likelihood that a person will commit a sinful act *(actual sin)* after baptism and so lose grace once again.[12]

Deadly Sin and the Sacrament of Penance

Less serious *(venial,* or pardonable) sin does not take away sanctifying grace; serious *(deadly,* or *mortal*) sin does, rendering the soul "dead" in God's eyes.[13] Thus baptism takes away Original Sin, but subsequent acts of sin, if they are deadly, put the soul in peril again. Recognizing this need, Christ established the sacrament of penance.

Penance (also called confession) was the sacrament through which sin could be removed and grace restored to the soul.[14] Penance involved calling to mind one's sins, being genuinely sorry for them, confessing them to a priest, receiving absolution (shrift) from him, and performing the penance he prescribed. (Note that the various names used to desig-nate the sacrament—penance, confession, shrift—derive from various aspects of the process as a whole.)[15] Anyone who has read Chaucer's *Par-son's Tale* about "contrition, confession, and satisfaction" will recognize these basic components. The essence of sin lay in the act of will by an agent who, knowing the difference between the real good and the false good, nevertheless chose the false. (One could not sin unawares.) The will was crucial also in the act of receiving grace and forgiveness: in addition to naming one's sins and receiving absolution, one had to be sorry for the sin, at least because it made one liable to damnation, and one had to have a "firm purpose of amendment," that is, genuinely intend not to sin again and seriously attempt to change one's pattern of behavior.[16]

Do the sacraments of baptism and penance offer Christians an easy and sure way to salvation? Or does the weakened human will, so inclined to choose false goods, leave them facing an insuperable task? The difference between confession and amendment is brilliantly dramatized in passus 5 of the B text as the people, having "confessed," mill about in confusion when the time comes to change their lives; and the wrenchingly melancholy cycle of sin and confession, sin and confession, leaves the Haukyn of passus 14 in tears. One can imagine the temptations for Christians to presume too much on grace or to despair altogether of obtaining it. Was it enough to confess without amendment, to go through the mere forms of the sacrament of penance by naming one's sins and receiving absolution?[17] If one kept sinning, could one ever be sorry enough for one's sins and intent enough on amendment to actually be forgiven?[18] And what if death came when one was in sin, in need of absolution?[19] In short, could baptized Christians consider themselves "safe," able to rely on the instruments of Christianity, on the sacraments as vehicles of grace? Langland dramatizes all these questions.

Sacramental and Actual Grace

So far we have seen that sanctifying grace enabled a kind of condition of the soul that, by virtue of the Redemption, rendered it holy in God's eyes and worthy of salvation, constituted it in the state of grace. Two sacraments, baptism and penance, were crucial in imparting and then restoring that grace to the soul. But the word *grace* has other meanings as well. All the sacraments, and indeed all other grace—all gifts of help from God—could be regarded as aids for preserving and strengthening a soul's grip on sanctifying grace. Each sacrament was regarded as giving its particular *sacramental* grace, God's supporting help to souls in their struggle to behave well. Besides penance, the Eucharist (the bread and wine consecrated at the mass and received in Holy Communion) was considered a particular source of strength of which Christians should take advantage.[20] But just as sorrow and a will to amend were crucial for good confession, so with the Eucharist the recipients' own disposition and spiritual condition were crucial for good effects. One had to be in the state of grace to receive the Eucharist, or else, rather than being nourished and strengthened in goodness, one committed a deadly sin of disrespect.[21]

God could also bestow a sort of ad hoc helping gift (*actual* grace) on humans, grace particularly associated with the Third Person of the Trinity, the Holy Spirit. The precise relationship between the human ability to choose well or to do well in a given instance and this kind of grace was a topic of intense technical debate in Christian theology over the centuries; for example, could someone choose to become a Christian without God's prior help (*prevenient* grace)? The technical arguments ultimately concerned how best to articulate the relationship between human effort and divine gift: the persistently dominant opinion was that however one finally expressed their correspondence, both were necessary. But Christians could easily find themselves waiting for, relying on, even presuming upon God's grace to instigate change, and Langland's poem urges his readers not to presume upon grace to the exclusion of effort on their own part.[22] One final, but vitally significant, topic relating to grace remains to be considered.

Purgatory and Pardons *a poena et a culpa*[23]

All grace was generally thought to have been won for humanity by Christ in his crucifixion. Christ was God the Son and so, being God, infinite in being and power. Therefore the effects of his sacrifice were also unlimited, infinite, and constituted an infinite "treasury of merit" (like a bank account with an inexhaustible balance) that could be distributed to humanity.[24] The sacraments of baptism and penance drew on this treasury. So did actual, or helping, grace. Pardons (also called *indulgences*) were another way of drawing on the treasury of merit established by the Redemption; understanding them is essential for understanding the famous "pardon scene" of passus 7, which generates the quest that occupies the rest of the poem.

As the present discussion will have reminded us, traditional Christianity conceived and expressed the relationship between deity and humanity in economic and legal terms, in a world dominated by hierarchies and stern notions of justice. The Redemption (the word literally means "buying back") reclaimed for God what had become the devil's "by right," because humanity had broken its contract with God in Eden and forfeited grace by the Fall; Christ's sacrifice countered by establishing the treasury of merit. Pardons bear especially on another aspect of this economically and legally conceived relationship: the "temporal punishment due to sin."

Sin was an offense against God that incurred a debt; justice demanded that this debt be repaid. The Redemption satisfied God's justice to the extent that through baptism and confession, humans could regain sanctifying grace and so be admitted to heaven despite original and mortal sin—which otherwise would have sentenced them to hell. But justice, as then conceived, demanded some further repayment by humans on their own part; in the terms of Chaucer's parson, this is the "satisfaction" that completes "contrition" and "confession."[25]

Baptism removed all traces of Original Sin. Confession, the instrument of sacramental grace, freed one *a culpa* (from the guilt) of actual sin and restored sanctifying grace. Nevertheless humanity was felt to owe something more, some debt to be repaid by suffering in return for having caused God to suffer.[26] Thus confession did not entirely free one *a poena* (from the punishment) due to sin. Acts of penitence could go a long way toward satisfying this debt: for example, good works that required effort and sacrifice; self-imposed deprivation, especially of sensual gratification; and the patient endurance of illness and poverty. But, sensitive to what they perceived as the infinite gap between humanity and a transcendent deity, how could humans expect their own penitential acts to satisfy an offense committed against God? Was not the debt commensurate with the one offended, thus infinite? Did people undertake enough penitential activity on earth to repay their debts? Could one ever rely on human acts of penitence to satisfy what was owing to divine justice? And so purgatory came to be conceived as the place in which those who died in a state of grace might, by enduring punishment, work off any debt still owed before they could be admitted to heaven.

This brings us back to pardons (the word comes ultimately from the Latin *per donum,* "by means of a gift"). As originally conceived, pardons were a "gift" intended to alleviate some of the suffering to be endured, whether in penitential acts on earth or in purgatory; they applied, to an appropriately prepared and disposed Christian, some portion of that infinite treasury of merit won by Christ.[27] We would, incidentally, err gravely if we discounted the seriousness with which the sufferings of purgatory were regarded. Although its torments, unlike those of everlasting hell, would be completed in time *(temporal punishment),* they were thought in every other respect to be as terrible as hell's, and one instant of suffering in purgatory was believed to be more intense than a lifetime of suffering on earth. One can see reflected in Langland's poem a deep concern about purgatory's pains and an anxious desire to pass through it quickly, if one could not avoid it entirely.[28] And so one can appreciate how welcome would be a *plenary indulgence,* a full pardon for all the temporal punishment due to sins. Originally such pardons were offered to those who performed some demanding feat of physical penance or undertook a difficult pilgrimage. (The first recorded instance is a full pardon granted by Pope Urban II to crusaders in 1095.) Full pardons became more common in the following centuries, and later the Church would be accused of "selling" them in exchange for generous contributions to the construction of the new St. Peter's in Rome. However, pardons were never officially offered as substitutes for the sacrament of penance (which removed the *culpa* of sin), and to benefit from a pardon at all (to get relief from the *poena*), one had first to make a sincere confession and dispose oneself for amendment.

It is only against this background that one can comprehend Langland's, and for that matter Chaucer's, attitude toward pardons and pardoners. In the worst case, pardoners were charlatans who sold meaningless bits of paper promising full relief *a poena et a culpa.* Such men perverted the entire dispensation of grace, exploiting the fruits of the Crucifixion in a dirty business that played upon the weakness of sinners. Not only did they lead people to indulge in the fantasy that, without confession or penance or any efforts at amendment on their part, their time in purgatory (the *poena*) would be reduced or eliminated; even worse, they led them to imagine that the guilt (the *culpa*) of their sins had been taken away, that they were in the state of grace when in fact they were not. Thus what was meant to be a spiritual economy of mercy and grace was cynically corrupted into a commerce of physical money, earthly complacency, and the eternal ruination of souls. The only pardon *a poena et a culpa* that Christianity really offered was through individual human beings' cooperation with the Redemption. The priest whom Langland depicts in passus 7 complacently expects to find in the pardon some formula by which one could easily and effortlessly latch on to grace; Langland relentlessly denies the existence of any such formula and prods his readers to undertake a more complex, and more demanding, quest.

Amendment: Reorienting Desire

We can appreciate the personal and social consequences, for Langland's world, of complacency in the expectation of grace and Redemption. If people think they can buy forgiveness, if they think even that merely by "being Christian" some external instrumentality of sacramental ritual, without any real effort on their own part, will save them, why should they change? Why should the corrupt dispense honest justice or the rich feed the hungry? As for the clergy, one can see how their perversion of the dispensation of grace into business—in effect selling denatured sacraments—would strike at the very heart of Christianity; unless they were to acknowledge their own individual need to reform their behavior, why should they bother to set a good example? Why should they risk forfeiting generous donations by telling their patrons the unpalatable moral truth?

Langland challenges all presumption of grace without human effort, of salvation without amendment. Some of the most intriguing episodes in the poem deal with those remarkable cases where God's immeasurable mercy and power seem to encourage human complacency; Langland, while conceding what orthodox theology requires, nevertheless urges against fixing on such special instances as models for ordinary behavior.[29] On the contrary, Langland intended to motivate his audience to *affective* change, moving them to reorient their feelings, dispositions, and inclinations so that they would *want* to "do well."

The name of his dreamer-persona, after all, is "Will." Sin was held to result from an act of the will; so were amendment and consequent virtue. As we have seen, a crucial part of the process of a good confession is not only being sorry for one's sins but also trying to change the way one behaves. Acts of penance through which the appetites are deliberately curbed work to repay the debt owed for sin, but they also develop habitual control over those appetites—they constitute both satisfaction and amendment. And amendment also involves changing the way one thinks about goods, examining and remotivating one's attitudes about what is truly desirable.

In our own time, we are familiar with the idea of "behavior modification." For example, if we want to stop smoking, we are told to try to change the way we think about tobacco, to visualize as vividly as we can damage to lungs in order to counter the sense of satisfaction smoking provides, to avoid occasions or places that present us with a particular urge to smoke. We all know that such things are more easily said than done, of course. And whatever we may think of sin or virtue, we still normally talk about the "willpower" of people who are able to make such resolutions to change and carry them out: to stop smoking, to eat less, to study harder.

Modern admirers of Langland (and I am sure Langland himself) would be appalled if they thought I were equating him with a modern self-help pitchman. Langland would regard such self-help resolutions, in themselves, as relatively banal, as details that derived any significance they have from a larger context. Anyone who reads him will instantly recognize his concerns as more complex, more generous, more nuanced, more honest, and more passionate. He addresses the total behavior of individuals who, acting in love of neighbor and of God, might form a just and fostering community in which each ultimately achieves the greatest happiness. The behavior modification he envisages can, moreover, count on God's helping grace to support human effort. It can, even more importantly, powerfully motivate itself by focusing on the actions of God toward humanity, and those actions, as perceived by Langland's world, overwhelmingly invite and inspire response. Although he speaks of the threat of eternal damnation, he everywhere stresses more God the Son's surrender of self in an act of love for humanity. Langland's poem is an attempt to excite and to arouse in his audience a desire to respond to that love in a manner he regarded as natural.

Also notable, in fact quite remarkable, are the ways in which the poem seeks to diminish, even obliterate, the notion that humans can be content with minimum change and limited response in this reorientation of desire and consequent behavior. The famous Dowel, Dobet and Dobest, which initially serve to suggest degrees of willing and acting well, evolve until they coalesce in the three persons of the Trinity, a boundless exemplar of love in interaction, and until the "lowest" grade, "do well," means no less than to imitate Christ, the manifestation in human form of totally selfless love. In passus 1 the dreamer anxiously asks Lady Holy Church, "Tell me, how can I save my soul?" This question can (and I think in context should) be heard as instinctively selfish and negative: it concerns "myself" and implies "keeping from" something—namely damnation. Langland certainly believed in hell as one of the fundamental facts of life; he makes fear of hell serve as a motivator. But just as he will not let his audience rest easy with minimal goodness, so he never lets them remain focused on individual salvation. Love, not fear, is his dominating message, and the conclusion of the poem, however one reads it, dramatizes the plight not just of one individual but of the entire Christian community.

The Nature of the Quest

A recurrent strain in Langland criticism is the notion that the poem is a quest for some kind of knowledge or understanding and that Langland, or his speaker and dreamer, is wrestling with intellectual problems and searching restlessly for their solutions. I believe this to constitute a fundamental misunderstanding of the poem.

Someone undertaking behavior modification in order to lose weight does not face intellectual conundrums. The problem is not a "knowledge problem," but an "attitude problem" and a "behavior problem." I argue that, similarly, the dominant "problems" *Piers Plowman* confronts are not problems of knowing but problems of willing and doing. To the extent that the poem deals with questions of propositional truth (e.g., Is it true that one is saved if one has been baptized?), the answers were not really in doubt. Any Christian who gave the question a moment's thought could answer it—though some might prefer to avoid the question, or attempt to postpone the inevitable answer, for instance by posing hairsplitting distractions to delay arriving at it. Rather, one's confrontation with and acknowledgment of truth were at stake, and the will's consequent response to that acknowledgment.

To define wisdom, Augustine, among many others, invoked a biblical phrase: *initium sapientiae timor Domini*, "fear of the Lord is the beginning of wisdom."[30] This beginning of wisdom is more than knowledge; it is a felt response, a reorientation of attitude and desire resulting from what is known. If one wishes to speak of *Piers Plowman* as a quest for understanding, it must be this sort of felt understanding. Indeed the poem continually exposes fundamental truths and confronts the audience with them, but it does this so that the audience can accept the consequences of those truths, forming and re-forming will accordingly. The truth that the poem seeks is not a proposition or a series of propositions that require only the audience's intellectual assent; it is a state of being and, ultimately, a state of loving whose only adequate model is Christ and the Trinity.

These themes may strike many modern readers as pretty solemn, and as relentlessly Christian, unlikely to engage our interest. Even someone generally sympathetic to such material might suspect that *Piers Plowman* presents a rather overwhelming dose of it. If the poem consisted of nothing but its subject matter, that could conceivably be so. But even the longer speeches, which make up a good deal of the poem, are never mere expository sermons, and if Langland heard us compare him with even the finest preacher of his day, I suspect he would be unpleasantly surprised. So let us turn our attention to *Piers Plowman* the poem.

Chapter Three

"All This I Saw Sleeping": Reading the Prologue

Piers Plowman is "poetry" for many reasons: Langland's skillful handling of his verse form, his extraordinary sensitivity to nuances of diction and syntax, his ability to generate vivid images out of bits of cliché and snatches of everyday life, his gift for creating dramatic tension and suspense, his evoking traditional genres and formulas only to extend or alter them, his deft blending of ordinary narrative with metaphorical modes (such as symbolic tableau or personification allegory), and his appropriating large conceptual constructs that combine to give his work a kind of dynamic, restless coherence. Restlessness and tension pervade the entire work, communicating their energy to the reader, who pursues the poet through juxtaposition and paradox and scrambles to keep up with associations linking scenes and episodes. The cumulative effect renders the familiar fresh, arresting and engaging both mind and feeling.

These very qualities that produce engaging poetry, however, create a text dense with challenges for the reader. Therefore this chapter and the next will each examine one section of the text closely. In this chapter, we consider the prologue, looking especially for Langland's strategies of selection and arrangement. My paraphrases of Langland's general sense will incidentally underscore the poem's brilliance, for the contrast between paraphrase and original reveals the color and vitality of Langland's language.

"On a May Morning": Beginnings

As the prologue opens, the speaker tells us how, in early summer and under a congenial sun, he set out to seek marvels. On a May morning, in the Malvern Hills, a wonder did indeed befall him that seemed from the magical world of Fairye. Weary from his wandering, he rested beside a pleasant-sounding stream, fell asleep, and dreamed (1–10). The Malvern Hills, straddling the border between Worcestershire and Herefordshire and suddenly soaring aloft from the surrounding countryside,

33

provide singularly striking settings for panoramic views of the surrounding world. In other respects, this opening evokes the beginning conventions of several kinds of poetry and consequently sets up a nexus of expectations.[1] For example, that the speaker seeks marvels—indeed says he experiences one quite beyond the ordinary—may briefly lead the audience to expect an otherworldly adventure,[2] but any such expectation is soon surprised, deliberately redirected toward a different kind of wonder. Lines 7 to 10 signal a dream vision, but again, expectations will be surprised, for other poems of the genre consist of a single dream and contain no dreams-within-dreams. The notion that such visions might derive force from something beyond the author's own opinions and ideas will certainly be kept in play by what the dreamer reports. Dream visions also conventionally indicate something about the narrator's inner condition.[3] This speaker, we learn, is a hypocrite, dressed "as if I were a sheep" (2–3). The next line restates the idea: he is clothed like a hypocritical hermit, one whose garment lays claim to a vocation his actions belie. The speaker, therefore, does not set himself up as a righteous moralist but suggests we should imagine him among the sinners he will describe.

As the dream begins, the narrator, finding himself in a wild, uncultivated region, looks east to see the sun and a high, well-built citadel. "Beneath" is a grim castle in a deep, dark valley. "Between" is the now-famous fair field full of folk who work and move about "as the world requires" (11–19). That we begin in a "wilderness" removes us from the familiar world and presents us, in effect, with a cleared stage, a blank canvas. That the sun is in the east may extend the narrator's "morning" (5) into the dream. But then the high citadel is associated with the sun and its light, in obvious contrast with the fearful, dark keep in the valley below. What began as a blank canvas of the wilderness now has humanity strewn across its center and framed, as if at its top right and bottom left, by the polarities in terms of which we are to evaluate their activities. The two poles have not yet been explicitly identified (Lady Holy Church will do this in passus 1), but high and low, light and dark can suggest only good and evil, heaven and hell, God and Satan.

"All Manner of Men": Folk in the Estates

Having thus set the stage, the poem now draws us closer. The scene crackles with bustling figures. But although their actions are vividly described, we see not individuals but types, "vocations," walks of life.

The acts we witness often represent typical behaviors, characterized and even caricatured with easily identifiable moral significances. Especially here at the beginning, the language of the poem emphasizes people's choice of professions and behaviors *(putten hem to, chosen hem to)*. Although there are some "good" people described, the "bad" predominate. Such negative characterization of society typifies the genre Langland employs here: estates satire, which surveys society according to its general categories in order to criticize the failings of each.[4]

The traditional three estates comprised *bellatores* (fighters, those who ruled and protected), religious (those dedicated to the care of souls or other formal service to God), and commons (those who labored). Within the first two estates, one can recognize hierarchy: in the religious, the pope, the cardinals, archbishops, bishops and abbots, their administrative subordinates (e.g., archdeacons and priors), and so on down to the lower clergy (parish priests, friars, pardoners), those in minor orders, and broadly speaking perhaps even some laymen (without vows or orders) who nevertheless especially dedicated themselves to a religious life.[5] The *bellatores* ranged from king to lowest knight. If this simple picture of the three estates had ever adequately categorized the actual medieval world, it had certainly ceased to do so by the later fourteenth century. It entirely failed to address the mercantile and professional classes, which were left hovering uneasily between lower nobility and upper commons.[6] But here Langland employs two general categories, "lay" and "religious." The laity comprises the commons as well as the nobility and knights, those responsible for providing the material wherewithal to sustain life and for administering law and justice governing the physical goods of this world. Religious, those in orders or under vows, bear responsibility for administering spiritual goods, revelation and grace.

As we approach particular folk (20 –22), we first meet the hardworking tillers of the soil whose labors earn what spendthrifts consume; Langland makes plowing the typical embodiment of work, of productive activity. England's economy was still agrarian, and agricultural labor was fundamentally important; the plowman's activity can serve, by synecdoche, to represent all labor providing the necessities of life (food, drink, and clothing) that Lady Holy Church will describe in the following passus. Contrasted with this productive labor is consumption by the unproductive *(wastours,* 22) and overconsumption *(glotonye,* 22). These lines are descriptive but far from neutral: workers "win" what the "wasters" use up through "gluttony." Some pursue honor and position, concealing their lack of real worth in outward trappings (23–24). Lang-

land uses language deftly here to establish patterns and associations
without becoming formulaic or tedious; repetition of *some putten hem to*
links lines 23 and 20, ensuring that we appreciate the contrast between
them. That "pride" is an abstraction makes us understand "apply themselves to" in a somewhat different sense, as a play on words if not quite a
metaphor. The contrast between plow and pride, between the tangible,
hard labor of the former and the insubstantial outward show (*contenaunce
of clothing*) of the latter, makes us sense sterile hollowness.

Many apply themselves to prayers and penance, for instance religious
solitaries who remain solitary—unlike the ones who wander the countryside in search of bodily pleasure (25–30). "Put themselves to" is
repeated again in line 25 but this time varied ("many" rather than
"some," placed in the second half of the line rather than in the first);
that variation gives added force to *preieres and penaunce* and so helps to
mark the transition from the secular (laborers, managers) to the religious. At the same time, we encounter the first explicit mention of living this life with an eye to the next, self-denial here for the sake of joy
hereafter (25–27). The language describing the good seems fairly neutral and indeed simply states what would be taken as normative for any
Christian. But as with the winners and wasters, the ideal is immediately
contrasted with failures to achieve it.

Then the focus shifts abruptly. Some choose to be merchants and
seem to thrive; some entertain for money, and that is acceptable; but
ribald entertainers who fake madness and put on fantastic skits do no
legitimate service, even though they could if they wanted to (31–39).
The poet is explicitly neutral about some minstrels (he reckons they are
"guiltless," 34) and implicitly neutral about merchants (they seem to us
to thrive, 32): as the proverb says, "fair exchange is no robbery."[7] But he
has no patience for those who abuse their wits and debase their patrons:
they are clownish charlatans, tellers of lewd stories. Calling bad minstrels "Judas's children" suggests they descend, morally, from the apostle
who betrayed Jesus with a kiss. The Latin quotation, allegedly from
Paul, is the first of many in the poem and must be considered at least
briefly. But before doing that, we might pause to ask how Langland has
been proceeding.

A poet writing estates satire could present us with a rigidly ordered
list, the estates one after the other (*bellatores*, clergy, commons) and,
within each estate, descending ranks (e.g., king, baron, knight). True, if
he were going to give a very detailed account in the latter part of the
fourteenth century, he would run into difficulties, especially where

upper commons and the other estates merged.[8] But such a list, even if one could construct it, would be artificial and tedious, and Langland creates no such impression. We might actually expect him to give us something of a jumble; we have, after all, folk working and moving about the helter-skelter world. The dreamer, we can imagine, observes and reports what happens to pass before his eyes or allows his eyes to dart about the bustling scene.

Nevertheless, beneath the skillfully created impression of the field teeming with people of all sorts lies a strategy for order, or rather strategies that interweave. One juxtaposes opposites: winners and wasters, good hermits and bad hermits, good minstrels and bad minstrels. In developing trains of thought, Langland uses such contrastive juxtaposition more often than any other single device. Another strategy distinguishes the secular and the religious realms. Temporal and spiritual goods and activities correspond metaphorically: hermits "work" and "produce goods" just as plowmen do. But more important, temporal and spiritual realms are fundamentally analogous and inherently related; activity in one realm both affects and illuminates activity in the other. For example, how a Christian uses wealth (generously, selfishly) cannot be separated from his or her spiritual state (virtue, vice). Langland begins with basic workers and "producers" in each realm: those who plow, and those who pray and do penance. Langland will resume a consideration of these two realms, going first up the ecclesiastical ranks (58–111: friars, pardoners, priests, bishops, cardinals, the pope); then, shifting from religious to secular, from pope to king, he will treat the secular hierarchy (112).

Why does Langland move from hermits to merchants and minstrels (31)? Here he seems to deploy yet another strategy, one based on the relationship between a vocation and goods. Having shown us producers in plowmen and good religious, he next describes two sorts of middlemen, those who do not produce but rather exchange: merchants buy and sell physical things; minstrels recite and perform songs and stories, intangible things. He will then go on to consider those who neither produce nor exchange but merely take: beggars and pilgrims (40–52). Both wander and seek, the former for tangible gifts, the latter ostensibly for intangible grace.

Langland's first Latin quotation occurs in line 39; Paul's condemnation of foul speech identifies ribald entertainers as servants of the devil, although the poet will "not venture to elaborate on it here." He does, of course, not need to elaborate, because the Latin serves to invoke both

Paul's authority and the accumulated and customary interpretation of Paul's words. In fact, the quotation does not come verbatim from Paul but rather distills his sense as commentators and preachers commonly understood it.[9] Such quotations import the authority of both Scripture and tradition into the poem, and knowledge of the surrounding context always enhances appreciation of a biblical quotation's force.

Next the dreamer notices beggars who travel about, acquire more food than they need, misbehave, bicker, get into trouble, and are habitually lazy (40 – 45). The collocation "bidders and beggars" (40) presents a lexical problem; it could mean "people who beg and, in return for a gift, promise to pray for their benefactors," but it could also denote those who beg insistently and annoyingly, whining beggars.[10] Those described here clearly abuse a legitimate practice and the charity of their contemporaries. They beg beyond need and out of sloth and so, in effect, steal.[11] As I have suggested, an underlying rationale for mentioning them at this point is the movement from producers to exchangers to those who take without giving anything in return. Some pilgrims who claim to seek the shrines of saints in far-flung lands are actually windbags and liars (46 –52) who misuse a religious practice. Instead of journeying to shrines with a devout disposition in search of spiritual favor, they are frivolous vagabonds who appropriate the external form of a pious endeavor without any spiritual intent or benefit.[12] Once again, pairing abuses in the temporal and spiritual realms sharpens awareness of the defects in each.

By line 53 we have returned to the fringes of the religious estate (laymen who falsely claim a religious calling). Beginning at these fringes, Langland progresses up the religious ranks. The image of sham solitaries (53–57) resumes and elaborates the bad religious mentioned at the outset (28–30). These strong, able-bodied loafers declare themselves to be hermits in order to avoid work. The lines are a particularly good illustration of the inadequacy of paraphrase. Hermits should have led solitary lives, in prayer and renunciation of physical indulgence. The lamentable state of affairs the poet perceives is vividly conveyed by the "heap" of them wandering about with their crooked walking staves, loose women traipsing after them. The specificity of Walsingham (in Norfolk, where there was a noted shrine dedicated to the Blessed Virgin) adds texture, as does the colorful diction: *grete lobies and longe, lothe* to work (55), who don *copes* (56). (Although *copes* could simply mean "outer garments," here it connotes clerical vestments, perhaps even those formal, ceremonial ones worn by ecclesiastical dignitaries, and so it emphasizes the ludicrous pretensions of these rogues.)[13]

Langland had another reason for portraying these loafing "hermits" here: They embody so dramatically failure in both secular and religious spheres. On the one hand, these loafers can, and should, work in an England that, in the aftermath of the plague, desperately needed able-bodied laborers (Baldwin, "The Historical Context," 70–72). On the other hand, they make a travesty of a way of life meant to be one of prayer and penance, of sexual abstinence and self denial, lived in order to honor God and intercede for their fellow humans. This same kind of dual failure appears in nearly all the descriptions of religious and consti- tutes a key dimension of the moral chaos Langland perceives: the acts that squander, abuse, or misappropriate temporal goods are at the same time acts that neglect, distort, or pervert spiritual goods, especially moral instruction and the dispensation of grace.

Friars, like false hermits, were considered a species of vagabond (Szittya, 228–29). The dreamer says that all four orders of friars were preaching for physical gain, explaining away Scripture just as they liked; to win prestige, they made their vocation into a business, what they should teach into "merchandise," Charity into a huckster. Their behav- ior has brought about many a horror in just a short time and, unless they and the church reach a better understanding, puts the world in the greatest danger (58–67). Even such a close paraphrase loses the force of the poem's language, especially lines 64 and 65. Charity means love and in this context implies God's love for humanity, manifested in Christ's redeeming death on the cross and resulting in the grace that can absolve *(shryue)* sins. Christians, especially the clergy, should be driven to share that love. The mendicant orders were established so that their members might imitate closely the life of Christ and minister to the needs of souls: to teach, preach, and move Christians to sorrow for their sins.[14] The abuse of the sacrament of penance by friars who "sell" absolution to unrepentant (and therefore unabsolved) sinners in exchange for money perverts the Christian dispensation and the friars' mission; the practice betrays sinners into the devil's hands and at the same time beguiles them into false security. Langland returns often to the friars' mercenary behavior in this perversion of confession.

Selling pardons perverted the dispensation of grace in similar fashion, and the dreamer next describes a pardoner preaching and claiming authority to absolve all sins. Uneducated people believed him; he fooled them with his authentic-looking documents and took their money (68–75). The passage contains a striking detail, figurative speech that, in small, employs the "allegory" typical of the poem. An imagined action perfectly captures and expresses moral "truth." Line 74 states that the pardoner thumped people on the head with his rolled-up "authorization," so that he made their eyes water. We are invited to visualize a physical blow actually blurring their vision and a moral one befuddling their judgment; at the same time, we might compare such merely physical tears with those that genuine sorrow for sins could have produced, sorrow without which even a legitimate indulgence would have been worthless.

The lines that follow compel us to consider the matter of the poet's voice: "Thus you, audience, squander your gold to support wretches who haunt gluttony and lechery" (76–77). The general fiction of the poem is "I had a dream and this is what I saw," but the narrator does not limit himself simply to reporting "what happened then." He readily turns aside from the narrative to address us directly, sometimes in a voice that we cannot confidently distinguish from the poet's own (cf. Pr.38, 66–67). One might compare this situation to a modern play in which a central character occasionally leaves others on stage to walk forward onto the apron and address the audience directly. Like many twentieth-century authors, Langland was not bent on rigidly maintaining psychological consistency in point of view.

The poet's direct commentary seems to extend into the following lines, which initiate criticism of the hierarchy and parish priests. You fools, he says, make pardoners possible by giving them your money, while bishops and priests are complicit in the deception. If the bishop were what he should be and deserved to have his two ears (i.e., if he took the trouble to be aware of what was going on), he would not let his authority be used this way in deceiving the people (the pardoner claimed to have the bishop's seal authenticating his documents, 69). It bothers the bishop not at all that such a rascal (*boy*, 80) preaches; he permits parish priest and pardoner to divide the take, money that the poor parishioners would keep were it not for this kind of "business" (78–82).

Friars and pardoners were usually journeymen, not part of the permanent and stable ecclesiastical structure that ministered to the people of an area. Parish priests should have been those ministers, shepherds to their flocks ("pastors," cf. Chaucer's Parson), and to those priests Langland now turns. Instead of faithfully caring for their parishioners' needs, they seek permission to leave their charges and take up an easier and better-paying life in London out of laziness and greed (83–86). Line 86, with its extra alliteration on the fourth stress (*swete*),[15] bites deeply. Simony (buying and selling ecclesiastical positions and their incomes) constituted a serious offense; the line bluntly accuses chantry priests of simony and suggests that they revel in it.

A bishop, who with his administrative and judicial staff presided over the larger unit (diocese) into which parishes were organized, should oversee and govern the spiritual affairs of his region. But bishops and other university-trained theologians, whose business was to preach, teach, care for the poor, and say their liturgical prayers devoutly, instead live in London and serve as secular administrators for the rich and powerful; one fears for their souls! (87–99). *Consistorie* (99) suggests in context an episcopal court where offenses against ecclesiastical law were tried; Christ's "consistory," on the other hand, suggests either his judgment of each soul after death or the collective Last Judgment. Thus the line very deftly overlays a jaded, earthly perspective (the courts of these worldly bishops) with a startlingly different one (Christ's court, where these bishops will ultimately be tried).

"About Court": Two Views from the Top

Langland has so far treated each of the religious ranks pretty consistently. He has described in vivid and straightforward language the failure of each vocation to fulfill its essential responsibilities, often with a ringing condemnation near the end of the section.[16] But as we arrive at the top, in lines 100 to 111, the tone and the method of presentation change. Langland does not simply describe someone's action or a series of actions. The passage is more oblique and requires us to recall the language of Gospel verses, to appreciate a pun, and to actively pursue the poet's imagination. Let us begin with a literal translation of the lines:

I saw, with respect to the power that Peter had entrusted to him,
[The power] to bind and loose, as the Bible says,
How he had left it with love, as Our Lord commanded,
Among four virtues, most powerful of all,
Which are called "cardinals," and closing gates
Of the place where Christ has his kingdom, to close and to lock,
And to open it [the kingdom] to them [the virtuous?] and show
　　heaven's joy.
But with respect to the Cardinals at the papal court who took that
　　name,

And took upon themselves the power to make a pope
Who would have the might Peter had—I do not want to challenge
    that—
For the election [of the pope] properly belongs in charity and learning.
Therefore I can, and cannot, speak more about "court." (100 –111)

The first two lines (100 –101) summon up Matthew's account of
Christ's giving "the power of the keys" to Peter (Matt. 16:18–19), a
passage commonly understood to show Christ making Peter his successor as well as specifically conferring on the apostles the power to absolve
the repentant from the guilt of sin through the sacrament of penance
(cf. John 20:23). Langland's imagination recombines and elaborates
Matthew's images of gates, keys, opening, and closing.
    What good does it do to unlock a gate unless it can be opened and
shut? And how can this happen unless the gate has functioning hinges?
The pun on the Latin *cardines,* "hinges," generates these questions. The
idea of hinge as that upon which something hangs, or "depends," underlies the traditional classification of the cardinal virtues, the most important moral strengths or powers on which other virtues depend. The
same rationale underlies calling the most important ecclesiastics of the
church "cardinals": they are "pivotal" figures in its administration. Cardinals should possess the cardinal virtues both because of their responsibilities and because of the name they bear. What use are cardinals without virtue? What use is the power of the keys if the "hinges" on which
the gates depend are weak and unusable? What would become of
Christ's dispensation of grace entrusted to feeble guardians?
    The keys unlock the kingdom of heaven, the place where Christ
reigns (cf. 105). Hell is explicit in Matt. 16:18 and implicit in these lines
of the poem, the alternative that remains for those against whom
heaven's gates are shut. The poem's language (*bynden,* 101; *closynge yates,*
104; *to close and to shette,* 105) forcibly states that they can be shut as well
as opened. Thus we are also reminded that the Christian dispensation
includes damnation as well as salvation, that heaven's gates can be shut
against the vicious as well as open to the virtuous: Let all Christians,
including cardinals, beware. One might also wonder if making fast the
gates of God's kingdom does not suggest the fortress of the church
firmly defended against its enemies (cf. Matt. 16:18). In this defense,
pope and curia played a crucial role; that they were actually fulfilling it
Langland's contemporaries had ample reason to doubt.

In contrast to his direct and biting criticisms up to this point, it may seem that Langland treats pope and curia with notable restraint, as he will subsequently treat the king. It is conceivable that the poet thought it impolitic to be explicitly harsh with these individuals at the summit of society; though he is utterly outspoken about bishops, abbots, friars, and mayors, who were both powerful and nearer at hand, those passages describe generic functions rather than single out an individual. But more likely Langland's tactic reflects his appreciation that king and pope presented the ultimate authority for enforcing good government, secular and religious, on this earth, authorities whose failure left all society vulnerable. Specific and difficult contemporary problems, for which there were no simple, pragmatic solutions, beset both. In the case of the papacy, the Avignon Captivity (1309–1377) and the Great Schism (begun in 1378) created turmoil and scandal.[17] Langland, rather than simply condemning the actual failures of pope and curia, chose to articulate an ideal model, a kind of moral paradigm; it implies formidable criticism of contemporary reality, but it also more emphatically (and more hopefully?) reasserts the ideal.

From the top of the ecclesiastical hierarchy, we cross to the top of the secular (112–22). A king, escorted by knights and supported by the people, rules. In accordance with natural intelligence (*kynde wit,* 114), the learned advise him in ruling for the common good, and the king, knights, and clergy are provided sustenance by the common people, who devise trades and crafts and ensure that there are plowmen to produce food. Finally, the secular community together, as intelligence directs, establishes laws and respect for the law so that each person may recognize what is justly his or hers (*ech lif to knowe his owene,* 122).

This section may seem to be another instance of "then I saw X do Y," since it begins "Then came there a king" (112). The lines may in fact allude to an actual procession; the passage suggests a king in the presence of a throng of subjects, who cry out to him and to one another. But the rest of line 112 ("knighthood led him") takes us into a different mode, a mode maintained by other personified abstractions (*kynde wit,* 114; *clergie,* 116) as well as by the very general, if not quite abstract, nature of the other parties (a king, the commons, clerks, plowmen).[18] Langland frequently combines abstraction with generalization in this fashion and thus articulates not an individual act or instance but a pattern, a set of relationships between general entities. As was the case with the papacy, we are again presented with a kind of ideal model, a moral paradigm, this time of how the three estates should cooperate in shaping the secular community in accordance with natural intelligence. These two passages, on papal curia and king with kingdom, stand somewhat apart from the rest of the passus, both in how Langland presents them and in their emphasizing the ideal rather than the actual. In both instances, ideal inevitably implies actual (we recognize how the latter falls short). Actuality reemerges in what immediately follows: in the case of cardinals and papacy in lines 107 to 111, here by four speeches (123–45) whose content and circumstances the poet juxtaposes to striking effect.

King, commons, and natural intelligence established law and respect for the law (121–22), and law and justice become the next theme. First a lean *lunatik* (123–27) respectfully expresses the wish that the king may rule justly and be rewarded in heaven. As wards of the king, lunatics were particularly dependent upon royal justice.[19] Yet one wonders if Langland might be recalling their special dependence upon it to suggest, simultaneously, that hoping for it is naive to the point of madness. In response to the lunatic's speech, an angelic voice speaks as if taking up the mention of "heaven" and representing God's perspective (128–38). The angel utters a traditional bit of Latin, which implies both authority and judicial force[20] and introduces a transcendent perspective: being a king is an accident of birth and will not necessarily last (certainly not beyond this life); moreover, an earthly king is a vicar of Christ the king, administers laws established by Christ (not simply invented by himself), and will be judged accordingly. As he exacts justice, he should remember that justice can also be exacted of him before the heavenly judge. As Christ acted out of love and mercy, so implicitly the king's duty in the Christian universe requires that he be compassionate as was Christ, his model.

This angelic admonition might render a well-intentioned ruler too cautious to judge at all. But then a literate, fast-talking scoffer (*a Goliardeis, a gloton of wordes*) shouts back in Latin that unless the king exercises his power, he will be king in name only (139–42). The scoffer's two lines of Latin, pushed to their extreme, not only counterbalance but overthrow the angel's warning. They employ an etymological argument but omit a key component so as to eviscerate the argument's natural moral: *king (rex)* comes from *rule (regere)*, and so a king should enforce his will.[21] As this stands, these lines constitute just the sort of plausible but abuse-prone defense of naked power one might hear from an educated but amoral advisor in a law court or royal council chamber. Finally, all the common people cry out a version of a legal maxim. This venerable Latin tag, brief enough for ordinary folk to have learned by rote, goes back to Roman law and expresses a timeless predicament: in effect, "the king's wish is our command" (143– 45).[22] That the people proclaim it themselves eloquently dramatizes their helplessness before king and legal system. Nothing in this section has satirized the king or criticized him directly. Rather, a series of juxtapositions have presented various "takes" on the king's relationship to the community. The effect is a tableau that makes us contemplate a range of possibilities for king as chief guardian of law and justice. Which image corresponds more closely to the audience's experience?

"Rats and Small Mice": The Fable

Then a throng of rats and mice scurries to a council to discuss their "common good" as Langland retells the well-known fable of belling the cat (146 –210). A "cat of a court" is on the loose and dangerous; a "rat of renown" suggests belling the cat, but the rats soon discover, to their chagrin, the crucial flaw in that plan. A mouse speaks up: not only would another cat simply replace one they were able to dispose of, but if the cat were replaced by a kitten, unable to hunt as effectively as an adult, the rats, and the mice too, would run amok. Langland retells the fable vividly, for instance in the description of the cat's depredations (150 –55). But he has also given it a wholly ironic cast (Schmidt, *B-Text,* 413, 146). Thus the complaint voiced at the beginning of the council lays bare the selfish motive of the rats: "We would be able to be lords on high and live at our ease" (157). The mouse gives a striking picture of how both mice and rats would behave if left to themselves (197–200); though he does not spare mice entirely (198), he is scathing about rats (201).

Characteristically, Langland deals out glancing blows along the way. About to recommend a collar with a bell, the rat of renown speaks of collars: he has seen people on the streets of London wearing "very bright necklaces" and "collars of skillful workmanship" (160 – 62). One imagines important officials wearing their chains of office, or servants of great lords wearing livery.[23] But these collars are also dog collars, and those who wear them unleashed hounds who prowl through rabbit warrens and uncultivated land (162– 63). The lines thus caricature the officious and oppressive functionaries who haunt the capital city.

The mouse ends the whole ironic scene on a thoroughly self-centered note: *Forthi ech a wis wight* [person] *I warne, wite* [guard] *wel his owene* (208). This concludes a council that began in quest of "the common good" (148). Line 208 echoes line 122, "Fashioned law and fidelity," *ech lif to knowe his owene*. Middle English *wite(n)* can mean both "know" and "protect, guard"; "know" parallels the earlier line while "guard," strongly suggested by this context, parodies it. We have gone from the ideal of recognizing what is justly ours to keeping whatever we can.

The fable complements and develops what has gone before. Langland left the idea of king and kingdom with the people helpless before the royal power. He then allows us to imagine the people, as it were, without the restraints of royal power. Neither scene satisfies, yet we recognize the real world in each. The first, on kingship, suggested an ideal model from which actuality deviates. The council of rats meeting for their common good seems a caricature from start to finish, its truth uttered by the mouse, and the poet-dreamer turns to us at the end (209 –10), inviting us to draw the obvious conclusions. He knows he has left us with unsolved problems. These topics, king and commons, the administration of justice in the secular realm, government under royal direction and government of the people by themselves, will be the focus of passus 2 to 6.

"Where the Cat Is a Kitten": Topical References

I have postponed until now any discussion of topical reference, something that lines 100 to 210 of the prologue obviously suggest. Many readers have found depicted there, in slightly disguised form, contemporary people and events.[24] The council of rats has suggested the failed "Good Parliament" of 1376, with the cat representing Edward III or John of Gaunt and the rat of renown Peter de la Mere; the kitten easily suggests Richard II, who came to the throne in July 1377 at the age of 10. The scene in which a king comes, led by knights (112), is usually understood as an allusion to Richard's coronation. It has further been suggested that the reference to cardinals electing a pope (107–11) was occasioned by the election of an antipope in 1378, the subsequent Great Schism, and even Wyclif's writings on papal elections. The last seems the weakest case, because there was turmoil and scandal surrounding the papacy throughout the latter part of the century. But it does seem inescapable that in the case of king and council, the poem reflects the specific concerns of the 1370s: the problem of an aged and ailing king who had a very young and not universally accepted successor, and the contention between Parliament, magnates, and royal power. None of these scenes (100 –210) had appeared in the earliest (A) version of the poem.

Nevertheless, concentrating on the topical would be a mistake, as would understanding the poem simply as "history."[25] For Langland, the timeless model of the ideal and the general significance of everyday inadequacies mattered most. As Kane says of him, "As soon as made, his topical allusions become in essence generic" (Kane, "The Text," 186). The paradigms of the ideal and the true that Langland created offered correctives; the contrasting failures he dramatized were significant because they were exemplary, representing actual behavior in order to make it morally identifiable and curable.

"Hot Pies, Hot!" Conclusions

The prologue concludes by returning to vignettes of particular but significant failures. A hundred lawyers (211–16) in their silk coifs loitered there, *serjeants* (from the Latin for "servants") who *serueden* only for money and confined (*pounded*, 213) the law. The transition from "parliament" to law courts may simply reflect the fact that "parliament itself was still primarily a court" (Bennett, 102, 210). But the rats' council has ended with the mouse's warning that everyone should guard his own possessions (208). What more logical than for the satirist to turn to the lawyers, who control the law and thus property? Especially if, as I have suggested, the mouse's conclusion parodies the earlier ideal: "The kyng and the commune and kynde wit the thridde / Shopen lawe and leaute, ech lif to knowe his owene" (121–22).

Langland's survey of the secular realm has thus descended from king as chief minister of justice through parliament (ordinarily the magnates and the knights) to lawyers. After an inclusive backward glance that encompasses aristocratic landowners, prosperous city dwellers, and serfs (217), the closing lines dwell on the folk at the foot of the secular ladder, especially tradespeople and laborers (219–24). The passus concludes with a vivid picture that takes us back to the full field at which we began, here envisioned as a clamoring bustle of touts and hawkers, the busy marketplace of the world where people scurry to buy and sell, to eat and drink what smells and tastes good. The concentration on food and drink, on physical sustenance and physical pleasure, will lead directly to Lady Holy Church's judgment opening the next passus (1.7–9).

In the prologue, then, Langland has introduced his dream vision, its narrator, and its subject. The wonder he sees turns out to be his world's shocking dysfunctionality. Drawing on many conventions of estates satire, he portrays that world by blending caricature with the depiction of fondly remembered ideals. His fiction creates a "realistic" jumble not obviously dominated by any artificial scheme; underlying it, however, are orders of various kinds.

These strategies of order arise from the application of logical thought (contrast, juxtaposition, division of a subject into its parts, hierarchical arrangement) to the categories of his age (the three estates, secular versus religious, temporal versus spiritual). He seems sometimes to have applied such habits of taxonomy and categorization to generate new categories (e.g., producers, exchangers, and takers of goods). The poem as a whole takes shape from large narrative units and conceptual structures, but as the prologue illustrates, Langland typically uses associative logic in developing individual scenes and speeches. Sometimes he associates likes: pardoners follow friars because they pervert the dispensation of grace in complementary ways. More often he associates unlikes in contrastive juxtaposition: good and bad or, better for what is to come, "true" and "false" generate considerations of their opposites. And he regularly pairs people or things that are temporal and spiritual analogues (plowing and praying).

The prologue displays other characteristics, many of them common to the period. The poet satirizes activities in terms that stamp them with an unmistakable moral identity, even to the point of caricature. He will often seize the opportunity for a trenchant satiric aside (e.g., the description of collars worn on the streets of London). At any moment, the narrator may turn toward us as if in the poet's own voice. Probably less familiar to modern readers is the ready mingling of different modes: Langland both describes the concrete acts of concrete agents and tells of a generic "king" being "led by knighthood." The poet regularly merges realistic exposition with this more allegorical mode, creating fictions that express abstract relationships or moral paradigms. In the prologue, we have seen a minute instance of this technique in the pardoner's striking his victims (74) and in the somewhat more developed section involving the king.

The rhetorical development of images and puns (keys, gates, hinges) constitutes another mode that modern readers are not used to meeting in narrative. Association and extension of traditional, especially scriptural, images was a fundamental habit not only of exegete and preacher but also of individual Christians meditating on the biblical text. Teasing the significance out of words, especially out of their etymology, was another habit that could be used to good effect (hinges) or to bad (the glutton of words on the meaning of *king*). Scriptural passages could be associated with one another on the basis of shared words, images, or topics and extended to words or images with extrabiblical associations; the "control" on this activity was the clear and explicit meaning of the New Testament and, usually, the received interpretations already offered by the commentary tradition.[26] Langland obviously knew the Bible intimately and had absorbed these habits of exploration and reflection, whether as private individual or as professional practitioner. Scripture, traditional authorities, and standard etymologies could thus offer him bits of narrative and conceptual structure; his imagination almost always recasts these and gives them new life.

Chapter Four

"What the Mountain Betokens": Lady Holy Church's Speech (Passus 1)

If the prologue of *Piers Plowman* can be regarded as its fanfare, proclaiming the state of Langland's world, then passus 1 is the poem's overture, recapitulating in carefully orchestrated language the themes of restoration that the rest of the work will explore. While employing strategies used in the prologue, this passus introduces the first major personification and then brings to bear two structuring sets of ideas. The first set provides a skeleton for successive narrative episodes, the second a unifying theme.

As the passus opens, the dreamer promises: "What the mountain signifies, and the dismal valley, / And the field full of folk I intend clearly to explain" (1.1–2). With these words, he introduces us to Lady Holy Church. Her speech (actually six speeches, responding to questions posed by the dreamer) occupies the whole of passus 1. In chapter 2 we considered the "home truths" that motivate the poet. One concise formulation put them as follows: "And if one asks why rational creatures were made, the answer is: to praise God, to serve him, to enjoy him."[1] Bearing such beliefs in mind and thinking back to the activities described in the prologue, distilled in the "hot pies!" and hawked wines of its concluding lines, we realize the force of Lady Holy Church's first words:

Son, are you sleeping? Do you see these people,
How absorbed they are in confusion?
The majority of the people who live their lives on this earth,
If they have honor and wealth in this world, they care for nothing
    better;
They take no interest in any other heaven than here. (1.5–9)

The world of the prologue matches the world of experience and stands the world as it "should be" on its head: earth was not heaven and those who treated it as such indeed wandered in confusion. Holy Church will go on to express these fundamental beliefs. But because Langland's audience already knew them, the challenge for the poet was to stimulate his readers to encounter these beliefs afresh, to stir them to feel and to act in accordance with the principles to which they gave abstract, intellectual assent.

"A Lady with Lovely Countenance": Holy Church

Why should Lady Holy Church speak these truths? Langland could have recited them in his own voice, by rote, as could most of his contemporaries. But a treatise, however lucid, does not engage thought and feeling the way a poem can, and one aspect of Langland's poetic strategy is to unfold what he has to say dramatically, here in dialogue between "teacher" and dreamer. Such a personified guide figure, suggesting authority beyond the poet's own, generally initiated the adventures of dream visions and so would have seemed quite natural to Langland's audience at this point. Making the teacher impressive and authoritative, and the dreamer dull and slow, guarantees a degree of dramatic tension.[2]

Granted that there is a motive for personification and dramatic presentation, why this speaker? Considered most broadly, "the church" is a powerfully comprehensive concept: the assembly of God's people incorporated into Christ's "body" by the sacrament of baptism. It includes the church triumphant (those now glorious in heaven), the church suffering (those in purgatory), and the church militant (those now living their lives on earth in pursuit of heaven).[3] But besides suggesting this collective historical witness, the term can also refer to the clergy, those in holy orders whose duty it is to teach, administer the sacraments, and conserve the tradition Christ entrusted to the apostles. In the prologue, Langland has just excoriated the behavior of the church, clergy and laity alike. In this personification of the collective church, he seems to reach beyond the feeble witness of church and churchmen in his own time for an ideal that transcends it, for the church as originally constituted and realized in more glorious but bygone days, the embodiment of the magisterial teaching and living of truth and morality. Such an ideal, in contrast to the actual, is enforced by the adjective "Holy." From the time of the Council of Nicaea (381), holiness was one of the solemn marks with which the church was supposed to be endowed, however flawed its contemporary realization. Thus Holy Church "came down from the citadel" on the mountain (1.4), as if sent once again by God to proclaim uncorrupted truth to his people.

Finally, why "Lady" Holy Church? The collective church was imagined from earliest times as a nurturing mother, *mater ecclesia,* and was often portrayed as a stately woman, for instance in debate with Synagogue (collectively the people of the Jewish faith). Perhaps influenced by Latin grammar that classified words such as *ecclesia, natura, ratio,* and *philosophia* as "feminine," traditional personification allegory regularly imagined such figures as beautiful, commanding women: the Reason of *Roman de la Rose;* the Nature of Alan of Lille, the *Roman,* and Chaucer; and perhaps most influential of all, the Lady Philosophy of Boethius's *Consolation.*[4] Lady Holy Church, then, both represents *mater ecclesia* and arises from a well-established tradition of idealized magisterial women who, in dreams or visions, instruct dull-witted pupils.

Shaping Concepts: "Goods"

The dramatic personification of Lady Holy Church and her sharp condemnation of the world portrayed in the prologue constitute two elements of the poet's strategy. A third is his organization of her speech, and much of the rest of the poem, around structuring ideas. The first of these is "goods," distributed through its complementary parts by "division."[5] Goods (things beneficial or desirable) divide into two main sorts: "temporal," used in this world to provide for humanity's bodily needs; and "spiritual," those beneficial for the soul rather than the body. Temporal goods are means to an end, to be used accordingly; spiritual goods are ends in themselves, to be pursued for their own sake. Temporal goods subdivide further into "natural" and "artificial." Food, drink, and clothing, required to sustain physical life, are natural; artificial are things such as money, gold, jewels, wealth in general, contrived or manufactured rather than the product of natural agriculture, surplus beyond what is required to sustain life. Spiritual goods, being intangible and transcendent, are more difficult to subdivide neatly, and the poem does not attempt to subdivide them here. The ultimate spiritual good is God, the end toward which humanity tends. God's revelation and the teaching of it, God's grace and the dispensation of it, both of which help lead one to God, are spiritual goods; so are the virtues, those internal habits or dispositions of the soul through which humanity fulfills its purpose on earth and reaches its intended end.

Having heard Lady Holy Church pronounce on the folly of those who treat earth as if it were heaven, the dreamer asks her to explain. She replies by speaking first about how and why God created human beings and gave them natural goods to sustain them while on earth (11– 42). Then the dreamer asks about artificial goods, "the money on this earth," and Holy Church briefly addresses the secular use of coins (give what is Caesar's to Caesar) and the prudent use of surplus (46 –57). After the dreamer learns who his teacher is, he shifts the discussion to spiritual goods and, abandoning interest in temporal "treasure," asks how he can save his soul (79 –84); in response, Holy Church speaks about spiritual goods, about "truth" (79 –135) and "love"[6] (136 –207).

Langland fills in the large headings of this outline, certainly familiar to his audience, with vivid particulars. But let us continue to consider how the division of goods provides underlying conceptual order for the poem. *Piers Plowman* is both a trenchant critique of society and an impassioned appeal for its reformation. Change in human behavior, in individuals or collectively in society, depends fundamentally upon the notion of goods because people's behavior depends upon what they value, desire, and pursue. Reform, if it could be achieved, would ultimately involve all the goods enumerated here, for as noted in the previous chapter, the uses of temporal and spiritual goods inevitably intertwine. But focusing on people as they pursue each particular type of "good" offers one way to come to grips with human behavior and with what changing that behavior requires. R. E. Kaske expressed the structure in the following diagram:[7]

Lady Holy Church	*Poem*
material goods	
natural goods 11– 42	passus 2– 4, the Lady Meed episode
artificial goods 43 –70	passus 6, the half acre
spiritual goods	
truth 79 –135	passus 8 –13 ?
love 136 –207	passus 13 ?–20

(natural goods and artificial goods lines cross-connect to the two passus lines)

Such an outline helps us visualize what Langland has done. Passus 2 to 4 consider the corruption, and the possible reformation, of the "kingdom," where secular society suffers because money and greed pervert justice (the Lady Meed episode). There Langland focuses on the use and abuse of artificial goods, on wealth and its attendant minions in the kingdom of this world. Passus 6 considers the "half acre," the agrarian community struggling to provide the necessities of life. There disorder reigns because greed and sloth impede honest work and cooperation. (That the poem subsequently reverses the treatment of artificial and natural goods we shall consider in a moment.)

Passus 2 to 4 and 6 explicitly address human life in the world, human society as it relates to the just acquisition and management of temporal goods. Passus 7, although readers have disagreed vigorously over its details, certainly marks the transition from the topic of the proper use of earthly goods to that of spiritual ones:

"I shall leave off my sowing," said Piers, "and stop working so hard at
   physical labor,
And not be so occupied any more with my livelihood;
My 'plow' hereafter will be the plow of prayers and penance. . . ." (7.122–24)

Passus 8 to 20 concern the goods of the spirit, although saying merely that does little to explain that vast tract of the poem. Nevertheless let me simply note, for now, that those passus concentrate on immaterial things, spiritual values, virtue and salvation, and the "society" concerned with managing them, namely the church and its institutions. That Lady Holy Church's discourse on spiritual goods and the poem's latter sections can be divided into a first part on "truth" and a second part on "love" is a view that will need further discussion. Kaske so divided the speech and suggested that at some point around passus 13 the dreamer's quest for truth turns into one for love.[8]

At this point, an apology to the reader may be in order. Although they are crucial for understanding the poem, discussing these broad generalizations about spiritual and temporal goods runs the risk of making the work seem deadly dull, hopelessly and lifelessly abstract. Just as a skeleton, however useful, cannot substitute for an animated body with organs, muscle, and flesh, so such generalizations serve only to suggest the underlying shape and organization of *Piers Plowman*. Anyone who has read in the poem will be sustained, even through a discussion such as this, by the energy of its spirit and the rich density and variety of its sinews and surfaces. But in this poem it is the underlying shape that seems most likely to elude modern readers and so to need description, and there remain a few more aspects of it to consider.

In her exposition, Lady Holy Church presents first natural then artificial goods, whereas the poem subsequently reverses that order. In her speech, Langland follows a logical arrangement (natural takes precedence over artificial); why did he transpose that order in the following passus? I think Langland deliberately controls his field of view in order to focus on consecutively smaller units of society. Beginning with the world in the prologue, he moves to the secular kingdom, then to the rural community of the half acre. As he proceeds, he considers the goods most obviously used and abused in each setting. Having anatomized human behavior and human society in both kingdom and half acre, he will leave us in suspense. The tentative reformations proposed for each seem to fail or, at the very least, to remain inconclusively tenuous. T. P. Dunning identified the most likely explanation for this and for the fact that beginning in passus 7, the poem's field of view narrows once more: "The reason is, I think, because the reform of society is not possible on a corporate basis: it is achieved when each individual reforms himself. . . . The pilgrimage to truth must be made by each of the folk on his own" (Dunning, "Structure," 232). In passus 8 and following passus, Langland concentrates on the individual human being and explores the ramifications of reform, the possibilities of amending behavior, in this most fundamental constituent of society. Thereafter the view once again expands by stages, finally encompassing the whole world once again. But this goes beyond the general structure based on goods we are considering here.

We have been attending to the conceptual skeleton of Lady Holy Church's speech; the sinew and the skin that flesh it out would reward a much more detailed consideration than space permits. Always central to Langland's strategy was the desire to elicit fresh response to familiar ideas, to combine the known and the surprising, to shock as well as to exhort or reassure. When Holy Church warns against overindulgence in natural goods, she seizes on drunkenness and on the graphic, "unnatural" sin of Lot (27–33), the stuff of today's tabloids.[9] Lines 34 to 41 vividly portray the tension between body and soul as soul tries to assert what is "dear" to it and impose moderation on the yearning body. Deftly chosen language (*good, goost, gut,* 36) combines with a vivid little allegory wherein the world, "a liar," in company with the devil, tries to seduce the flesh.[10] In his almost casual dismissal of artificial goods (46–57), Langland must have jarred much of his audience (most of whom certainly, in the words of line 44, valued money). London was an international mercantile center, throbbing with commerce and flush with wealth. Yet by his choice of Gospel text the poet wrenches attention away from any interest in commerce and capital for their own sake, practically dismissing money as belonging to another world, of concern to Caesar but not to Christians. His only favorable remarks concern the cooperative husbanding of surplus against hard times (54–57), and *tresor* in the following lines (e.g., Judas's silver, 67; Wrong's betraying treasure, 70) reinforces the negative verdict. Notice, finally, that each of these first two passages, one on natural and one on artificial goods, consists of a discursive part and a biblical borrowing. In one passage, that borrowing follows exposition, in the other it comes first; one is from the Old Testament, one from the New. This kind of variety in symmetry typifies Langland's writing.

Earlier we considered the impact of making Holy Church the instructor of passus 1; are we to conclude anything from the fact that she is identified only at line 75? Here Langland seems to have succeeded in creating complex effects with a single stroke. At the beginning of a dream vision, with the first guide approaching the dreamer, and the audience anticipating a crucial, motivating encounter, what might have been our initial reaction if the poem had immediately identified the lady as the church? Can we not imagine the eyes glazing over, the stifled yawns? But besides avoiding this potential rhetorical anticlimax and creating some measure of suspense, postponing the identification generates other effects.

"Nature" and Beyond

What the lady says up to line 61 need not issue from a theological authority in order to carry weight: her message consists of the most basic and (for its age) most obvious of truths, albeit truths often conveniently pushed well to the back of the mind. Expressed concretely and forcefully, they arrest attention as fundamental truths rather than as supernatural doctrine. But having her utter them before she is identified seems also to reflect another familiar notion made to bear fresh significance: human life and behavior can be considered from two complementary points of view, as "natural," and as "supernatural" or "Christian."[11]

"Natural man" refers to humanity without particular reference to revelation and Redemption. Using natural intelligence (*kynd wit*), humanity, it was believed, could recognize its status as creature and apprehend some essential truths about its creator, its soul-in-body nature, its ultimate earth-transcending end, and the fundamental standards that, in consequence of all this, should govern its behavior: the "natural law." Thus what the lady says about the use of natural goods

(12–26, 35–39) and artificial goods (54–57) should be recognizably true to any human, and those parts of the poem that examine this aspect of human existence will focus on behavior in natural, temporal society, the secular kingdom and the agricultural half acre.

Without any outside help, natural intelligence might realize something of humanity's vulnerability to passion and its inclination to violate law; but without revelation, the fall of Lucifer, the subsequent fall of humanity's first parents, and the consequent intervention by God in human history would all be unknown. When the Lady comes to explain the *castel of care* (61), therefore, she begins to address specifically "Christian man," humanity as revealed in the Bible, as seduced by Satan and redeemed by God. At line 75, she identifies herself as Holy Church and reminds the dreamer of her role in the promulgation of Christian teaching and the dispensation of grace, and beginning with passus 7, the poem comes to concentrate on the interaction between humanity and these Christian goods.

To note this distinction between "natural" and "Christian" is emphatically not to suggest that passus 2 to 6 concern an exclusively natural world while the remainder of the poem treats one exclusively Christian, nor is it to imply that everything Lady Holy Church says down to line 61 is merely natural. Quite the contrary. She is presented, even before being identified, as an emissary sent by Truth. When speaking of natural goods, she invokes an Old Testament warning (Lot, 27–33) and cautions against the devil (40), and when discussing artificial goods, she immediately appeals to the Gospel (46–53). Langland, I think, would have found inconceivable a world that was merely natural, for he inhabited the thoroughly Christian one of the fourteenth century. He did imagine those who lived beyond the pale of the world that revelation and Christianity had penetrated, but in his own world, the natural and the Christian were essentially complementary. Far from replacing natural law, revelation assisted fallen humanity, with its corrupted natural reason, to apprehend it. More significant, revelation explained the Fall, humanity's endlessly manifested inclination to moral failure, and the Redemption offered grace, God's help, without which fulfilling even the natural law seemed beyond human grasp. The Redemption also showed God going beyond natural justice, according to which humanity would all have been condemned, to divine love, which gave them another chance and asked of them a higher, fuller response. The last speeches of Lady Holy Church will demand this response. The poem, then, seems to remind us of the notional distinction between natural and supernatural and, at the same time, to deny its practical viability: on one hand, humans cannot succeed in the natural world without the grace of the Christian one; on the other hand, the facts of Christian Redemption render merely natural goodness inadequate. Put another way, one ought "naturally" to be just in the kingdom, to perform honestly in the half acre; but could one, and if one could, would that be enough?[12]

Truth

Lady Holy Church's last speeches introduce the second set of structural concepts and, by demonstrating the unity of "Truth" (85–137) and "Love" (140–74), supply the poem with a powerful unifying theme. The dreamer had asked about earthly *tresour,* and Holy Church has just warned against the *tresour* of Wrong (70). When the dreamer learns his teacher's name, he immediately says: Forget "treasure," tell me how I can save my soul! (83–84). But Lady Holy Church does not leave *tresor* behind; instead she seizes on that very word, and the way she transmutes it into treasure of a different kind is symptomatic of the way she replies to the dreamer's question. Some critics have complained that her answer is not clear. But everyone already knew it: Keep the commandments of God and of the Church; receive the sacraments; when sin inevitably intrudes, repent, confess, and try again. Persevere.

Medieval sermons preached this message constantly. Writing about the relationship between *Piers Plowman* and such preaching, Siegfried Wenzel has remarked that in their underlying structure, Lady Holy Church's last two speeches are the most sermonlike section of Langland's poem.[13] But, as he goes on to say, the mode and progression of the speech are decidedly not sermonlike; rather they are reminiscent of meditative prose, exhibiting Langland's "fascinating association and compression of images" (168–69). The poet's imagination takes Christian commonplaces and transforms them into an intellectually and emotionally charged minefield, each section capable of erupting into significance when probed by the reader.

Truth versus False

Lines 85 to 137 announce that when all treasures are tested, Truth is the best (85). What is Truth? The Latin quoted in line 86 summons up the First Epistle of John and forces the reader to ponder the relationship between truth and charity, and we shall return to it. In exploring truth the next lines (88–110) ascend a hierarchy: the commons (and "everyone"), the clergy, the nobility, a biblical exemplar and touchstone of nobility (David), and the ultimate exemplar in heaven. Here even the apparently most simple statement repays pondering. The common folk (88–89) should speak the truth, act accordingly, and have evil will toward no one—a deceptively bland injunction that experience tells us goes unfulfilled and that would produce startling consequences if obeyed: those who do this would be "gods" (90–91).[14] Clerks who know the truth should make it known (92–93). Of course they should! What teachers should teach is truth; the clergy should teach Christian truth. Then why this injunction? Because "clerks" do not know it? How, then, can they be what their name implies? And should they simply "make truth known" by word of mouth? Or should truth be taught by example? And are Christian teachers any better at this than non-Christians, and if not, why not? Next (94–97) come the *bellatores*, king and knights; ideally they should fight to maintain justice in the world, but the lines suggest that they fail to "keep" truth just as clerks fail to teach it. *Transgressores* (violators, 96) likely derives from the Epistle of James (2:9) and its immediate context: those who administer justice must not favor the rich while treading upon the poor (James 2:1–7); the "law" of Scripture is "love your neighbor" (James 2:8). David (98–104) is the biblical ruler who established a model for kingship over God's people.[15] His example both sanctions kingship and knighthood (99–100) and removes them from the merely natural world into the one of sacred history. At the same time, the lines demystify a chivalry cloaked in quasi-liturgical ceremonies and priestlike status. Upholding justice is chivalry's true function, not aping the customs of other "orders"; a knight who fails in that is an "apostate" (104), one who breaks faith with and renounces his true and divinely sanctioned vocation. Finally, from biblical exemplar we arrive at the ultimate exemplar, the King of Kings whose "retinue" of ranked angels in heaven can be imagined as knights faithfully serving their lord. Taking as his point of departure that relationship of fealty, Langland gives a striking definition of truth and its opposite.

Traditional theology held that God created the angels out of the generosity of his love. Some were traditionally regarded as his messengers (the meaning of Greek *angelos*); but their main occupation was simply to enjoy God, face to face, in heaven (cf. 110). This direct vision of God ("the beatific vision") was considered the ultimate goal of every intelligent being, the "heaven" to which humanity aspired, fulfilling every desire; it is the "salvation" that the dreamer wants. He is about to be reminded that some who possessed this vision deliberately turned their backs on it and so invented hell. In good homiletic fashion, the passage stresses that Christians can choose to follow Lucifer-Satan to hell or to join God and his angels in heaven (128–33). Indeed, more than half of the passage concerns the fall of the angels and their consequent damnation, and certainly Langland intended to steer his audience away from hell as well as incite them toward heaven. But the most compelling implication of the passage concerns the meaning of "truth."[16]

Because all the angels saw God clearly (109), they knew him as their Creator and knew themselves as his creatures. Yet some refused to comply with this reality of their existence and turned away. Lucifer "broke buxomness" (113): the phrase means "disobeyed" but here also suggests rejection of the willing and gracious compliance that his existence naturally entailed. Countless others "leapt out" after him (117); the language emphasizes the deliberateness of their departure. And Lucifer utters his own decision in a statement whose language we must closely observe: *Ponam pedem in aquilone & similis ero altissimo* (119), "I will place my foot in the north and I will become like the most high."

The Latin comes from Saint Augustine, a speech assigned to Lucifer-become-Satan as he rebels against God. Langland has made a small but telling alteration to it. Augustine actually wrote *Ponam sedem*, "I will place my *throne*," a phrase that represents Satan establishing a kingdom to rival God's. Langland substituted *pedem*, "foot." He did not do this just to make Satan's action more concrete. Elsewhere in his writing, Augustine had established "foot" as a metaphor for love and desire, and that metaphor had become well known and widely used.[17] This apparently minor substitution thus serves to underline Satan's setting his own love and desire, his own will, against the Creator's. Consider the implications for Langland's use of "truth." Satan did not lack knowledge: he saw God face to face and so knew Truth (111). His fall was occasioned rather by his choice, by his will; he chose not to act in accord with the truth he knew.

The Whole Truth

We call a statement "true" if it corresponds to the facts, a lover "true" if he or she measures up to our expectations of faithfulness. "Truth" fundamentally means appropriate correspondence between words and the things they purport to describe, between behavior and the code governing it, between imitation and exemplar, between what is and what should be. For Langland, being "true" meant being, unlike Lucifer, *buxom,* willingly responsive to the facts of one's nature, choosing to measure up to what one was created to be. That may seem a very broad generalization, but it carries enormous power because it establishes the full force of Langland's sense of truth.

The absolute model for truth in the poem is God. God speaks truth and teaches it to humanity (cf. 12–13). But more fundamentally, God *is* truth because he both sets the standard for goodness and corresponds to it perfectly. The Middle Ages understood God to be, always and completely, everything good that can possibly be: "pure act" in the terms of scholastic philosophy, "The one who is" in God's words to Moses (Exod. 3:14). In medieval philosophy, God, as creator and shaper of "natures," thereby authored the patterns that creatures enact and established the standards for creaturely truth. Revelation added that God is—quite specifically—the exemplar that human beings should strive to imitate, for he created them in his own "image and likeness" (Gen. 1:26). Climactically, the idea of the Trinity, to which the poem specifically refers here (109, 133), added rich dimensions for imagining God as model for human truth. In trying to fathom the doctrine that one God comprised three "persons," Augustine articulated analogies between the Trinity and the human soul.[18] As Father, Son, and Holy Spirit mutually cooperate in dynamic interaction, they set the standard for human cooperation and love.

Deus Caritas

The final speech of Holy Church elaborates this theme, but it has already been put in play at line 86:

> When all treasures are tested truth is the best;
> I call on the text *Deus caritas* to show the validity of this assertion.
> It is as precious a love-gift as dear God himself. (85–87)

The meaning of these lines is neither instantly clear nor straightforward. Why does Holy Church quote, in support of her claim that truth is the best treasure, a phrase from the First Epistle of John that says "God {is} love" (1 John 4:16)? The following line raises more questions: How is truth a love-gift? Are we to think of God as "dear," "precious," or as himself a love-gift? To these questions, the rest of the present speech

(88–137) offers no explicit answers. Readers might wait for the follow-ing speech to resolve their questions; alternatively they could fill out what must have been Langland's meaning by reference to the biblical context from which he drew the Latin phrase.

John's letter develops the idea of God's redeeming love for humanity and the appropriate human response to that love. "In this has the love of God been shown in our case, that God sent his only begotten Son into the world that we may live through him. In this is the love, not that we have loved God, but that he has first loved us, and sent his son as a pro-pitiation for our sins" (1 John 4:9–10).[19] God has sent to humanity Christ-Truth precisely as a love-gift. The epistle does not explicitly enjoin Christians to love God in return; it simply takes for granted that God's love demands reciprocity and goes on to address what that response should be. For example, "For this is love of God, that we keep his commandments" (1 John 5:3); "He who says that he knows [God] and does not keep his commandments, is a liar and the truth is not in him" (1 John 2:4). Therefore God's love demands human love in return, "love" means keeping God's commands, and keeping those command-ments renders Christians "true."[20] The phrase Langland actually quotes comes from a line that sums up the entire nexus of God's love and human response: "*Deus caritas* [God is love], and he who abides in love abides in God, and God in him" (1 John 4:16).

We might well have heard something negative in the dreamer's "How can I save my soul" (84): how can I not lose it, how can I avoid the *castle of care*. He might approach truth as justice in a legalistic and minimal way: I owe this much but no more, I must not speak untruth, I must not wish evil upon anyone (cf. 88–89). But for Langland, humanity was in no position to demand justice as its measure. By the Fall, humanity had lost original integrity and, according to justice, deserved hell. An out-pouring of divine love rescued it and set it a new standard of truth: the two "great commandments" to love God above all and to love neighbor as self.[21] Lady Holy Church will address both in her last speech.

Kynde Knowyng

The dreamer protests (138–39) that he has no *kynde knowyng* of truth; by what power does it originate in his person, and where? For instance, might one get hold of truth by intellect, by assenting to propositions in one's head? The phrase "kynde knowyng" (138), used a dozen times in the poem,[22] merits careful attention; understanding its rich and interconnected senses is crucial for grasping the poem's concerns.[23] The basic Middle English meaning of the adjective *kynde* is "natural," and thus *kynde knowyng* means "natural understanding." As modifier, "natural" yields a number of complementary senses: to know what it is natural for a human to know; to know it in a way natural for humans; to know (so far as possible) in accordance with the nature of the object known. Yet another range of meaning is triggered by an extended sense of *kynde:* "having normal affection or disposition, well disposed; benevolent, generous, loving"[24] (the latter giving the modern meaning of the adjective). *Knowyng*, in its turn, has a semantic range that includes "knowing, perceiving" and extends to "being familiar with" and, in Middle English, "making something known, teaching, showing."[25] And so *kynde knowyng* includes the following implications: to react naturally to what is known; to understand lovingly; to manifest love in response to love perceived. "Knowledge" thus surpasses mere conceptualization and not only becomes "intimate, practical and personal" (Davlin, *"Kynde Knowyng,"* 13) but also passes from apprehension to reaction, to response to what is known, to feeling, desire, and love.[26]

Lines 148 to 174 of this last speech address the latter range of meanings, love and desire.[27] Holy Church begins with a remarkable assertion about *kynde knowyng:*

> It is a "natural knowing" which teaches you, in your heart,
> To love your Lord more dearly than yourself,
> To do no deadly sin, even though that cause you to die:
> This I believe to be truth. . . . (142– 45)

Thus Lady Holy Church asserts that *kynde knowyng* means love in the heart. The pun in line 144 *(dedly, deye)* values spiritual life over physical life. The demand she makes (die rather than offend God) reflects familiar New Testament injunctions that are neither very appealing nor likely (baldly asserted) to make much impression. Therefore Langland, in a series of highly crafted images, describes the reciprocal: God, out of love for humanity, let Christ die rather than see humanity lost forever; the natural response of humans should be to return God's love.

Truth of the Trinity

Lady Holy Church depicts Truth as Christ come to save humanity. The first images picture a healing ointment (148–52) sent to medicate wounded humankind; these undoubtedly create more effect in an audience familiar with the phrases of Scripture and liturgy that they incorporate, evoking a densely textured fabric of associations.[28] The images of lines 153 to 159, also rich in associations, work effectively even on the surface. God's love is so "heavy" that it spontaneously "fell" from heaven (153) and cast itself in a mold of earth by taking on flesh and blood (154–55).[29] Then, extending the paradox suggested in line 153, instead of being captured and coarsened by flesh, God's Son transformed flesh, making it as light and agile as a leaf: rather than divinity being debased, humanity became elevated. Lines 158 and 159 probably refer both to Christ's harrowing of hell after the Crucifixion and to his leading the liberated souls back to heaven, but the language, so lively in itself, permits other associations: Whose heart should not be pierced by the needle point of God's love, what stubborn heart could shut him out, how should those behave whose Leader is Love?[30]

From images of wound healed and weight transmuted, the poem shifts to one of debt both forgiven and repaid (160 – 62). The Original Sin of Adam and Eve, inherited by all humans, was an offense against the Almighty that incurred a debt beyond humanity's ability to repay. Serious sin committed by individual acts after the Fall had added to the impossible enormity of that debt. A mayor mediated between king and people; he could offer to interpret the law and assess and levy fines. Similarly Christ mediates between God the Father and humanity, "shaping" the law and imposing the deserved "fine." But this mediator, Christ, by his gift of self entirely rewrote the law of justice into one of mercy and became, himself, payment for the debt. The play on *mercyment* is powerful because under the circumstances we cannot fail to see "mercy" in a word that means "penalty to be paid in cash." Then what does it mean to say that "Christ levies the fine upon man for his misdeeds"? Christ took away the debt, redeemed it through the Crucifixion, but are Christians not to understand that they owe something for this Redemption and must somehow respond to Christ's mercy in order to benefit from it?

The next, and climactic, section elaborates on Christ's gift of self, this time in a way that invites us to see the entire Trinity, Father, Son, and Holy Spirit, participating in the Redemption. The dreamer had earlier been told that Christ taught the angels to know truth "through the Trinity" (109) and that "truth is in the Trinity" (133). Here the language suggests that the truth of the Trinity is love: love in the concord among the three persons as they cooperate in the Redemption, love collectively extended toward human creatures as Christ dies for them on the cross. The Father restrains his power in permitting mere humans to put his son to death; the Son submits meekly and invokes no revenge upon his persecutors; rather he begs Mercy (here suggesting the love and grace traditionally associated with the Holy Spirit) to take pity on them.[31] God in the Trinity has offered humanity an experience of God's love for it, an act that, in setting aside divine power in meekness and mercy, should powerfully stimulate a natural response of love returned.

We have been emphasizing the poem's conceptual density and resulting evocative force. At the same time, Langland deploys language masterfully to achieve aural and emotional impact. He can combine complexity of reference with simplicity of diction to striking effect. For example, in the midst of the Trinitarian passage, with all its lofty reference, we read:

[the Father] Looked on us with *l*ove, and *l*et his son die
*M*eekly for oure *m*isdeeds to *m*ake us all whole.
And yet he *w*ished them no *w*oe who *w*rought him that torment
*M*eekly with *m*outh *M*ercy he besought
To have *p*ity on that *p*eople who *p*unished him to death. (167–71)

Here, it seems to me, plain words, picked out by the alliteration, convey the "humanity" and vulnerability of the divine experience.

The concluding lines of this last speech apply the divine model of truth particularly to the rich (175–87) and the clergy (188–201), that is, to the custodians of temporal and of spiritual goods.[32] The rich must do more than win their wealth "justly" (179), the clergy more than abstain from sex (188–89). Active love for others is required of all, and love is what releases God's grace (202). The language is wonderfully vigorous and concrete (e.g., 184, 188–89) and is marked by Langland's typical wordplay (e.g., on *deed, dede* in 187).

Our appreciation of Langland the poet arises most naturally from his wit and dexterity with words, images, and ideas. Puns arrest our attention and confront us with paradoxes (*dedly, deye,* 144; *mercyment,* 162).[33] When God becomes a lord surrounded by angelic knights, human institutions render the deity imaginable while encountering their defining analogue. Satan's "foot" striding away from God enlivens a traditional story while vividly dramatizing "False." Moral truisms appear in contexts that surprise them back into life (88–91). It is easier to overlook how effectively Langland manipulates larger structures of thought and image. By dividing goods, he generates a thematic rationale for the following episodes. By fusing truth with love, he creates a core resonance for truth modeled in the Trinity that will remain the poem's principle of coherence and the goal of *kynde knowyng*. For Augustine, the knowledge of the Son by the Father generated love, the Holy Spirit, expressing the relationship between the two. Truth is a way of being and of behaving; and natural, affectionate "knowing" means working to live in harmony and love.

Chapter Five
"Hard . . . to Bring This About": Kingdom and Half Acre (Passus 2– 6)

The preceding chapters considered successive passus of the poem, concentrating on shaping ideas and on some of the ways in which Langland crafts his verse. We must now move more briskly. Henceforward each chapter will offer an interpretative tour of a larger section of the poem, treating aspects of Langland's presentation and picking out thoughts and moods significant for the overall development. This chapter focuses on the events of passus 2 through 6, on Langland's use of personification allegory, and on the theme of reforming secular society.

Passus 2 to 4 and passus 6 are companion pieces. The former dramatize the problems of artificial goods in the secular kingdom, how wealth tends to corrupt justice and the law. The latter highlights natural goods, the problems of getting people to cooperate in producing the necessities of life and using them equitably. Between these two episodes, passus 5 anatomizes the causes of society's failures.

"What Is This Woman?"
The Lady Meed Episode (Passus 2– 4)

Passus 2 to 4 are perhaps the best-known part of Langland's poem: the betrothal of Lady Meed, her interrogation by the king, and her subsequent intervention in a legal case.[1] In response to the dreamer's request that Lady Holy Church show him "the false" (2.4), she points to a woman dressed in expensive clothes and fine jewelry: Lady Meed, wealthy and therefore much desired as a wife. Unfortunately, she is betrothed to False, and people like Deceit and Liar, along with False's other rich retainers, rejoice at the impending marriage. All three estates are complicit in the match (2.58), but corrupt officers of the law are especially prominent (e.g., 2.59 – 67), and the venal ecclesiastical officials Simony and Civil sanction the union in exchange for a bribe

(2.67–68),[2] then join in proclaiming a marriage contract offered by Guile. When a character named Theology suddenly appears, objecting to the marriage and insisting it be submitted to judgment in London, legal officials scramble to profit from the proceedings and influence the outcome. As this entourage sets out for London, word of them reaches the king, who orders the arrest of False and his fellowship and commands that Meed be brought before him. The venal throng learns this and scatters, leaving Meed alone to face the king.

Passus 3 opens with Meed in the king's custody. While she awaits interrogation, people about the court woo her eagerly: judges, clerks, and a strikingly corrupt friar-confessor. When the king confronts her, he rebukes her for having taken up with False but offers to forgive her if she will "marry" Conscience instead. Meed agrees quite willingly, but Conscience cries "God forbid!" The rest of passus 3 consists of a debate between Meed and Conscience about Meed's merits. She argues that Conscience has harmed the king, whereas she is useful to him because he must reward retainers and servants. But Conscience declares her to be inherently untrustworthy, a "loose woman." His concluding speech reminds the king that the reward that really matters is not earthly but heavenly.[3] As for money, wages appropriate to work in a society justly ruled are acceptable, but earthly wealth has no significance. Conscience ends his last long speech with a reminder of how a biblical king was punished for wanting wealth contrary to God's commands and how justice and law uncorrupted by wealth should be the norm in a true kingdom, exemplified by the Kingdom that will arise at the Second Coming. Meed's conclusion, quoting a verse from Proverbs out of context (which Conscience immediately corrects), serves as a emblem of her entire self-presentation: incomplete, inadequate, and unsatisfactory.

As passus 4 begins, the king tries to end the debate by having Meed and Conscience kiss and make up, but Conscience still resists. Unless Reason urges it, he will have nothing to do with her. The king dispatches Conscience to find Reason, and the two return to court, where Reason is welcomed. What follows further dramatizes Meed's untrustworthiness: Peace bursts into the court of Parliament with a complaint against Wrong, who, Peace says, has beaten him, violently injured members of his household, and stolen his goods. Again, as the case unfolds, we see legal officers and intelligent individuals succumbing to Meed's winks and blandishments. "Wisdom" tries to get the king to accept a cash settlement, Meed offers Peace a bribe to resolve the case, and clerks and confessors try to construe Reason's advice so as to bring the king financial profit. But Reason argues that cash settlements will not put an end to Wrong, that until people are prepared to act with justice and truth, until Meed is under control, real punishment is necessary. At the end of the scene, all the just, "most of the common people, and many of the power-ful" (4.159) agree that Wrong should be punished and Meed condemned as a whore. The vignette of inveterately corrupt individuals, caricatured in lines 167–70 as the courtroom scene draws to a close, is a characteris-tic touch by Langland; so too is the conclusion of this entire episode, which refuses to assure us that all is now well. We shall return to it.

Personifying Concepts

When we encounter figures such as Lady Meed, False, Conscience, Rea-son, Peace, and Wrong acting as they do in these passus, we recognize personification allegory. Langland employs this mode throughout the poem; we have already encountered varieties of it in Lady Holy Church and Truth. Because readers are sometimes struck by apparent inconsis-tencies in Langland's use of this form of allegory or by the way he com-bines it with nonallegorical elements, it merits examination.

It would be incorrect to call *Piers Plowman* a personification allegory; rather, Langland uses personification allegory along with other modes. As this mode's name implies, it depicts an abstraction as a person engaged in human activities (speaking, proposing marriage, riding for help), often interacting with individual or generic human beings (Bette the Bedle, sheriffs). These activities suggest in context some other signi-fication, for example, a corrupting interdependence between dishonesty and wealth or a desirable coincidence of secular leadership with just judgment.[4]

At the beginning of passus 2, as Lady Holy Church describes herself and Lady Meed (2.5–39), Langland personifies two women who seem to compete for our favor. Meed wears a robe of rich cloth embellished with gold ribbons and jewels, a cloak trimmed with fine fur, a crown as splen-did as the king's, and on her fingers gold rings set with the most pre-cious stones. The very sight of her captivates the dreamer: Whose wife is *she?* he asks. He learns that Meed has often harmed Lady Holy Church, has spoken ill of Leaute (fidelity)[5] and lied about him to lords responsi-ble for upholding law, and is intimately known in the pope's palace. Moreover, she is a bastard, daughter of the ever-deceitful False (who, one infers, inevitably failed to make her mother an "honest woman"), and she has inherited her father's bad habits. As for her husband, whoever marries her will lose any scrap of "charity" he might otherwise have had. On the other hand, Lady Holy Church has, along with Leaute her beloved, been victimized by Meed and must contend with her for attention at the pope's palace. All this has happened despite the fact that Lady Holy Church should be accorded a higher place than Meed; for, unlike Meed with her dubious lineage, Holy Church is not only legitimate but God's own daughter. When it comes to marriageability, God has given her Mercy as a dowry, and she stands ready to marry any merciful man who will love her faithfully; such a man will possess her forever as his beloved in heaven.

How are we to digest all these details? Let us begin by considering very briefly two useful analyses of Langland's practice. The first argues that personification allegory's "essential characteristic is that it uses abstractions as though they were concrete substances—people, places, things."[6] The characters, identified by their names (Meed, Conscience), are not themselves allegorical and do not need translation into some second meaning, but their names control our reading, and we must understand what they imply in the author's experience or culture. The allegory proper, the other significance, arises when we find the "second meaning for the pattern of relationship and activity in which the personifications are placed" (Frank, 245)—when, for example, we appreciate what a "marriage" between Meed and False implies.

Another analysis distinguishes between two kinds of allegory characterized as the "picture model" and the "disclosure model."[7] The picture model presents a static image from which abstract meanings are "read off"; its procedure is relatively wooden, typical of much medieval exegesis, encoding "truth" already "known" in an image (or finding it already encoded there) then decoding again. The picture model conveys proposition under the guise of image, like kernel under shell or fruit under chaff.[8] Thus we might decode a picture of blindfolded Justice, whose one hand holds aloft a balance scale while the other grasps the hilt of a lowered sword, as follows: she is blindfolded because Justice recognizes no favorites, holds scales because she honestly weighs out right and wrong, grasps a sword because she will, when necessary, punish severely.

The disclosure model, by contrast, is not just a shell used to encode a truth already known. Rather than beginning with a discursive proposition, independently understood, the disclosure model uses figurative language as part of the process of discovering truth. Langland uses both picture models and disclosure models, but the poet relies upon the latter for crucial passages later in the poem (especially in passus 16 and following).

What can we say of the beginning of passus 2 in light of these two sets of generalizations? First, to what extent can we find the "second meaning for the pattern of relationship and activity in which the person-ifications are placed" or "read off" the encoded "truth"? Here is one ren-dition: As for Lady Meed, her lavish dress suggests wealth to the highest degree. Such wealth has often led churchmen astray (harmed Holy Church) as well as enticed lords to fail in the enforcement of justice (slandered Leaute to them). Even the papal court (where Meed is so familiar) has succumbed to wealth and put the church's best interests aside. But such wealth is not "legitimate"; it is produced (accumulated, "gotten") through lies and deceit, and it "behaves" accordingly—it leads to unjust and deceitful acts. Anyone who seeks permanent union with and control over (to be husband and lord to) this sort of wealth, such ill-gotten gains, will not possess the love that Christians are bound to man-ifest (and so will not finally "abide in God").

As for Holy Church, how Meed has harmed her and her beloved Leaute and displaced her at the papal court is clear from what has already been said. Churchmen should give higher priority to their duties to the church than they give to getting rich. The church was instituted by Christ through the mercy that moved the Godhead, and as a result, mercy for humanity is available, through the church, to all who will be faithful to her. If they are themselves merciful ("and forgive us our tres-passes as we forgive . . ."), they will be beloved in heaven.

Does this reading render the "other meaning" completely? Certainly not. And, a closely related question, does this reading decode truth already adequately known but simply hidden in the images? Yes and no. The large truths, the fundamental propositions of Christianity, must be taken as given, as the fundamental *data* underlying Langland's poem; his allegories do not "discover" them in the process of poetic expression. On the other hand, the way his imagination realizes their interconnections and explores their moral implications for human behavior is continually revealing and provocative. His allegory is more rhetorical than epistemo-logical, dramatically leading readers to appreciation and response rather than to mere concepts or simple propositions. One could go back repeat-edly through the passage just considered and "read off" more apprecia-tions: for example, the way that Holy Church's father, "the source of all favors [grace and Redemption]" (29), contrasts with deceitful False, who seems in Meed to have begotten favors of an entirely different sort.

Langland's personification allegories are anything but static. One does not find a simple, literally consistent image that translates into a simple series of propositions. At the beginning of passus 2, for example, the image is full of literal inconsistencies. Lady Holy Church calls Leaute her beloved but soon offers to "marry" not just someone else but everyone who meets certain conditions. As for Meed, how could she marry any number of humans (suggested by line 34) and yet be about to marry the abstraction False (40 – 41)? Meed, moreover, is both familiar at the pope's palace (therefore living either at Avignon or Rome) and residing here in England about to be wed (40). And one might be incidentally distracted by the presentation in close parallel of two such different personifications (the collective institution "Church" and the abstraction "Meed"): earlier Lady Holy Church seemed the lofty and nurturing *mater ecclesia;* here the images present her as one of two women vying for our affection.

But to look for that sort of consistency is to misdirect one's attention.[9] Each concrete detail in this passage should be viewed not as a piece of a literally consistent "story" but as one in a series of associated and complementary images, each a thrust toward realizing an implication of the ideas being considered, in which words such as *marriage, daughter,* and *father* suggest relationships to be appreciated. The big truths are givens; the new truth that the poem creates lies in the vivid realization of how abstract doctrine comes alive in human experience and how human behavior appears under doctrine's light.

Frank emphasized that in order to understand personification allegory, we must properly identify its name. By this he certainly did not mean that we simply know the meaning of an allegorical figure from its name independent of the allegorical action. *Meed* and *Conscience,* for example, are words that have more than one sense in Middle English, and only the larger context in which they appear allows us surely to identify them. The Middle English word *Meed* can mean anything from wages, income, or reparation to gift or bribe (*MED,* s.v. "mede n."). When Theology objects to Meed's marriage, saying she is "legitimate" after all, is he contradicting Holy Church's assertion that she is a bastard? As the episode continues, Meed speaks up in her own defense, offering a favorable picture of herself. Even Conscience allows that she might have good points. Is Langland's Meed tantalizingly ambiguous after all? No; Holy Church introduces her in response to the dreamer's desire to learn about "the false," and what we see there is wealth in the service of False, Deceit, and their ilk. Theology later speaks of wealth's potentially good uses and protests against society sanctioning a permanent and formal "marriage" between wealth and dishonesty. Temporal goods are in themselves neutral; morality arises from how people use them. But Langland, as we have seen, has little patience for wealth and chooses to emphasize how fallen humanity seems horribly disposed to corrupt wealth and to be corrupted by it (thus we see Meed both seduced and seducing). As the episode unfolds, it makes this emphasis clear.

Conscience is another complex word; its Middle English senses ranged from "awareness, sensibility" to "excessive scrupulosity." In earlier theological discussions, the word most often signified sensitivity to the morality or immorality of one's behavior, along with the ability to recollect what one has done, both good and bad, and consequent awareness of innocence or guilt.[10] In the scholastic philosophy of the thirteenth century, the word developed a more technical sense: an act of the "practical" intellect that judges a choice to be right or wrong.[11] And we must note, especially for later episodes of the poem, that conscience is fallible—it can misjudge. But the word's central meaning in an ethical context was "a sense of right and wrong" (as instructed by Reason), and that meaning seems generally appropriate here.[12]

Of all these abstractions, Reason presents the greatest challenge to modern readers because of its distinct medieval senses.[13] The word could mean the human rational capacity, but it did not usually denote a subjective process, human intelligence puzzling through a problem. More often it implied an objective standard, the order established by God the Creator. Human intelligence can perceive that order and when so perceiving can rightly be called Reason. Behaving "reasonably" means conforming to that order (and so Reason has an intimate relationship with Truth). In *Piers Plowman*, Reason implies this standard. Of course, human intelligence and cleverness are free not to conform to Reason; thus throughout passus 4 "Warren Wisdom" and "Witty," particularized perversions of intelligence, dramatize guileful attempts to subvert Reason, Conscience, and justice.

Aers spoke of the sense in which Langland's allegory discovers truth. The poet's imagination brilliantly discovers details that enliven his allegorical fictions and lead him to explore fresh implications. For example, the "marriage charter" (2.69–107) parodies marriage contracts and similar formal documents to expose the motivations behind the union of Meed with False while dramatizing and caricaturing its circumstances and consequences (Tavormina, 20–23). When False's entourage first sets out for London, the "saddling" of "mounts" (2.162–83) dramatizes the grotesque relationships between corrupt petty officials and falsely wielded money. When "Dread at the door" overhears the king's com-

mand to apprehend the villains (2.208–12), Langland captures with a
stroke the fear such a decision would inspire in the corrupt and, simultaneously, the presence of such corruption even within the king's own
household. There are dozens of such moments throughout the poem,
more than I could possibly discuss, and I can only urge the reader to
watch for and savor them as they appear.

Finally, I would emphasize that Langland seems not in the least concerned with consistency (much less wooden consistency) in details at the
literal level of his personification allegories. Such details are means,
devices to be exploited as opportunity arises. The ideas he is putting
before his audience are not new and therefore do not require such consistency. He is concerned to characterize vividly good and evil behavior,
moral valuations that he wishes to drive home. He willingly explores
new associations in the process of developing allegorical actions and dramatizes them in turn. But his overall focus stays fixed on moving his
audience to fresh responses to, fresh recognition and application of, old
and familiar truths.

"I Shall Provide": The Half Acre (Passus 6)

In the Meed episode, Langland considered temporal artificial goods; in
passus 6 he takes up humanity's behavior with respect to temporal natural ones: food, drink, and clothing.[14] The dominant figure is Piers the
Plowman. He strides onstage at the end of passus 5, remains there
through passus 7, then disappears until later in the poem. A much richer
and more complex figure than personifications such as Conscience, Piers
seems to comprise a series of interrelated manifestations of "humanity at
its best." We will later see him as humanity before the Fall, as Christ
incarnate in human nature, and as Peter leading the apostolic church in
its pristine age. Here, in the realm of natural goods, Piers represents the
honest laborer, living and acting as Truth would have him do.[15]

Piers Plowman first offers himself as one who can lead milling and
irresolute humanity on a "pilgrimage" to "Saint Truth," in a context we
shall later examine. But his pilgrimage is postponed, or rather tem-
porarily transformed into the life of work that necessity and Truth
demand of humanity on earth. The basic action of the passus portrays
Piers plowing, sowing, and tilling the soil through one farming season,
from spring through harvest.

As Piers postpones his pilgrimage to perform his labor and others ask
what they should do in the meantime, Langland creates an opportunity

to remind everyone of the rationale for the division of labor according to estates: women should weave cloth and make clothes, knights should protect workers and control crop-threatening vermin, and religious should perform their offices in prayer and detachment. Piers tells those who ask, in effect, to perform the tasks required by their vocations and teach their children to do likewise: his own "family" exemplifies that lesson (78 –82). His "last will" (83–104), which one might make before setting out for a distant shrine, keeps the image of pilgrimage alive, and Langland uses this testament to dramatize a life lived in truth and justice. Although Piers gladly provides for all true folk and for the needy and incapacitated (16 –20, 136 –37), he rebukes the many loafers, fakers of disabilities, and religious idlers who dot the landscape, and Langland heightens the tension until Piers faces the aggressive "wasters" (152–58) who threaten simply to take what they want by force. When knighthood cannot control them,[16] Piers turns to the figure of Hunger.

If we hasten to fix Hunger with a label such as "famine," we will run into difficulties. For example, Piers summons Hunger to force the idlers to work but keeps them alive, despite Hunger's ravages, with "fodder" foods.[17] And why should Piers ask "famine" about how to avoid bellyaches from overeating? We should instead understand Hunger as the "natural need" that natural goods satisfy.[18] Such need compels Piers to work in order to remove the lack of such goods; need should be satisfied with enough, but not with too much. In other words, people should make deficit into sufficiency but avoid excess, and Piers, in the process of his labors, confronts all three conditions.

As for those who do not supply this need for themselves, if they are truly needy or the victims of misfortune, Piers should help them; if they are true religious or perform any other useful work, he should provide for them; but if they are able-bodied beggars who simply refuse to produce, Piers need give them no more than mere sustenance, meeting their minimal natural requirements in a way calculated to stir them to productivity.

When Piers invites Hunger to leave, Langland once again dramatizes dysfunctional human society. Hunger says he wants to eat his fill before departing, and Piers supplies such lean pickings as he can between harvests (280 –98). Then harvest comes, people "feed Hunger with the best" (300), and need is filled to excess. Wasters and beggars, having in their several fashions availed themselves of plenty, refuse again to work, and wageworkers will accept in return for their labor only the choicest food and the highest pay. Perhaps Langland dwells, at the end of this

scene, on landless folk who must live by their labor because they so
aptly image human "pilgrims" living in this transitory world: they will
neither work until compelled by need nor be content with such recom-
pense here as natural need requires. The prophecy with which the passus
closes serves as a reminder that this human drama unfolds in the context
of salvation history and that humanity has an ultimate end (Schmidt, B-
Text, 434, 320). Hearing the prophecy, Christians might repeat words
that Christ, in another context, spoke of himself: "I must work the
works of him that sent me, whilst it is day: the night is coming, when
no man can work" (John 9:4). The passus's final lines express fear of
"death and dearth," emphasizing society's peril yet holding out the hope
of a "truce."

"Then Repentance Ran": The Confession of the Deadly Sins (Passus 5)

In passus 5, between Meed's trial and the adventures at the half acre,
Langland presents the confession of the seven deadly sins. This justly
famous episode invites us to examine once more the poet's use of personification allegory and then to consider the role of the confession scene in
the *Visio*.

Personifying Sins

In discussing Langland's portrayal of the sins, gluttony is a good place to
begin (5.296–384). Although not typical of these portraits, it nevertheless fairly represents what modern readers expect. A Glutton sets out to
go to confession but easily succumbs when invited to stop at a tavern.
Great Oaths (306) goes in with him, and inside they find townsfolk of
many occupations. They play a game called "the new fair" (319–35), in
which they apparently gamble away the clothes off their backs.[19] Thus
they sit and carouse until evening, by which time Glutton has drunk himself sick. He relieves himself (where?), breaks wind noxiously, wobbles to
the door and falls down. When a companion heaves him up, he vomits on
him. Finally his wife and servant girl manage to get him home to bed
where he sleeps right through the weekend until Sunday night. (Not only
did he never get to confession, he has also missed Sunday mass.) And
when he wakes up, the first thing he cries is "Where's the ale cup?"
    One's reaction to this vignette should be twofold: "How revolting!"
and "Yes! That's gluttony!" The graphic details, the sounds, smells, and

sights, make the excesses of the abstract "sin" vividly concrete and disgusting. That Glutton stands for all gluttons is clear, not only from the name but also from the similar behavior of his drunken companions and from Great Oaths, who serves deftly to associate the traditional "tavern sins" with the scene.

The relationship in such writing between concrete and abstract, between literal detail and general significance, merits reflection. In one sense, general significance is paramount: Langland did not set out to describe the actions of an individual named, implausibly, Glutton; he wanted us vividly to imagine and appreciate what the generalization gluttony means. At the same time, he intended to characterize the behaviors that he describes *as sin*. A bidirectional dynamic operates: to make the general vividly comprehensible, and to identify the particular as belonging to the general category.

In this instance, personification allegory describes a complete and consistent action: we have, if you will, one Glutton's lost weekend. But it would not have mattered for personification allegory if the action were incomplete or inconsistent. And as it continues from line 363, the depiction in fact becomes less consistent: rebuked by his wife and moved by Repentance, Glutton finally confesses his sins, mentioning as he does some excesses not described in the previous scene (366–77). And so the portrait has become a composite one, including not just this sinner's behavior, which we have witnessed, but that of all gluttons.

Glutton, though generic, is nevertheless the name of a human agent. Other sins are presented as personified abstractions, as when Envy asks for absolution (75). Langland from the outset depicts this sin (75–134) as a composite, for he does not portray a sequence of acts by any one individual. Instead he gives a physical description (77, 81–82), followed by an inventory of envy's characteristically dyspeptic behaviors. The physical description is both personification and allegory: its concrete detail helps build the personified image, but because it amounts nearly to caricature, it leads us beyond any mere human individual. The habitual attitudes (e.g., sorrow at others' profit and at one's own loss) are those that could arise in any farmer or tradesman (91–104), in any villager (110–15), in any merchant (130–34). On the topic of sorrow, we see the first of a number of exchanges between Repentance and the penitents that, with wry humor, give expression to the weakened dispositions of sinners.[20] In response to Repentance's "Be sorry for your sins," Envy replies that he is always sorry, for he never avenges himself adequately (126–29).

Wrath illustrates the most explicit sort of personification allegory. The sin declares itself and speaks in the first person: "I, Wrath" (137, 148, 151, 162). This self-portrait might well strike us as especially disjointed and inconsistent as well as decidedly selective. After a brief physical caricature (135–36), Wrath's confession successively represents anger among friars, parish priests, nuns, and monks. Such focus results from satiric intent: love, not anger, should motivate these vocations. The lines vividly sketch angry intolerance, malicious gossip, and open quarrels in convents of nuns (153– 65), and they clearly invite one to visualize an angry monk being corrected by a monastic discipline that makes anger unwelcome in monasteries (172–75). They also portray friars and parish priests angrily contending for the "business" of penitents (144–52), and the shocking sense emerges that preaching, teaching, and hearing confessions can be driven not by love of God and fellow humans but by wrath.

The opening image in Wrath's confession (137– 43) presents several difficulties. As a gardener in a friary, he grafted slips onto stocks, that is, lies onto friars licensed to preach and teach in universities. The general process that the growth metaphor depicts is easy to visualize. Friars who had managed to gain access to large audiences then engaged in lax teaching so as to make themselves attractive, especially to wealthy and influential people; thinking to find them easy confessors, people abandoned their regular priests and came to the friars. Grafting slips was too ordinary to be understood as necessarily evil, but it may here suggest misappropriation of an otherwise valid practice: what are mendicants, who are supposed to lead lives of simple evangelical poverty, doing with established convents, gardeners, preaching concessions, and university posts?

But the suggestion, if we take the image seriously, that Wrath originates and motivates the process of corruption requires some thought. One could readily understand how greed, for instance, might have led the friars to encroach on the parish priests' territory, so that wrathful competition resulted. But Wrath, the image clearly says, not only is the end result of the process but also lies near its illegitimate "roots" as cause. Langland seems here to be in the tradition that, by the fourteenth century, imagined friars as the devil's minions, sent by his hatred to overthrow the church; according to this tradition, the four mendicant orders descended from Cain, who slew his brother out of wrath.[21]

The presentation of these sins through personification allegory has in no case consisted of "realistic" narrative. Even in the case of Glutton, the most straightforward, the sinner became a composite by the end, and most of the sins are composites throughout; this was, in fact, typical of the description of the sins in popular manuals.[22] Moreover even gluttony's portrait alludes to something outside the immediate fiction: its traditional association with "tavern sins" (Great Oaths and gambling). The portrait of Wrath contains not only a striking and historically conditioned emphasis on anger among religious but also an allegory within an allegory (the grafting image within the confession) that seems to depend on a particular view of the friars' origins. Understanding these allegories requires a sense of the controlling historical and conceptual context.

Confession and Repentance: Moral Anatomy

In fact these various components of passus 5 make up a larger personification allegory within an enclosing conceptual framework. Chief constituents of that framework are two ideas of confession that would have been evoked by what Langland presents. On one hand, confession was the Christian sacrament: *shrift*, the act of going to confession and receiving penance and absolution from a priest-confessor. On the other, *confessio* was a literary device, a revelatory monologue in which a speaker revealed its "character." Thus in this passus we have a series of confessions that are both revelations of human sinfulness and instances of penitential action.

That the characters portrayed here confessing are the seven deadly sins is appropriate to confession in both senses. The deadly sins constituted a traditional and useful set of categories under which all human failings against God and neighbor could be gathered and cataloged. Penitential manuals written for lay reading and instruction (e.g., Chaucer's *Parson's Tale*) were in large part inventories of sin organized under these seven headings, each with its subdivisions ("branches"); they thus both itemized all possible sins and served as an aid for penitents, helping them recognize and recall any sins they had committed. Penitential manuals written for priests were similarly organized and were used by the clergy both as sources for sermons against sin and as aids to confessors:[23] a priest was expected to prompt and quiz penitents in order to help them identify sins. This parade of the seven deadly sins, then, besides standing as a manifestation of sin in general, carries with it an aura of sacramental confession and associated penitential themes.

All seven conventional sins appear here (63– 460): pride, lust, envy, wrath, covetousness, gluttony, and sloth. We ease into the series not with an abstract "pride" but with a proud woman (*Pernele proud-herte*, 62) who renounces her finery. The second figure is just one notch more abstract, not Lust but Lecher (71). Covetousness gets most attention (108 lines), followed by Gluttony (89), Sloth (76), Envy (61), Wrath (52), Pride (8), and Lust (4). Emphasis falls especially on those sins that most impact human social interaction and the distribution of temporal goods ("distributive justice"); the lines devoted to Covetousness occupy the middle of the section. After the initial physical caricature of this composite person (188–97), we hear him confess having cheated at various trades and admiringly describe how his wife has cheated too (198–225). At this point Covetousness offers to leave sin and asks the Cross of Bromholm to "bring me out of debt" (228), initiating a topic that will haunt the remainder of the confessions. Repentance asks if Covetousness has ever repented or made restitution (230). He replies that he once stole from peddlers, and if that's not "restitution," well, it sounds like a French word to him, and he knows no French! (231–37). Although it may seem funny here, the quip reflects sadly on this character's attitude. And the deeply troubling problem of restitution will soon return in a totally serious vein.

Getting Free of Sin: Restitution and Satisfaction

What will become of Covetousness's ill-gotten gains? Perversely, he does not use them himself. The opening caricature (196–97) says that his clothing is so old, its weave so worn, that lice must leap from one thread to another. Yet, as Repentance goes on to remind him (260–78), his winnings cannot legitimately be used by anyone else: not by his heirs or executors after his death nor by some religious house (which might, in return for a bequest, pray for his soul). He cannot be absolved unless he makes restitution (270–72), and anyone who accepts those goods from him also owes restitution (274–75): a chilling thought for any thoughtful Christian in a world where goods are constantly being exchanged, deeded, bequeathed. And so this confession ends by returning to restitution.

Church law required restitution before sins that deprived others of their goods could be absolved.[24] If one stole a horse, one had to return it before one could be forgiven (or one received absolution on condition that one did everything in one's power to restore it). Covetousness reacts to Repentance's words with despair (279). How, after a career of cheating and stealing, could he possibly decide what to restore to whom? And what would he have with which to repay that was not stolen from someone else? Repentance offers him a demanding solution (281–95): Leave off buying and selling, because the only honest capital he has is his hands and his wits. That is, begin again with nothing. As for the property you now have, if you cannot decide whose it really is, give it all to the bishop and let him distribute it for you. (Then *the bishop* will be held accountable, 292–95.) Faced with restitution, the sinner who amassed property through avarice is asked to undertake a total change of life. And in a larger sense, as we shall see, what is true for Covetousness is true for all.

Sloth, the slowest, is last in this series of sins (Wenzel, *Sloth*, 135–47). In the first caricature of him (385–91), he says he has to sit down to make his confession and then immediately falls asleep. This confession too creates a composite catalog of failings: a Christian's spiritual duties shirked (393– 414), those of a parish priest carelessly left undone (415–21), slovenly behavior as a neighbor and employer (422–39), a wasted youth resulting in the lack of a trade (439 – 40). Repentance asks if he feels sorrow for his sins; but this is Sloth, who has, appropriately enough, fallen asleep once more (441). At this point a new figure appears: *Vigilate the veille* (442), "Stay-Awake, the watch keeper." *Vigilate et orate*, "Stay awake and pray," Christ had said to the apostles in the garden of Gethsemane (Matt. 26:41), words traditionally interpreted as a command to repent (Alford, *Guide to the Quotations,* 48), a command appropriate for any sinner reluctantly facing penance and reform. Note that Vigilate warns Sloth against *wanhope* (444), "despair," the disposition of those who could not bring themselves even to attempt repentance. Despair was regarded as the inevitable end of those who abandoned themselves to sin, sloth as spiritual torpor. The character Sloth thus appropriately comes at the end of the catalog. Whereas Vigilate dramatizes the injunction to repent, Sloth's behavior dramatizes the general human tendency to avoid the process.

No sooner has Sloth vowed repentance than we meet Robert the Robber (461–76), who looks at Reddite ("Pay back!") and weeps, "for he has nothing with which to repay."[25] A thief like Covetousness, Robert must make restitution; one could, in fact, be called "robber" simply for failing to restore ill-gotten goods. Langland, concerned with the use of temporal goods and fiercely advocating social justice, cared about restoring to people what was justly theirs. Without restitution, contrition was a sham. But true repentance required something more, something distinct from but analogous to restitution: *satisfactio operis*, making up to God for the offense of sin. Satisfaction included carrying out the penance assigned by the confessor and trying seriously to amend one's life.[26]

And so the series of confessions ends at Robert. A thief, he thinks of those thieves crucified with Christ (Luke 23:39 – 43) and especially of the one who exclaimed to Christ, *Memento,* "Lord, remember me when thou shalt come into thy kingdom" (5.466, Luke 23:42). Christ responded, "This day thou shalt be with me in paradise" (Luke 23:43). Dismas (the traditional name of the good thief) became the classic case of successful "deathbed confession," of snatching salvation at the very end by crying out to Christ for mercy. Because Dismas was a thief, he should have made restitution, something that under the circumstances he was hardly in a position to do. In another sense, he and all humanity are "robbers" before God: they have offended and need to make good their debt to him. Yet the Gospel says Dismas was saved. Juxtaposing Robert the Robber and Dismas asserts a delicate balance between grace and works. Langland (the "I" of lines 471–72) cannot say for certain what became of Robert, observing only that the robber confessed his sins and acknowledged that he should spend the rest of his life doing penance (imaged as a penitential pilgrimage, 474–75). No sinner can presume on Dismas's good fortune.

"Hope Seized a Horn": Sin Overcome?

Repentance concludes the series of confessions with a prayer (477–505) recapitulating salvation history. No simple narrative, the lines present a highly allusive blending of phrases from liturgy and Scripture suggesting a formal prayer (Alford, "Repentance," 22–26), proclaimed by an officiating minister interceding for the congregation of sinners. Yes, the words say, humanity is fallen, its inclinations depraved. But in response to Adam's fall ("A sickness to us all," 482), Christ became man and died in a human body. This union of deity and humanity, this intimacy between God and humankind, seems such a positive thing that the sin that instigated it becomes "happy fault, necessary sin" (483a, words from the Easter hymn). The sorrow of death was overcome, heaven reopened, and this was accomplished expressly for the sinful (epitomized by Mary Magdalen, 497–98). In the face of human weakness and sin, of the painful process of restitution and satisfaction, this prayer joyously and eloquently reaffirms the possibility of mercy and restoration. There is reason to hope.

Now Hope appears (506 –509), aroused by Repentance's prayer and the people's penitential mood, reciting psalm verses appropriate to that mood. In this dense and suggestive allegory, Hope's *horn* probably derives from Psalm 17:3, "God . . . is my protector and the horn of my salvation, my support" (Schmidt, *B-Text*, 429, 507). It becomes an instrument proclaiming God's saving power, one that can be activated ("sounded") by the penitential actions of humanity: Psalm 31 (line 507) was one of the penitential psalms associated with repentance;[27] it speaks of those who acknowledge their sins in seasonable time (verses 5– 6). Hope's seizing and blowing his horn suggests a moment of response by humanity, a gesture at cooperating with grace through prayer and penance. Acknowledging this gesture, those already in heaven join, like a cosmic chorus, in beseeching God's mercy for all sinners still on earth.

The vigor of Langland's imagination, which gives us leaping lice and slumbering Sloth, Envy's "sorrow" and Covetousness's "restitution," Wrath's grafted trees and Hope's horn, stimulates imaginative involvement and reaction. For an audience familiar with liturgy and Scripture and intimately aware of these larger themes, a tour de force such as Repentance's final prayer must have been quite moving. For all the flashes of humor and irony, for all the brilliance of detail, the episode results in a vivid, comprehensive impression: human sinfulness, the promise of redeeming grace, and the question of whether humanity will manage to respond in deed.

"Unless the Commons Will Agree": Conclusions

What role does the confession scene play in the whole of the *Visio*? The first dream, exploring the possibility of justice and the elimination of bribery and venality in the kingdom, ended inconclusively. In response to the king's declaration that "I will have fidelity to law" (4.180), Conscience replied, "Unless the commons will agree to this / It is very difficult, in my opinion, to bring this about, / And to lead all your people thus equitably" (4.182–84). The king repeats his intention to rule according to Reason and Conscience. But can Reason prevail? Will the commons consent?

As passus 5 begins and Reason preaches, the poem considers these questions. The scene is once again the field of folk (10). Reason, in the presence of the king and holding a cross, prepares to address the entire kingdom like a bishop, whose ceremonial cross (crosier) signified his office of teacher and spiritual leader. Formal sermons by bishops before kings were a fact of English life, but besides suggesting this sort of occasion, what else does the scene accomplish?

It is reasonable, in fourteenth-century terms, to understand that diseases and natural disasters occur in response to the unreasonableness of human behavior (13–23); reasonable people should take such occurrences as indicators of their sins, intended as warnings and correctives. Reason's sermon goes on to describe in practical and obvious terms what reasonable behavior ought to be (24–59): for common man or woman; in domestic discipline (wife, child, servant); for priests, prelates, and religious; and for king and pope. The sermon ends (52–59) directing lawyers to long for truth (justice) and pilgrims to seek Truth (God), complementary objects of the human quest; no walk of life, whether lay or religious, can deny truth and be saved. The entire speech has, in fact, been about truth, for to acknowledge and conform to Reason is to be true and to arrive, finally, at Truth in heaven.

This implied confrontation between the people and Reason, between humanity in its actual state and the measure (stated in everyday terms) of what it should be, activates Repentance: "Then Repentance 'ran' and repeated Reason's theme / And caused will to weep water from his eyes" (60 – 61). As in the actual confessions, we can imagine Repentance either as another cleric, helping Reason the preacher, or as a disposition arising in people who acknowledge their failures. *Ran* (60) can mean "hurried, hastened, moved about quickly," and in this sense it suits Repentance the confessor; but, the word can also mean "become current, be present,"[28] and this sense suits repentance the disposition. The senses are complementary. Similarly "Will" (61) can be a name (common as Tom, Dick, or Harry) or suggest *voluntas,* "the human will," the aspect of the soul that loves and hates, sins and repents, and chooses from what the intellect presents to it. The confessions of the seven sins take place in this context of "repentance" moving "will" to weep.

When the confession scene has ended, poised between Robert the Robber's fear of Reddite and Hope's blowing his horn, the people seem disposed to change. A thousand thronged together and asked for the grace to "go to Truth," but no one knew the way, so "they blundered about like dumb beasts over dales and hills" (510 –14). Robert the Robber had acknowledged that he should undertake a life of penance, a penitential pilgrimage (474–77). At the end of his opening sermon, Reason had enjoined pilgrims to seek "Saint Truth" (57–58). Here the image of pilgrimage appears once again, capturing the alternatives facing the people and dramatizing the difference between confession and reform.

Pilgrimage could represent two very different activities. As a difficult journey to a distant shrine, undertaken with a reverent and prayerful disposition and in the face of physical hardship, pilgrimage constituted a genuine act of penance. Traveling through the world while making minimal use of its comforts, bent on arriving at a sacred destination, offered a model for life on earth: all Christians are pilgrims on their way to the New Jerusalem. On the other hand, the poem has, from its outset, satirized so-called pilgrimages that are merely physical journeys undertaken for worldly motives by pilgrims and palmers who seem most bent on tall tales and lies (Pr.46 –52), the self-declared hermits who go to Walsingham with their wenches (Pr.53 –57), and those fakes who journey about the land in search of bodily satisfaction (Pr.29 –30). Such travel is, at best, busywork that obstructs genuine spiritual activity and preempts the real and difficult tasks of restitution and satisfaction. Penance and reformation require the changing of attitude and behavior.

If the people had better teachers, if priests and religious set good example, there would be someone to "show them the way." The lack of such example and sound teaching is a theme echoing through the poem. Here, Piers Plowman is about to make his first appearance. He will try to direct the people in the "way" required of them, a life led according to the Ten Commandments and the laws of the church, lived according to their Christian faith, which will produce truth within themselves, sitting in their hearts (5.561– 606). Anyone who has read the confession scene thoughtfully will realize this is no easy way; people do not eagerly undertake a journey to that "country."

The end of passus 5 typifies Langland: a mixture of satire and sardonic humor, of sublime Christian optimism and a refusal simply to invent a happy ending. A pickpocket and a monkey-training entertainer recognize no "kin" among the virtues in the country Piers described (630 –31).[29] Piers adds one more word of encouragement (634–38). In the place he spoke of, Mary-mercy is a maid all-powerful, close kin to all sinful, as is her Son; one can confidently expect grace from them—if one asks in time. But instead of asking, a pardoner retrieves his worthless indulgences, and a prostitute follows him offstage—and Langland's "I" does not know what became of them. Does this cast of unsavory characters represent the whole people, all the commons, by a kind of synecdoche? That is the question Langland poses, the challenge he issues, and the answer depends ultimately upon the lives of his audience. Meanwhile, the experience of the half acre, as it unfolds, shows that the commons have not yet found the way.

Chapter Six

"Come If We Would": Pardon and Quest (Passus 7–11)

"Truth Heard Tell Hereof": The Pardon (Passus 7)

Passus 6 ended with an apocalyptic warning about the failure of the half acre, about how the human community, flawed by wasters and idle takers, will fail to sustain itself with natural goods—"unless God, out of his goodness, grant us a truce" (6.331). As if to supply that truce, passus 7 opens with Truth/God responding to Piers's plight, "purchasing" for him "a pardon *a pena et a culpa*" (7.1–3). Langland is about to play a trick on his audience, seeming to offer easy answers only to reject their efficacy.

Toward the end of passus 7 (174–84), Langland's speaker will remind himself of the doctrine of pardons (indulgences); chapter 2 discussed it in some detail. Even a full pardon (plenary indulgence) could not, by itself, remove the guilt of sin, and prerequisite for relief from punishment was a good confession, which included honest resolve to sin no more. Pardon *a pena et a culpa* had been "purchased" only when Christ died on the cross. Availing oneself of that pardon meant receiving the sacraments (especially baptism and confession) and living according to Christ's teaching. Educated Christians formally believed this, but the understandable human longing for easier terms spawned the activities of the pardoners excoriated by Langland, Chaucer, and others.

Langland's dramatic announcement of Piers's pardon thus has a twofold effect. In a world where lax clerics offer easy indulgences, it momentarily suggests some reprieve from the daily battle against fallen nature and the struggle for virtue. At the same time, it makes his audience take a fresh look at the Redemption, which was indeed the most momentous pardon imaginable. The tension between too facile hope and genuinely remarkable deliverance simmers through the whole passus to reach a rolling boil when the pardon's "text" is read and rejected by the priest (107–18).

Until that point, a reader might cling to the wish for a less-demanding reprieve, for the poem speaks of the pardon as a document, a writ of indulgence *(bulle)* that specifies and excludes beneficiaries according to estate and profession (5–106). The pardon includes laborers, kings and knights, bishops and church lawyers, and the image of a writ underlies details such as the "many years in the margin" granted to merchants. But at the same time, the attentive reader notices how the writ includes people not because of externally determined estate or profession but because of behavior: workers who work, kings and knights who preserve justice, bishops and church officials who teach and correct, merchants who generously share their profits. Lawyers who, in exchange for using the wit God gave them, extort fees from poor innocents enmeshed in lawsuits have "very tiny pardon" (40 – 60), while beggars who fake infirmities (65 – 69) or, worse, breed bastards and then maim them to render them more pitiable (90 –99) have no pardon at all.[1] Pardon corresponds to deeds.

When we finally see this pardon's text, we find no reprieve independent of human effort. The Latin, quoted from the Athanasian Creed, simply says: "and those who have performed good works will go into eternal life; but those who [have performed] evil works into eternal fire."[2] The priest translates accurately enough (116 –18), articulating for the first time the *do wel* that the next passus will pursue. The explicit words of the pardon ("eternal life," "eternal fire") and the priest's rendition (it tells who shall "have thy soul," 116, 118) point to death and judgment. Indeed, in the creed from which they are drawn, the pardon's lines refer not only to judgment but to the Last Judgment at the Second Coming.[3] The opening lines of the passus frequently refer to death and judgment (e.g., 11–12, 17, 37, 51, 99). The pardon is the Redemption, its text the creed, and Langland reminds his audience of what they intellectually acknowledged as the inevitable "last things": death, judgment, heaven, and hell. The pardon reasserts perspective.

Granted this perspective, does the pardon actually offer any "pardon" at all? The passage evokes the vacuous, indeed betraying, blandishments of pardoners only ruthlessly to deny them efficacy. Affirmed in their place stands the real truce, the desperately needed pardon of the Redemption. Before the Redemption, without sanctifying grace or helping grace, humanity was incapable of doing well. Now, through and with grace, it can. And, Langland reminds his audience, every Christian soul, for its own dear sake, had better try. The pardon is real, but conditioned.

Has Langland thus abandoned temporal kingdom and half acre? The people's desperate need for a truce at the end of passus 6 arose in the context of society in this world; has that truce now become Piers's pardon, wresting our attention in an entirely different direction? No, but Langland believed that the restoration of secular society employing temporal goods depended finally upon Christian society using spiritual ones, so he has forced a fundamental shift in perspective. The inability of people in passus 5 to leave sins once acknowledged and pursue Truth ensured that the community would fail to assent in the justice required for the kingdom, fail to cooperate in the labor required in the half acre. Underlying the logic of the poem's development is the idea that remaking temporal society depends upon the moral restoration of its individual members. That restoration requires a laborious process and all the grace the Redemption makes possible, all the effort with which humanity can respond, and consequently all the motivation the poet can supply. Those unmoved by pleas for social justice and love might yet be stirred by forceful reminders of how enormous are their personal stakes when they consider life from the perspective of eternity. These truths are medieval commonplaces; the poem has led the audience, caught up in the frustrations of the half acre and yearning for truce, to confront them anew.

The priest's reaction to the pardon should disturb: a minister of the new dispensation of grace expects indulgence and, implicitly but unmistakably, rejects the terms of the Redemption. Although the Christian community depends upon him for instruction as well as for the sacraments, he will clearly not provide crucial teaching, certainly not teaching by example. Piers's "unmitigated vexation" (*pure tene*, 119) and tearing of the document reject not the Redemption but the priest's too comfortable expectations.[4] The Redemption offers neither the blanket dismissal of sin wished for by the priest nor a guarantee that weakened nature will never sin again. Rather, the Redemption presents a path to forgiveness and effortful reform. Piers seems to understand these terms immediately. The quotation from Psalm 22:4 (120–21) expresses confidence that, at the point of judgment ("in the midst of the shadow of death"), Christ the Good Shepherd will support him, but Piers understands that he must cooperate. The previous verse of this psalm describes how the shepherd has led his flock "on the paths of justice" (Ps. 22:3), and Piers undertakes to attend more closely to contrition and repentance (122–35). Reflecting the poem's shift in perspective from natural to spiritual goods, Piers will henceforth pay more attention to the "bread" of penitence and less to his physical livelihood.[5] Even Piers, the manifestation of the best in human nature, sins and must do penance.[6] The *Visio*'s second dream closes on juxtaposed responses of priest and Piers to the possibilities of Redemption and restoration.

What, meanwhile, has become of the pilgrimage to Truth? In granting the pardon at the opening of passus 7, Truth bade Piers "stay at home
and plow his fallow fields" (5). At the end of the pardon scene, Piers does
not say he will stop plowing altogether, but he will not devote all his
efforts to it: "Work not so hard, nor be so busy about my livelihood"
(122–23). Earlier, he said that "now old and hoar," he would set out on
"pilgrimage" (6.83–84). Nevertheless, although this recalls a literal penitential pilgrimage, it turns out to be his "pilgrimage" at the plow
(6.102, 105), just as the poem had called him "pilgrim" in his vocation
(6.57, 64). As Piers's reaction to the pardon illustrates, and as all the
poem's urgings to moral behavior confirm, the pilgrimage denotes the
journey from this life toward Truth in the next and, meanwhile, toward
truth in one's life on earth. The journey to that personal truth, in pursuit
of spiritual goods, becomes the new subject of the poem.

Introducing the *Vita*

We noted as far back as the prologue that the speaker-dreamer's voice
can merge with that of Langland. This happens again in the interlude
between the second and third dreams (7.145–8.66). Some lines show
the poet very sure of what the pardon means, addressing his audience
directly (e.g., 7.187–206). This voice declares that people must act well,
that to any pardon they must add penance and prayers (7.183), and that
what they do "day by day" (7.196), the "works" that they "work"
(7.204), will determine how God will finally judge them. But just as
clearly we hear the voice of the speaker (e.g., 7.145–53, 8.1– 66), and
some lines could come from either voice or from one becoming the other
(7.154–86).

The poet, of course, seeks not merely to intone truth that his audience already knows. He intends to dramatize its discovery and to
orchestrate its emerging implications through the adventures of his protagonist. And so we never entirely lose sight of the speaker-dreamer,
mulling over what he has "seen" as his thoughts and feelings become
engaged in the fate of Piers and the nature of his pardon (151).

"For to Seek Dowel": Beginning a Quest (Passus 8)

As the poem opened, the speaker traveled about to "hear wonders"
(Pr.4). Now, in the prologue to subsequent adventures in passus 8, he
roams "in order to seek Dowel" (8.2). His quest, though not yet neces-

sarily personal, is nevertheless focused. Although we sense that Langland the poet knows very well what "do well" means, the speaker does not. The verb plus adverb (do wel, 7.116) of the pardon quickly becomes an abstract noun, dowel (7.174), and, by passus 8, even a personification: where does "this man" Dowel "lodge" (8.4–7), where does he "live" (13)? When Langland personifies an abstraction such as "covetousness" (passus 5), he renders it more palpable and vivid. Here, personification serves as the last stage of abstraction, making the concrete and palpable (acts of good behavior, already described in numerous concrete instances) into a vague generalization whose meaning must be rediscovered. By this tactic, Langland invents a problem motivating a quest.

But what audience would care about a wholly artificial quest? Indeed, it is also real. First, although personification serves here to create an abstraction, the search for "this man Dowel" makes perfect sense if understood another way. For how can human beings know Dowel naturally unless they see actual people doing well?[7] Second, the priest's reaction to the pardon reflects a recurrent Christian query: If the Redemption has given humanity God's grace, then what need we do? If God is with us, who can stand against us? Any Christian baptized into the dispensation of grace must wonder just how much personal effort "do well" requires. Third, as we think back on the first two dreams, we recall that humanity, even though redeemed, exists in an appalling state; society is rent by selfishness and sin, and even the dispensation of grace (Christian teaching and the sacraments) lies in the hands of mercenary wretches. Why has the Redemption so little impact on human society? Any member of Langland's audience, having accepted the truth conveyed by the poet's voice at the end of passus 7, could still care a great deal about what the dreamer might discover concerning Dowel. And each could see, modeled in the dreamer's reluctance and resistance, his or her own reactions and responses. Most people, when told that the world is wretched, are quick to point at those others who make it so; told that they themselves are the problem, they resist acknowledging it; forced to acknowledge their own culpability, they respond grudgingly and in minimal fashion. And so we follow the speaker-dreamer with both sympathy and curiosity.

The Friars' "Example"

The speaker first questions two friars (8.8–61). To their claim that Dowel dwells with them, he has an explicit and an implicit rebuttal:

implicitly, Dowel cannot be among them because (as we have repeatedly seen) friars are sinners;[8] explicitly, the Bible says even the just fall seven times daily, so at least sometimes Dowel must be elsewhere (20–25). Beneath the zesty surface of this challenge lies a serious question: If humans are sinners, how can they do well? How are Dowel and sin compatible?

Unfortunately the friar's explanatory "example" (26–56) serves to obscure the issue utterly, blending truism with self-justifying nonsense. It asserts, first, that what may appear as sins induced by world, flesh, and devil are merely venial, falls of the soul-man knocked down within the body-boat, and that serious sin results from acts of the will, which remain interior and invisible. Dowel becomes "charity the champion," strengthening and teaching within (45–46, 56), not only invisible but portrayed as some external force (Christ? grace?) rather than any virtue or quality generated by the individual.[9] Because observable acts are not deadly sins (a nonsensical generalization), the friars are not serious sinners. But the unspoken consequence of this position is that their lives can illustrate Dowel no better than their "example" can. No wonder the speaker gets no "natural understanding" from them (57). Although the farewells appear amicable, one can easily read sarcasm in the speaker's parting words: May Christ "give you the grace to *become* good men" (61).

The Inward Journey

The encounter with the friars suggests the dreamer will find little help in his waking world, even should he travel through it widely (something at which both he and the friars excel). And so, still seeking Dowel, he wanders on and once more falls asleep (62–67). As the new dream unfolds, we follow the dreamer on a kind of inward journey; he now seems to travel not widely through the world but more introspectively.[10] His experience is not subjective, involving the dreamer's unique, personal inner life. Rather the dream surveys what Langland regarded as commonly available, shared human experiences and potentialities. We now learn that the dreamer's name is Will and are invited to associate him with the human power of choice. We see him encounter mental processes, abilities, and vulnerabilities represented by Thought, Wit, Study, Clergy,[11] Scripture, and finally Ymaginatif. How does "will" respond to knowledge, the knowable, learning, and what learning can manipulate? What are the relationships between knowledge and Dowel? The focus of the poem gradually narrows to the individual

human being, the "atom" of society. The dreamer will end in a fundamental self-confrontation, become personally involved in his quest for
the first time, and emerge a changing man.

Thought: "Dowel, Dobet, and Dobest the Third"

Beginning his journey within, Will encounters Thought, a man "like
myself" (70), so intimately familiar as to suggest identity.[12] Thought
seems to represent the notions, opinions, and frame of mind one might
discover upon first seriously turning one's attention to a topic—the
dreamer first "taking thought," considering such notions as might occur
"off the top of his head."[13]

No sooner is Thought asked about Dowel than he introduces the
"three do's" that have so preoccupied students of the poem. Dowel,
Dobet, and Dobest illustrate a fundamental technique of human thinking, that same sort of hierarchical *divisio* that produced the categorization of goods discussed earlier. They also reflect a deep instinct of
human nature, measuring and delimiting moral imperatives (I must do
this much, I need not do that much—how high must I jump?). But
once Thought has put them into play, subsequent figures use them as an
extraordinarily versatile device for exposition and argument, one capable
of proposing comparisons, relationships, interactions, and tensions.[14]
Critics once believed Langland sought to define through them three different states of life or standards of perfection. Now they generally agree
that the poet employed them as a rhetorical and expository tool destined
to suggest not separable alternatives but complementary stages of a
continuum.[15]

Thought's presentation of the three do's (78–110) suggests both internal and external characteristics. They are virtues close at hand (79), ranked
in excellence and scope: Dowel corresponds roughly to justice (80–84),
Dobet adds humility and generosity (85–95), Dobest the correction of
others (96–99).[16] But Thought's presentation also inevitably suggests
another, more external, triad: laity, clergy, and episcopacy. Rather than
finding this inconsistent, we should appreciate how it expresses a continuum: while the laity should be just, even more is required of the clergy, and
most of bishops.[17] The idealizing quality of Thought's do's stands out in his
portrayal of society and its rationale (especially 100–110) as Dowel and
Dobet establish kingship to protect Dobest—a theocracy in which secular
power serves the City of God. Reminiscent of the establishment of kingship
in the prologue, Thought's formulation nevertheless presents a distinctly

spiritual point of view; in contrast to the *Visio,* images of society in the *Vita* will consistently see it from this perspective.

Thought's account of the three do's contains no errors, but his concluding words emphasize an external hierarchy in which clergy, episcopacy, and king are prominent. No wonder the dreamer asks how "Dowel acts among the [ordinary] people" (114). Wit comes along to address that very question, indeed to consider how Dowel acts *within* people.

"Man with a Soul": Wit (Passus 9)

With Wit, Langland seems to be saying: Very well, let us step back from these first-order reflections of Thought. What, more generally, can human intelligence, Wit, tell us about human beings and how they should behave? Operating by itself (natural intelligence) and with help from revelation (here the book of Genesis), what "big picture" does Wit see?[18] Once again, Langland intends to affirm Christian truth: A human being consists of immortal soul in mortal body, placed on earth eventually to be recalled to the Creator. Therefore soul and body, indeed the entire microcosmic "society" of powers within the human being, should cooperate for the soul's ultimate good; human intellect, aware of the soul's end, should guide that interior society accordingly. Exterior society, notably that most basic and natural institution, marriage, should foster the interior one. Once again, the poet presents truth not as bald assertion but through a combination of concept, image, and scriptural quotation. The individual sections of passus 9 seem vivid and straightforward; let us focus on how tightly, and how powerfully, they interact.[19]

The nature of human being as soul in body is neatly conveyed by the opening image (1–24) of beloved lady Anima (soul) in protective castle *caro* (body). The Dowel, Dobet, and Dobest of these lines, personified as people who have duties about the castle, represent behaviors that function to protect and support Anima—the clear implication being that "doing well" means precisely taking care of this lady. Dowel is the duke in whose land the castle stands, Dobet a lady-in-waiting for Anima, Dobest a resident chaplain and spiritual guide. Their relationship is consistent with Thought's depiction of them, though in this image they are internalized, part of the interior society of the castle.

On the other hand, Sir Inwit (18), who governs the castle, clearly represents a particular power, or faculty, of the soul. In medieval psychology, *soul* was the term for the entire spiritual entity, while various aspects of its operation (e.g., memory, intellect, will) could be conceived of and named *as if* they were separate beings.[20] Thus although Anima actually "inhabits" the entire body (56), Langland is free to associate her most closely with heart and desire (57)—she is, after all, Kynde's beloved—while emphasizing Inwit's governing operation "in the head" (58–59). *Inwit* might best be translated as "intellect," for he represents the human rational ability applied to taking care of Anima's best interests.[21] Intellect was imagined as containing both male and female components, one concerned with eternal things, the other (its "helpmate") with earthly things (e.g., nourishment).[22] As long as these two cooperate, "wife" attentive to "husband" and "husband" to God, they exist in "chaste wedlock," but when intellect is seduced by carnal desires, the couple reenacts Adam and Eve's Fall.[23] Thus "first wife" (19) suggests the pristine union, the harmonious integration of the soul, in the state of natural justice before the Fall; it reminds us of the origins of marriage and contrasts with the decline from it by Adam and Eve and their descendants (9.121– 47). The couple's "five fair sons" suggest the five senses well used (the functions of *caro* well "begotten" and well "fostered").[24] So within the microcosmic household of the human body-soul there should exist a microcosmic marriage and family cooperating in harmony, governed by an intellect aware of its nature and duties.

Wit's first speech ends with Anima in the castle awaiting *kynde* (24). As the dreamer interrupts asking about *kynde*, Langland reminds his readers of a fundamental principle already underlying Wit's images, that people should naturally act according to what they are: *Kynde*/Nature (God the former and shaper) endowed humanity with a *kynde*/nature in conformity with which it should *kyndeliche*/naturally function. God gave humans a spirit derived from the Godhead, life that endures; his creation *caro* is "man with a Soul" (47–51). But the language further endeavors to engage by reworking a familiar idea.

In the Genesis account, God created with his word (*dixit et facta sunt*, "he spoke and they were made," line 33a). Only when creating humanity did God say *faciamus*, "let us *make* mankind to our image and likeness" (Gen. 1:26, quoted at lines 36 and 43). Commentators on this verse regularly seized on "let us make" (plural) and "image" (singular) as revealing the Trinity, three persons in one God; they went on to ask how humanity was particularly like God, giving central place in their answer to the immortality of the soul. Langland reminds us of all this and that humanity, created in the image of the Triune God, resembles God precisely in its immortal soul and so should treasure that soul as its distinguishing characteristic and glory. But the poet seems to suggest something more. The persons of the Trinity cooperated actively in creating their human image: the assertion that "work" or "workmanship" must be added to "word" sounds throughout the passage (38, 44, 45– 46, 52). So the society within the image must act cooperatively, adding act to being, performance to nature, thus realizing the likeness of the actively cooperating Trinity that created it.[25]

The next section of the passus (61–109) pursues the idea of Inwit and develops the theme of natural fostering. Given human nature, what must Inwit do? It must not overindulge the body, imitating the devil rather than God. On the other hand, many whose Inwit is ineffectual lack adequate nourishment for castle *caro* and guidance for Anima, and Christians (singled out are godparents and bishops) have an obligation to use Inwit to provide for the temporal and spiritual needs of those in their charge. Given Kynde's purpose and humanity's *kynde,* temporal goods and the fruits of the Redemption (*cristes good,* 89; *patrimonium christi,* 94a) are an inheritance (patrimony) from Creator and Redeemer, left to all his children. Not to dispense and share them according to nature is to show no respect for Kynde—to "do not well" (95). Thus the section closes by recasting the three do's with which Wit began: to act according to *kynde* out of fear for God's wrath is at least to respect nature; to act according to nature out of love is much better; best of all is to employ fully one's intelligence and energy, not only to provide temporal goods for castle *caro* (107–9) but also to strengthen and encourage Anima as it awaits its end (100 –106).[26]

Inwit is one strand tying Wit's speech together; another is family. As Tavormina notes (66, 70), the middle passage just discussed also concerns the larger "social family" of Christians. And beginning with line 110, Wit focuses on literal marriage: part of God's creating human *kynde,* and part of his image in humanity, was his creation of Eve as help- mate and his institution of marriage (115–20). As Tavormina aptly comments, Adam and Eve, like the Trinity, are plural persons in one nature, and "the cooperation of the divine persons in human creation finds its image in the mutual help of man and woman in human procre- ation" (60 – 61). Husband and wife do well to propagate the species in "good time" and for the right reason and to foster their children. Such marriage is "the natural, divinely-established 'production plan' for Dowel's continuing presence among human beings, the dynamic process whereby Dowel is constantly regenerated along with the species" (Tavormina, 82). Marriages for money or for lust (e.g., marrying off young girls to spent old men, 166) are unnatural; they recall Adam's

begetting Cain "out of season" (121–25, 187–88) and the bad marriages, described in Genesis 6, that brought down God's wrath in the
Flood.[27] The sexual drive, so likely to rage out of control, should *kyndeliche* be harnessed within a loving and productive marriage (182–86a).
The Fall originated human vulnerability to passion; succumbing to passion replicates biblical Fall and bad marriages and deserves Kynde's displeasure.

Wit closes by returning to the three do's. At the beginning of his
speech, they were imaged as three separate agents, though all seemed to
assume roles within the human castle. Midway they were degrees of
respect for Kynde; finally they are three complementary stages of love.
Dowel is to love and restrain oneself according to law (the law of nature
seems especially appropriate here); Dobet adds generosity to restraint
("to love and to give," 204). Dobest in turn adds that active and ener-
getic care for others that "brings arrogance low . . . that is, wicked will
which ruins many works and drives away Dowel through deadly sins"
(208–10).[28] Throughout the passus, human desire opposing *kyndeliche*
behavior has begotten sorrow and chaos; Wit asserts that active love
must keep "unnatural" will at bay.

"So Shall You Come to Clergie" (Passus 10)

Dame Study opens passus 10, bursting in to deliver a diatribe against
her husband, Wit, that draws on the convention of shrewish wives
(5–139). The dramatic interplay between the characters is lively, and
Study's indignation finds expression in vivid and colorful language, but
while savoring its liveliness we should note the underlying logic. Study
personifies industrious effort to apply human ability and intellect for
whatever purpose, and so we witness the idealized application of human
capability belaboring human intelligence for allowing itself to be misdi-
rected.[29] Wit's reaction to Study and to Will (140 – 46) perhaps recalls
dramatically that according to medieval psychology, the human will
actually governs application of intellect. Study's speech continues the
examination of human conduct while Wit's recommendations are still
fresh in the audience's mind. How do people actually behave? For what
ends do they actually expend their effort, their industry, and their zeal?

Study begins by castigating humanity's pursuit of the wrong objects.
Too many study to acquire and maintain wealth but not to use it properly. The sort of study they patronize is that of ribald entertainers rather
than of honest minstrels, of advisors skilled in sharp practice and dis-

honest trickery rather than in justice. Such patrons support not teachers of plain truth about the Redemption and the charitable management of wealth but false friars who preach clever, misleading sermons and so confuse folk rather than lead them to firm faith and penitence. Thus the "study" of most—both patrons and patronized—is locked in a vicious spiral of selfishness, abusing goods both temporal (wealth) and spiritual (intellect and faith). In this context, study of the Christian faith descends to "slobbering" over religious subjects, corrupted just like the overindulgence in food and drink at the tables of the rich (57–58). The lord and lady who dine in separate quarters lest the hungry disturb them, while chattering inanely and self-indulgently over garbled theology, vividly illustrate the moral and intellectual isolation of such people.

Responding to this diatribe (and to Wit's discomfiture), Will humbly asks Study to instruct him about Dowel, and Study directs him to Clergy: thus we turn to "study" specifically as pursuit of learning. What follows might best be read as a paradigm rather than as biography. That is, rather than allegorically suggesting the dreamer's academic career, the poem presents a consideration of how well-disposed will might apply intellect in order to generate useful learning.[30] In response to the dreamer's request for directions, Study describes the "high road" to Clergy: real learning demands that one set aside interest in wealth and self-indulgence. In response to Will's request for some token by which he might induce Clergy to receive him, Study offers a description of Clergy's lineaments and history, the background information that might induce a teacher to accept a new student.

Clergy represents the learning that Study has established through history, from the seven liberal arts, which constitute learning's foundation, to the higher sciences, with theology at their summit.[31] Scripture represents learning's product, writing in general, and particularly theology's wellspring, Holy Scripture.[32] Human study has produced not only the works of classical learning (Aristotle, "Cato") but also the accumulated skills of building in wood and stone and even the "bad" sciences (212–21) that, upon reflection, should be rejected as merely deceiving. Notice Study's evaluation of Theology, queen of the sciences (185–92): overly subtle delving into mysteries vexes and misleads; only the fact that the central message of the New Testament is, inescapably, love of God and neighbor has kept theology on track. Dowel is love, and this core sets Christian "science" off from that of the pagan classics.[33]

Properly approached, Clergy and Scripture prove hospitable. Given Study's caution about Theology, we should not find Clergy's version of the three do's surprising. As if to avoid all intellectual excesses, science (and theological science at that) defines Dowel as something that exceeds its grasp, as faith in what it cannot demonstrate: an ordinary way of life, accepting the articles of the creed and that specifically Christian mystery, the Trinity (238–56). Dobet adds accepting all consequences such faith demands—including an injunction, with a Trinitarian ring, to realize in action the image of the Trinity in which it was made, to practice what it professes.[34] Dobest follows logically: Correct others only when you live correctly yourself. Most appropriately, Clergy proceeds to address the clergy, priests and religious within whose domain literacy and learning especially resided and whose task it was to teach and guide people, to "work" God's word. Clergy upbraids them for their hypocrisy and threatens apocalyptic disenfranchisement unless they reform their lives.[35]

In defining Dowel as "to bileue" (238), does Clergy depart from the consistent refrain of all the dreamer's informants thus far that Dowel is behavior, is love? I think not, for three reasons. First, to believe "in conformity with law" (*lelly,* 240) already implies more than mere intellectual assent. Second, the emphasis on the Trinity, and on Augustine's account of it, must recall how the Trinity created human nature in its image and that to realize this image, humanity must add performance and action to being and belief; moreover Christ, witness to the Trinity and center of Christian faith (252–52a), is the working of divine love incarnate. Finally, the exchange between Will and Scripture that follows explicitly defeats any attempt to understand belief narrowly.

Will's apparently naive and literal-minded response to Clergy (336), although superficial, is not entirely silly. Clergy has concluded by describing, at some length, Dobest as an avenging king: are Dowel and Dobet lower degrees of this kind of secular power, for example, lordship and knighthood (*dominus* and *knyghthode*)?[36] Scripture steps in to correct Will, and from this point, driven by Will's contentiousness, the tone becomes that of clerkly debate. As the fundamental wellspring of theological learning, Scripture plays a vital role in religious argument: text generates proposition, opposing proposition countertext. The broad lines of her first speech (337–48) invoke a famous Pauline passage[37] to argue that wealth (implicit in rank and power, *dominus* and *knyghthode*), precludes Dowel; other writings both biblical and classical (Ecclesiastes and Cato) agree. Patriarchs, prophets, poets, and apostles (thus all the works of the Old and New Testaments) urge "poverty with patience" instead.[38]

In turn, the dreamer responds with his own verse from Scripture (350), articulating an extremely comfortable position: To do well and be saved is simply to be a baptized Christian. This attempts to trivialize Clergy's Dowel (*to bileue,* 238). Scripture replies with a characteristic theological rebuttal, a distinction that—quite correctly in terms of medieval doctrine—denies that the verse means what the dreamer wants it to except in the case of those baptized at the point of death (*in extremis,* 352). Her urging of love and generosity (e.g., 357, 360 – 68) and the biblical verses she cites are powerfully apt. The "two great commandments" appear in 360 – 61; the quotation at 359a, "If you be risen with Christ" (Col. 3:1), introduces a chapter all of which is directly pertinent to her theme: If you be risen with Christ, put aside all sinful behavior, above all things have charity, fulfill your roles in life out of love for the Lord and one another. Then you shall receive your rightful inheritance (Col. 3.1–24; cf. "Eritage," 347). But those who do injury shall be punished, for "there is no respect of persons [of wealth, rank or position] with God" (Col. 3:25).

This second speech by Scripture concludes with a difficult passage (369–76) requiring familiarity with the biblical contexts cited. Helping "heathen" (369) is an extension of charity urged in Col. 3:11.[39] The surprising quotation of "Thou shalt not commit adultery" (*Non mecaberis,* 372) in support of "slay not" (371, 373) derives from James 2:11—"For he that said, 'Thou shalt not commit adultery,' said also, 'Thou shalt not kill.' Now if thou do not commit adultery, but shalt kill, thou art become a transgressor of the law." That is, if you avoid "impurity" but injure your neighbor, you do not do well, for as Holy Church had said earlier, "Chastity without charity will be chained in hell" (1.188, 194).[40] Scripture closes by quoting Romans in support of rendering good for evil rather than responding to evil in kind (see Rom. 12:19–21). Thus Scripture has rejected the dreamer's assertion that to do well, to be saved, is merely to be baptized, urging instead living in love and sharing one's goods.

The dreamer next falls back to another effort-saving position, articulated explicitly at the beginning of his last speech of the passus (379–83). Theology, he claims, teaches predestination: even before people are born, they are destined for salvation or damnation. Therefore it does not matter whether one acts well or not: authors of wise works, such as Solomon and Aristotle, are damned, the good thief got into heaven by a deathbed confession after a life of sin, and other great sinners were saved (witness Mary Magdalen the prostitute, David the adulterer and murderer, Paul the persecutor). God's grace is what saves (e.g., 422–23, 457), and so Dowel cannot mean "behave well." In the course of this argument, the dreamer rejects learning as useless, even dangerous, thereby rejecting the instruction he has been receiving from Wit, Study, Clergy, and Scripture. Humans, he argues, cannot judge Dowel at all, because only God can evaluate the moral qualities of human acts. Indeed, the evil that sinners commit, because it teaches good by contrast, might even have won some sinners salvation (436 – 43). No one, in fact, behaves well in this world of sinners, who all must rely on God's grace (444– 47).

Langland seems to have realized that this was a tangled speech, for he substantially revised it in the C text.[41] On the one hand, we are meant to recognize the dreamer's error about Dowel, both from what precedes and follows in the poem and from the matrix of medieval theology (Adams, "Theology," 99 –100). On the other, the speech asserts much truth about the limitations and dangers of learning. For example, Langland's voice warns clerics and teachers to practice what they preach lest they be lost like the carpenters who built Noah's ark, and the speech ends implying that from those to whom much has been given, much will be expected. But what I believe constitutes the narrative backbone of the speech, and of the passus, is the dreamer's reluctance to accept for himself the clear and repeated admonitions of all his teachers that to do well is to live in active love. Here and throughout, the poem urges that although the truth about Dowel can be clearly and forcefully stated, in order to know it *kyndeliche,* people desperately need to see Dowel in action, to be taught by example.[42] At least equally central is the theme that a human will resists changing its own pattern of behavior, focusing on what is wrong with the world rather than on what is wrong with itself.

"To See Much and Suffer More": The Inner Dream of Passus 11

Will, resisting all the complementary exhortations about Dowel, is finally brought up short by Scripture's rebuke.[43] Stung to tears, he falls into the first dream-within-a-dream (11.5– 406). Whatever other purpose might underlie this device, it serves both to set off and to unify the three episodes that follow: Will's view of himself in the "mirror called middle earth" (7–139), an encounter with Trajan (140 –319), and another view from the "mountain called middle earth" (320 – 405).

The first episode affords Will an imagined "autobiography," a life spent in self-indulgence following Fortune and her handmaids, lust, greed, and pride, into the "land of longing."[44] Abusing his wit (45, 16) as he pursues lust, then greed, he brushes aside thoughts of old age or sober advice about treating good fortune judiciously while accepting advice from the likes of Recklessness and Childishness. Foolishly relying on Fortune,[45] he forgets Dowel; after all, he can get easy absolution from a lax friar-confessor, and by purchasing a burial plot from the friars, he can ensure their prayers and masses for the repose of his soul (52–58). But when old age comes and Fortune flees, the friars reject him. Feeling trapped and distraught, he castigates them and, still the contentious Will, articulates yet another fallback position: at least he has been baptized (no thanks to the friars), and because Original Sin has been thus removed from his soul, an act of contrition can save him, can it not?

This marginal stance, relying on the formal letter rather than the spirit of the Christian law,[46] elicits the appearance of Lewte ("fidelity to law," 84–106), who both laughs at Will and gives him a hard look. Will wants leave to proclaim his dream, that is, to rebuke the friars (he does not yet appreciate his own faults). Lewte can quote Leviticus (88) to justify correcting others, though Will points out the friars might quote Matthew back at him (90). But what good is law if lawbreakers cannot be condemned (91–106)? We can see in these lines Langland's sensitivity both to his own position as satirist and to Will's dramatically ironic situation.[47]

Scripture, who has just provided texts to defend correcting others, supplies one more that makes Will tremble: "Many are called . . . few are chosen" (112–14). Wit, Study, Clergy, and Scripture had all defined Dowel as love in action, whereas the dreamer struggled to define it superficially as being a baptized Christian. Will now pushes his argument to the extreme (123–36). A Christian purchased by Christ's blood is Christ's "property"; even should he want to renounce his fealty, he could not. Like a runaway serf he would be brought back home. Punishment he would deserve, even purgatory until the end of the world, but after that he would still get to heaven. After all, Scripture also says God's mercy is the greatest of all God's works (139).[48] Here Trajan suddenly breaks in.

This famous Roman emperor, whose story appeared in many collections including the *Legenda Sanctorum*,[49] offers himself as antithesis to the dreamer's complacent reliance on Christianity's external apparatus. This *vncristene creature* (143), outside that apparatus, attained salvation not through priestly prayers or the saying of masses but through his love, fidelity, and lawful judgments (145, cf. 147, 152). His case constitutes a stark, if extreme, counterbalance to the dreamer's exaggerated reliance on his formal Christianity: love and works versus merely "being Christian."[50]

In the space available here we cannot really explore the dense passage that immediately follows (154–319). Editors and critics do not even agree on who speaks what lines.[51] But let us attempt to point to some principal threads and consider how they relate to the poem's development. Trajan's opening barrage sets love in action against "Clergy," both priestly ministry and the learning, particularly knowledge of Latin and Scripture, required in that ministry. The New Testament law of love, which adds love of enemies to love of friends,[52] acts as transition to the topic of poverty (183–84). The poor like the newly impoverished dreamer may well feel hate for the rich like the friars; but all well-to-do Christians should love the poor, whom they would not normally consider their familiar friends.[53]

Poverty and riches acquire spiritual dimensions. Through the Redemption, all Christians share both "noble" lineage and "Christ's coffers" (199–204); bought back (redeemed) by the *Red-emptor* ("buyerback," 207), they are rich in grace unless they choose the serfdom and beggary of sin (204). Riches include Christianity and grace as well as physical goods; poverty includes sinfulness and lack of instruction and grace as well as material want. All Christians are members of the same family, are liable to lose both wealth and learning at any time, and are all flawed; therefore they should bear with one another rather than lash out in criticism (210–15). Better to rely on poor and simple faith, accompanied by humility and repentance,[54] than on the letter of Christianity ("logic and law") and run the risk of being judged by that letter (228). People should examine their faults rather than other "mysteries" (231)—let all accept their spiritual need.

Meanwhile, Christianity requires love in action: whosoever gives not, loves not (180). Christ came as a pauper and recognizes "his own" by how they treat the poor (185–89). Christians recognize their paradigm not by his appearance (richly—or clerically—clad) but by an act commemorating his self-immolation (232–42). Christianity demands love and patient poverty. Finally, Christ enjoined those who would follow him to "go sell what thou hast, and give to the poor" (274). And so the passage concludes (279–319) by urging the clergy to be content with their livings, not to extract further fees for their services. Priests given titles to pastoral care should be supported,[55] just as are knights made by reasonable kings, and such priests should be willing and able to execute their functions (e.g., praying the mass and divine office) properly. The relationships between clergy and grace, love and being Christian, wealth and poverty in goods and in grace, money and clerical function weave tightly throughout the passage. All of it bears directly not only on the friar-confessor and his situation but also upon the dreamer and his spiritual condition.

The third part of the inner dream (321– 405) begins as Will views the world one more time, now guided by *kynde* (nature) and from a "mountain." He sees creation as remarkable and admirable, the behavior of all creatures ingeniously appropriate to Reason[56]—except for that of "man and his mate" (331–34, 369 –72). Accusing Reason of not shaping human conduct as he does that of other creatures, the dreamer receives another sharp rebuke (376 – 44). Reason stresses the need for "sufferance," adds to the cautions already spoken about blaming others, and suggests that if people could become sinless simply, they would all do so instantly. All creation serves humanity, yet of all creation, humanity has most to bear of temptation and cannot help sinning sometimes: "No one lives without sin" (404).

Numerous clues indicate that the inner dream's third part counterbalances its first. Fortune and nature are paired and contrasted at Fortune's expense, a commonplace.[57] Earlier Will looked at middle earth as if in a mirror, the object of his lust and greed; here he sees it from a vantage point allowing perspective on his, and all humanity's, activities. And as that earlier vision left him in fear for his own salvation, this one leaves him ashamed. Why?

All God's creation was "good" (398 –98a), and moreover God endowed his image with an immortal soul possessed of intellect and free will. But God "suffered" humanity to exercise that free will, humanity fell, and it "suffers" the consequences. Passion and temptation assail it; it fails to adhere to Reason. The human procreative act, all the more necessary now that humanity experiences death, suffers the fervor of passion.[58] Every single human being bears this burden, and even though, viewed in the context of the rest of creation, humanity behaves aberrantly, God suffers it. Humanity has no choice but to suffer it as well. Will, so used to declaiming the sins of those around him, finally accepts his personal sinfulness and so awakens from the dream-within-a-dream.

As the *Vita* began, the speaker told the friars that Dowel could not be living with them, for "the just one falls seven times daily." The dreamer has since then been reminded, in numerous and complementary ways, of what humanity was created to be, what it has become, and what effort Dowel requires of it. In passus 11 Will has finally reacted personally, his fear and shame aroused. Change now becomes possible.

Chapter Seven

"On the Verge of Doing Well": Can Will Change? (Passus 12–15)

Near the end of passus 11, awakened from the inner dream, Will makes a striking claim: within it he learned Dowel as he never had before (11.408–9). He cannot mean he received new and better conceptual definitions of Dowel; the term occurred only twice, both times emphasizing Will's total neglect of it (11.48, 51). Questioned by a new presence, identified for now merely as "one" (*oon,* 410), Will says Dowel is "to see much and to suffer more" (412). Though affectively disposed for change, he has by no means undergone transformation. The new guide figure quite sharply tells Will that had not his resistance, his pride, and his ingrained habit of blaming others led him to oppose Reason, he might have learned a great deal more (413–23).

The theme of the Fall, prevalent in the last section of the inner dream, reappears in the reminder (417–22) that Adam lost paradise for wanting to know the wrong things and learned to his chagrin about good, evil, and shame. The example of the drunkard in the ditch (427–34) underscores the sort of knowledge emphasized here: where no conceptual discourse might reach, basic personal experience (hangover, hunger, filth) causes the drunk to "know" (*woot,* 434) his fault. These images reinforce Will's own altered disposition, and a new informant can now deal with arguments that the resisting Will had earlier offered in defense of his status quo.

This interpretation of the last 200 lines of passus 11 depends on a hard scrutiny of the text. But it receives considerable assistance from the commonplace nature of the medieval moral psychology here described. In that psychology, vice and virtue arise in the affective faculty, the free will. The will, weakened in consequence of the Fall, resists what the intellect more readily accepts as true, creates spurious obstacles, and seeks alternatives to change.[1] Langland dramatizes that resistance in the dreamer while bringing him gradually to accept familiar conclusions. Will becomes a model in whom the audience can recognize themselves and whose new "knowledge" they might share. One might even suggest a specific analogy: the audience see themselves in the dreamer just as Will saw himself in the inner dream.

"I Am Ymaginatif" (Passus 12)

As passus 12 begins, Will learns his new guide's name: Ymaginatif. Because this figure had been deferred to earlier as an expositor of theological propositions (10.117–19), because he appears where the earlier A version ended (some have thought due to the author's doubts about how to proceed), and because he seems to settle issues previously raised, Ymaginatif was long thought to represent some special, almost prophetic, power. This presupposition collided with the modest role that "imagination" played in medieval psychology. Imagination was one of the "internal senses," responsible for retaining impressions caused by physical objects in the absence of those objects (thus one could still "see" a tree after one had left the garden); it could also recombine impressions, thus imagining a mermaid (woman and fish) or a centaur (man and horse).[2] Many have attempted to find some other theory of imagination on the fringes of medieval psychology that might account for the faculty's "exalted" role in the poem.[3] But what Ymaginatif has to say, though it concerns difficult issues, is quite straightforward rather than prophetic or exalted. What makes the figure appropriate here is not the source or content of his speech but the state of the dreamer.

Will can now hear, and take in, what he refused to accept before. Rather than rejecting advice that makes demands on him, he can attend to it more openly. Ymaginatif, then, represents the condition of Will as receptive to considering the inevitability of his own death and his need for penance and amendment (12.3–15). Insofar as Ymaginatif has to do with recalling or projecting experiences (what Will has done, what he must face), the personification reflects well enough the basic function of medieval imagination: recalling and potentially recombining experience. I think the name also emphasizes Will's condition: the form of the word (equivalent to Modern English "imaginative") helps reinforce our perception of a new psychic state in the personally aroused dreamer.[4]

What does Ymaginatif say? He begins (12.29) by reaffirming Dowel in a manner reminiscent of earlier definitions. Dowel is faith, hope, and charity, but especially charity; be faithful, "true," to your vocation or state in life. Taking up the series of objections the dreamer had raised against Scripture's Dowel in passus 10,[5] Ymaginatif asserts balance and moderation. As for intelligence (40), it along with wealth or other endowments can be used well or badly; wealth and natural intelligence can encumber (45, 55). Wise words without deeds, knowledge not acted upon, are like wealth hoarded. Grace (59), which helps govern intelligence and wealth, lies beyond their absolute control, but in a receptive human disposition (58– 63), it grows like a healing herb. As for the relationship between grace and the apparatus of Christianity (71), *clergie* (priestly ministry) plays a crucial role. But the dispensation of grace can cut two ways: it can damn those who fail to acknowledge their faults and who abuse the sacraments just as surely as it can save those who receive the sacraments well.

Ymaginatif insists that learning (application of intelligence, 99) has value because it transmits and articulates revelation, and the clergy (using learning and Latin) perform functions only they can (113). Natural knowledge on its own, however (139), cannot save: salvation was initiated by God's direct intervention (139). Its benefits are received and made fruitful in the well disposed: the simple and some clerks, true seekers after it. The ignorant are not better off than the learned (155), for those who have knowledge of Christian teaching can better help themselves. As for predestination and the good thief (192), there are some things humans cannot know any more than they can know why birds build their nests as they do or why Adam fell. People can draw moral lessons from nature (236), as from peafowl and larks. They cannot know (270) whether pagans such as Aristotle, who seem to have been just, are saved.

Thus far Ymaginatif has affirmed familiar medieval truths. When the dreamer says all Christian clerks believe that non-Christians are damned, Ymaginatif counters, still orthodox[6] but most emphatic (281): When the Bible says, "The just shall barely be saved," it does nevertheless say they shall be saved. As for Trajan, the "book" (presumably the *Golden Legend*)[7] puts him in heaven. Christian teachers acknowledge three kinds of baptism; "baptism of desire" might reasonably have applied to some righteous pre-Christians.[8] Finally, Ymaginatif insists, we must believe that God, who is Truth, values truth in humans, so those who follow truthfully the best law they know have grounds for expecting Truth to reward their truth.[9] And so human intelligence and wisdom have served human communities very well in the past. This whole concluding passage gives the fullest possible value to behavior that does its best to establish an understanding of truth and then to live up to it; by analogy, those lucky enough to access the Christian "faith" had best profess it "faithfully."

The foregoing paragraphs summarize what Ymaginatif says but do no justice whatsoever to how Langland has him say it. Consider, for example, how his Dowel (29–39) demands the audience's involved response. He quotes Paul (1 Cor. 1:13, a verse familiar to most of Langland's readers): "And now there remain faith, hope, and charity, these three: but the greatest of these is charity." By this point in the poem, the reader has been conditioned to think in triads: Dowel, Dobet, Dobest. Is one to see them as these three virtues? Ymaginatif goes on to discuss married life, religious life, and the state of virginity: Dowel, Dobet, and Dobest again? One is made to consider the possibility and then to conclude "no." The quotation about faith, hope, and charity climaxes a short chapter of 1 Corinthians commending charity: Charity must animate every virtue, it excludes every vice. Dowel is Charity. Previous definitions of Dowel have emphasized the loving fulfillment of Christian "law."[10] Let love, as well as fidelity, animate good marriage, the observance of religious rule, and sexual abstinence voluntarily undertaken or endured.[11] Dowel requires no more exotic pilgrimage. Contrastive juxtaposition, moving from Dowel to do evil, then supplies the transition to the next topic (Lucifer et al., 40).

Or consider the section on Christ's *clergie* (71–98); these lines deal with the dispensation of grace through the sacraments, which requires literacy, Latin, and some knowledge of theology for its exercise, as well as the spiritual cooperation of those who receive the sacraments. The gospel scene of the woman taken in adultery provocatively frames these issues. It sets New Testament off against Old[12] and shows Christ using *clergie* (writing) while confronting hypocritical executors of the law's letter (Old Testament "clerics"). Standard commentaries on the scene explained that Christ wrote the deadly sins of the accusers in the earth before challenging those without sin to cast the first stone.[13] Thus Christ's *clergie* condemns sinners and hypocritical clerics while liberating the repentant.[14] Augustine, in his numerous elaborations on this scene, emphasized how Christ, while preserving justice and truth, preserved also his mercy; while the Old Law had been written on unyielding stone, the New was written in the "earth" of human hearts so that it might bear fruit; for this to occur, each person must enter the tribunal of his own conscience and acknowledge his sins.[15] Thus the confrontation between Christ, woman, and accusers clearly models the balance between sacramental grace, Christian response, and the Latin apparatus of the sacraments: Christ's *clergie* can damn as well as save (90–91).

As this instance illustrates, Langland must have counted on his readers' familiarity with Scripture and its commentary to render some touches more resonant. We sense this with *pastores* and *magi* (139–54),[16] but it also occurs where we are less likely to notice. That no clerk can explain why only one of two thieves responded to the unique opportunity of asking Christ for grace (214–16) is driven home by the terse "Why did it please him? Because he willed it" (216a). Any of Langland's readers who recognized the biblical source of this Latin would appreciate the powerful reinforcement its context provided for the sentiment expressed.[17]

Ymaginatif's entire speech bristles with vivid juxtaposition, analogy, and example (the two men in the Thames, the peafowl and the lark). We recall how Ymaginatif began by accusing the dreamer-poet of wasting time "composing" (12.16–19); should we therefore reflect on the role of imagination in poetry's devices, in this passus or in the poem as a whole?[18] No simple answer presents itself. Almost every speaker employs such devices at one point or another; Ymaginatif uses, and demands we use, thought and analysis as well as imagination. *Poet* is a word Langland applies not to verse makers but to ancient philosophers and authorities,[19] and he partially dismisses his "makings" as recreational play (20–24).[20] The dreamer closes his defense (25–29) by returning us to Dowel, but in the process he suggests that something about "making" plays a crucial part in discovering the object of that quest.[21]

"So Hard It Is": The Fourth Dream (Passus 13–14)

As passus 13 opens, the protagonist wakes from the long third dream that had begun (with Thought) back in passus 8. What are we to make of the interlude (13.1–20)? Why should he feel "nearly without intelligence," "ill-starred," and go "as a beggar" (1–3)? As he thinks back on his dream, he takes to heart especially the lessons of passus 11 and 12: life rushes past, earthly fortune fails, friars betray people's complacent expectations, and the laity too often depend on unskilled and greedy clergy. The highly compressed lines 15 to 19 reflect the speaker's acceptance of Ymaginatif's teaching that humans, fallen, sinful, and culpable, should nevertheless not blame this state on a generous and evenhanded Creator and that the "just" shall be saved, though "barely."[22] The speaker thus finds himself in a wrenchingly difficult situation. He bears responsibility for his own moral fate; he has no simple recourse to automatically efficacious *clergie* (either "knowledge" or "ministry"). Well may he feel himself witless, unfortunate, and profoundly needy, as may any reader who has intimately shared his journey.[23]

The poem does not tell us exactly when the next adventure occurs, only that Will endures this state "for a long time" (*many yer after,* 3). Eventually he lies down and dreams a fourth dream, comprising two episodes: a dinner at Conscience's palace and an encounter with a character named Haukyn, "the Active Life."[24] Having accepted his own need for moral change, Will now learns about the process he faces.

"Conscience Called for Food": The Dinner (13.21–214)

In this process of change, Conscience plays a central role. Accepting the premise that he (like everyone else) sins, Will must next recognize his own particular sins. Only then can he behave differently: recognition can lead to sorrow and repentance; repentance can gradually help him control and correct his tendencies to sin. Thus he will need Patience as well as Conscience. Conscience, moreover, requires help, because it is a practical judgment made by the intellect, or a pattern ("habit") of such acts: "This particular deed here and now is right, that one then and there was wrong." But the intellect can judge only in the light of what it knows and understands: conscience needs practical moral instruction. And because these judgments concern not abstract theory but concrete decisions about real choices, acts of conscience involve not only intellect but also will; disciplining desire contributes to forming judgment. Conscience, one of the diners as well as the host, needs "nourishment."[25]

Small wonder that Will, feeling himself witless and needy, eagerly accepts an invitation to dine at Conscience's house. We would expect Clergie and the learned theologian, who also attend, to offer moral support for Conscience and Will. (We might understand Clergie as collective Christian learning and ministry, the theologian as a contemporary instance of them.) Patience, necessary even if these two did support Conscience, is all the more imperative given the theologian's behavior.

This doctor[26] becomes an object of biting satire. Far from speaking so as to encourage Conscience and Will in concrete moral truth, even further from providing example by his own life, this self-indulgent hypocrite recalls the mercenary friar who wooed Lady Meed (3.35), the "theology" that provoked Dame Study (10.185), and the gluttons who mangle doctrine while overindulging at table (10.52). As we first see him (37– 45), he rejects the solid "meat" (40) of the Gospels and their traditional interpreters. He demands instead fancier fare, Christianity pounded and mashed into purees (41) in which, implicitly, straightforward moral teaching has been "glossed" to death, explained away.[27] The densely packed image closing this description portrays a teacher-confessor who, rather than encouraging folk to contrition, restitution, and penance, instead deludes them with easy absolution in exchange for a share of their ill-gotten gains. Such confessors "eat the sins" of their charges,[28] and the accompanying "sauce" will be torment after death (*post mortem*, 44) for both master and pupils.

This image, though it does not mention the word *penance,* nevertheless puts the topic in play. Penance embraces both specific acts of reparation or satisfaction assigned to penitent by confessor and, much more broadly, the general practice of prayer, self-denial, and discipline. The scene next directs our attention to Patience: the disposition to suffer and endure equably what must be endured.[29] Accordingly Patience "nourishes" himself with scriptural texts prayed by penitents, takes a similar text for his *pitaunce* (57, an additional gift such a guest might carry off with him), and basks in "merry" dinnertime entertainment in the same vein (58).[30] He personifies the virtue in full flower: he rejoices at this harsh fare (52, 59 – 60) and so reminds us of Piers, who accepted the terms of the pardon (cf. 7.128). Patience models the behavior required of all Christians, for to be human is to sin, sin requires penance (in both narrower and broader senses), and penance perseveringly endured gradually repairs fallen nature's proclivity to sin and so begets amendment. Patience, as pilgrim, stands counter to the official teacher; the doctor will seek to banish him from this household, and Conscience, leaving Clergie behind with the doctor, will choose to follow Patience. The departure dramatizes another sense in which Christians must suffer and endure: they lack inducement and example, particularly from their priests, who effectively marginalize those who would really do well.[31]

In his present state, Will becomes Patience's "mate" (35). Although bursting to confront the doctor's hypocrisy (64–85), Will nevertheless allows Patience to restrain him (86, 99, 113).[32] The topic of penance, as much as the doctor's hypocrisy, claims his attention. He exclaims (so only Patience can hear) that he witnessed this man preach on penance just the other day, quoting Paul's description of sufferings endured (2 Cor. 11, where Paul asserts, through these sufferings, his claim to be a true apostle). Who is this glutton to appropriate such words to himself? Among the dangers Paul says he suffered were "those among false *fratres* (brothers *or* friars); let him preach on that verse! He "has no pity on us poor" because he does not practice what he preaches (78−80); this complaint indicates that "poverty" denotes more than lack of physical nourishment. But after expressing his disgust privately to Patience, and venturing one fairly restrained sally aloud (106−11), Will falls silent and remains Patience's observant companion.

Will and Patience make penance the topic of the after-dinner conversation (85, 98, 103). Perhaps they pose penance as Dobest because real penance is the last thing they expect this doctor to recommend. The doctor's first Dowel (104−5) teaches the minimum, negatively stated: Do no evil. Will's rejoinder (106−10), claiming the doctor has in fact done evil by consuming all the food, makes us realize again how Langland uses allegorical frameworks to generate independent bursts of significance: the doctor's food as earlier portrayed was nothing to long for; here emphasis falls on the doctor's consuming the best himself without offering to feed Patience and Will.

As Conscience then invites doctor, Clergie, and Patience to speak in turn,[33] we hear three new definitions of the do's, which we now evaluate against the new background of penance. The doctor's "teach, learn, practice what you preach" (116−18) guarantees his own Dowel (he *is* a teacher, however bad) and consigns what Christians most need from him (teaching by example) to the highest (and last) place, as if he never expects to achieve it.

Clergie's teaching is much richer, more suggestive, even mysterious sounding. It points forward, and it effectively eliminates the possibility of isolating Dowel as a minimum. Clergie says his seven sons (the human arts) have discovered no adequate definition; Piers Plowman has declared them all worthless (124). We cannot resolve this surprising appeal to Piers by reference to what we have already seen of him. Piers's "science" of love (125−27) points to Christ, who stands as the central mystery of Christianity.[34] Piers's judgment (128−30) that Dowel and Dobet are two infinities that seek out Dobest, a third like themselves, suggests a triad who interact as intimately and dynamically as the persons of the Trinity: all exist simultaneously in one entity, their limits no more definable than those of the Godhead in whose image humanity was created.[35] But such notions surpass human comprehension, and faced with defining Christ and God, Clergie can only gesture inadequately. Christians need to learn these do's naturally by seeing them enacted by God incarnate, and so Clergie says, "let us pass on till Piers come and exemplify this in deed" (133). Until then they can only wait patiently—and until then Patience's teaching will have to suffice.

Patience's "learn, teach, love your enemies" (137) neatly replaces the doctor's lesson. Learn to love and value your soul, teach it to love, and love those who hate you; bear with enmity, smother and beat it down with love—a lesson as befitting Patience as the famous riddle that follows (150 –56). Patience seems to expect a solution to the riddle and challenges the doctor to "undo it" (157), but despite learned attempts to untie its knots, Dowel remains bound up in Patience's words.[36] Somehow this seems appropriate. Clergie cannot pin Dowel down, Patience will endure and order its affections as the Gospel says, and Christians endure their bafflement as they persevere in love, for that is surely the thrust of Patience's words.[37]

The doctor, after totally misconstruing Patience's closing statement, would have him sent packing. Patience does indeed depart—accompanied by both Will and Conscience. Conscience thus leaves his own "house" and, for the time being at least, separates from Clergie. Thus Conscience seems to have absorbed the preoccupation with penance and so to represent especially the penitential contemplation of past deeds.[38] Accordingly he finds in Patience the appropriate instructor and in Will the appropriate disposition:

But the will of the person and the will of people here
Has moved my disposition to mourn for my sins.
The proper disposition of a creature has never been purchased with
     money,
For there is no treasure equal to a true will. (190 –93)

These lines, though difficult, seem to say that Patience and Will are disposed to a life of penance and reform, that this disposition holds immense spiritual value, and that Conscience will seize the opportunity to be guided and shaped by it. Having been "perfected" by Patience, Conscience can return to Clergie, at which point they could remake the whole world (206 –7).

"My Name Is *Activa vita*": The Example of Haukyn (13.220–14)

Leaving Clergie and the doctor, Will, Conscience, and Patience encounter Haukyn. How does he present himself, and what is his function?[39] Obviously, he somehow represents "everyone," each Christian.

The parade of Haukyn's sins recalls passus 5, and his earnest business recalls Piers's efforts to feed the people. But though he counts himself among those who help Piers (236 –37), he is no Piers, and several details reinforce this.

He is a "minstrel" (221, 224) but no minstrel (227–34). The word can mean "servant" as well as "entertainer," but the fact that Will's party immediately identifies Haukyn as a minstrel suggests they see in him something of the oddly clad vagabond.[40] He calls himself a "waferer," literally one who makes and sells thin cakes, and he certainly does supply food (235, 240, 241– 43, 260 – 62). But wafers seem somewhat more luxurious than bread, and waferers had an unsavory reputation.[41] Finally, "Haukyn," though a legitimate name, might suggest "hawker" and "hawking," the activity of an itinerant peddler somewhat on the fringes of the economy.[42] All of this might have served to cast Haukyn just a bit beyond respectability. Similarly, his self-identification as "the active life" begins to shade into "the hyperactive life," a life totally enmeshed in the affairs of this world.[43]

What Haukyn would have from the pope underlines his preoccupation with this world and contrasts him strikingly with Piers. Although Haukyn speaks of how people need to become "worthy" before blessing can take effect, and of how pride calls down famine in punishment, he talks of physical healing and redress (247– 49, 254–56), of the exercise of those miraculous powers the Gospels say Christ left to the apostles. He expresses little interest in an actual indulgence (245– 46), a spiritual rather than a temporal benefit. Piers, on the other hand, had instantly realized the pardon's implications: "I . . . shall not work so hard, and not be so busy about my livelihood" (7.122–23). Quoting Psalm 22 (7.120 –21), Piers implicitly expresses his faith that the Good Shepherd will supply verdant pastures and living water. Patience will have a way to go before Haukyn contemplates any such thing.

Haukyn thus represents all those Christians absorbed in their struggle for the world's goods and preoccupied by life here. Because of the Fall, they must endure sickness and death and must earn their bread by the sweat of their brow. They also bear the burden of fallen nature, so inclined to sin that even the just fall seven times a day and "shall barely be saved." Baptism washed their souls clean of Original Sin, gave them a spiritual mark, a spotless "coat of Christendom" (13.273). That coat will always be with them, but simply having it is not enough; they face the inevitable and unrelenting task of cleansing it. And so Will to amend, Conscience to accuse, and Patience to endure the consequences come to study Haukyn's garment.

In passus 5, the seven sins obstructed remaking society. In passus 13 they challenge every Christian in his or her personal life. Langland's presenting the sins again makes the audience confront them anew, perhaps this time in a mood more conducive to individual examination of conscience: before contrition can occur, one must recognize that one has sinned. The presentation renders the sins of all, not just those of a waferer,[44] and depicts them brilliantly (for example, covetousness at 370 –74, lust at 344– 47). The staging keeps the march of the seven from becoming rote: first Will notices some, Conscience exclaims about others, Haukyn "turns" to reveal yet more, Will looks more closely, Patience also sees. And, ironically, those sins quickest seen are exactly those by which Haukyn would show himself as other than he truly is (278 –79).

Langland returns to Haukyn's coat at the end of the passus after two apparent digressions: on despair (409 –20) and on commendable "minstrels" (421–56). In passus 5, sloth came last in the list of the deadly sins, for succumbing to spiritual sloth leads to *wanhope* (despair). Langland elaborates this idea again (406 –8)—the voice now seems the poet's own—so as to make it particularly relevant for penance. The "branches" that lead to *wanhope* are absence of contrition, failure to perform assigned penance, failure to give alms (frequently an assigned penance), and so on—*lack* of penance. One bound for despair indulges the appetites and enjoys ribald entertainments, and describing these leads naturally to the associated digression: whom should lords and ladies have to "entertain" them? Not fools, flatterers, and liars, but the poor, sober teachers, and the infirm. Reward these, and at the end you will fall not into *wanhope* but into *welhope* (453); such "minstrels" contribute to the atmosphere of sober, penitential behavior that leads to penance and amendment.

Passus 13 ends as Conscience gently rebukes Haukyn for not having washed or brushed his coat, and 14 opens with Haukyn's defense: he has but one garment, he must wear it constantly, he has a whole household to deal with,[45] he just cannot keep it clean no matter how hard he tries. The coat seems to me best understood as referring still to his "coat of Christendom" (13.273), his soul as cleansed of Original Sin and garbed in the once white garment of Christianity, now stained and soiled by countless actual sins.[46] Haukyn says he has observed the Lenten fast and has been chastised by sickness and loss; these alerted him to his wrongdoing and goaded him to contrition and confession (5 –11), and he subsequently performed the penance his confessor assigned. But he quickly sins again (12 –15), and so his coat is always fouled.[47]

Conscience urges the three parts of penance: contrition, confession, and satisfaction. The first two can restore Haukyn's coat to its baptismal cleanliness—devoutly undertaken can redye and rebleach it by sorrow and absolution in the sacrament. Satisfaction can keep it clean yet makes the most difficult demands: *satisfactio* in this sense means that life of "penance," of prayer, self-denial, and discipline that over time can lead one to real amendment, to resisting sin successfully. Patience offers to free Haukyn to pursue such a life: Do not worry about food; here, eat *Ne soliciti sitis.* ("Be not solicitous for your life, what you shall eat, nor for your body, what you shall put on . . ." [Matt. 6:25].) Haukyn scoffs, and Patience launches into his long recommendation of poverty.

The texts Patience offers to nourish Haukyn urge humanity to trust that God will provide ("Whatsoever you shall ask the Father in my name, that will I do," 46a; "thy will be done," 50). The latter clause, from the Lord's Prayer, comes just before one that says "give us this day our daily bread." But Patience does not speak just of physical food: "Not in bread alone doth man live . . ." (46a). We realize that Patience does not promise plenty or speak of a cure for world hunger. He says, in effect, this life does not really matter: "Don't worry about food, drink, or clothing; . . . die as it pleases God" (57–58); "If you live according to God's teaching, the shorter life the better" (60)! These startling pronouncements harmonize perfectly with the "truths" underlying Langland's poem, expressed since Lady Holy Church's speech.[48] Nevertheless they jar us, and they cannot have failed to startle Langland's audience; indeed they seem calculated (like the example of Trajan) to underline a principle at its extreme. The message Patience wants Haukyn to take away is moderation in the use of temporal goods, "detachment" from them (55–56, 72–75, 82). If everyone practiced measure, the needy would have enough (71). Acting according to these values that faith professes, armed with this disposition, Christian conscience can judge effectively; contrition and confession can function as they should; and satisfaction, the process of prayer and self-denial that gradually purges the soul from its desire to indulge in sin, will leave the soul healed (83–97).

What prompts Haukyn to ask, "Where is Charity" (98)? The word has not been mentioned since the dinner (which Haukyn did not attend). If the question reflects some plea by Haukyn for relief from the radical detachment and effortful penitential life that Patience advocates, some hope for benevolence or beneficence,[49] Patience disillusions Haukyn straightway: charity arises from *him,* from his truth, detachment (poverty of heart), and forbearance.[50]

Patience's answer to Haukyn's next question (is poverty more pleasing to God than riches honestly won and reasonably spent?) allows Langland to make the case for detachment from the opposite side. He has spoken about those who feel want; now he warns the haves while consoling the have-nots (104–273). The satirical first line sets the lively tone ("Can there be such a thing as riches combined with justice!"), and the speech subsequently darts back and forth between rich and poor. The argument, clear and trenchant, needs little commentary, but one should appreciate its various strategies.

For example, tight deductive logic underlies lines 111 to 121: all creatures were created for joy; the poor have had no joy here; therefore they must have a right to it hereafter. Unhappy experiences with workmen paid before the job is done animate the suggestion that the rich enjoy their reward too soon (126 – 43). The image of preparing the parchment required for a letter of remission eloquently enforces the idea that individuals must be inwardly disposed in order to benefit from the Redemption (192–201). Early in the series of contrastive juxtapositions, a brilliant transition poses Satan and the Gospel "rich man" (*dives*, 122–23) as ominous touchstones for those who had joy and then were damned. One meets striking paradox (riches rob men's souls, 132; have pity on the rich! 168) and puns (e.g., the one on *riche,* "kingdom" and "rich(es)," at 179). The speech's closing lines revisit the seven deadly sins, arguing that poverty defends against them, whereas riches make one more susceptible.

Langland had to have been aware that in praising poverty and urging moderation in the enjoyment of physical goods and detachment from them, he was going against the human grain. And so when Haukyn asks Patience to define poverty, an "authoritative" quotation appears. The difficulty of explaining it in English (278) arises from the unappealing topic rather than from hard Latin. Patience nevertheless addresses the phrases gathered in the quotation. Five offer the poor freedom from the risks and responsibilities faced by the rich; three offer positive boons to those compelled to moderation. The very first arguably has the most impact. Its paradoxical expression ("hateful good") perfectly suits the rhetorical situation, and Patience employs deductive logic and analogy in a tightly reasoned explication (280 –87). Pride hates poverty, and whatever pride hates must be good; just as sorrow for sins paradoxically solaces the soul, so poverty complements sorrow by chastising the body and leads to the soul's health.

Haukyn recognizes (as Will looks on) what Conscience and Patience demand. Alas, his soul and his once spotless coat almost inevitably suffer the stains of sin in daily living. It is "so hard to live and commit sin" (325) because one must consequently endure contrition, confession, and satisfaction. Being responsible for one's own personal behavior is burden enough (327–31). Christian life, for one who would do well, means repeatedly falling, getting up, and going on. Dowel is not an idea contemplated, nor a condition passively experienced, nor even a conversion undergone in one moment. It is undertaking, patiently and perseveringly, the penitential life that *satisfactio* demands.

Haukyn's bitter tears of contrition wake Will and so end the fourth dream. Any reader who took Langland's Christianity seriously, who accepted that Haukyn modeled Will's (and everyman's) plight, would have reason to feel as sorrowful and as isolated as Haukyn. Will seems to. The poem will soon offer real consolation and community. But the next dream begins by continuing the exploration of isolation, need, and struggle. It protests that countless others endure similar isolation, and such consolation as it offers results chiefly from excoriating those responsible.

"In a Dark Manner": Dream Five Begins (Passus 15)

The fourth interlude (14.335–15.11) shows Will as we would expect to find him—still struggling. As a rebuke early in the coming dream will point out, he remains "imperfect" (50), and such "understanding" as he has is insecure.[51] His refusal to bow and scrape to the rich and powerful suggests some detachment from worldly goods (though perhaps a chip on his shoulder as well). And if "natural knowing" of Dowel implies experiencing it practiced around him, the ensuing dream helps explain why such knowledge is so hard to come by.

When Reason has pity on Will and rocks him to sleep, Anima appears. This new guide speaks on behalf of the redeemed "soul" (16 –21), the soul that constitutes humanity's distinguishing characteristic, what a person should love above all else, immortal and destined for heaven. The nine Latin names of "soul" emphasize its many activities; Anima's translation elaborates all but the first three into moral applications particularly relevant for the soul's doing well. In this passus, which emphasizes what the soul needs from the clergy (real moral teaching, good example), "sense" becomes what Anima learns from others (29 –30); and "spirit" (breath) becomes its final "exhalation," its inevitable departure from the body at death, bound for judgment (35–36).

Anima's address concentrates on a set of closely related topics, all present in his first long speech (50 –148). Clerics (friars, priests, bishops and other prelates, even the pope) fail to live the *clergie* they know, fail to nourish and strengthen the folk with good lives and example, fail to spread the gospel as they so easily might. The same themes dominate the last half of this long passus: "There is a defect in those people who are in charge of the faith" (347), on account of which the faithful have become like counterfeit coins, Christian on the outside but full of bad alloy within. The striking image of Mohammed as selfishly ambitious Christian priest gone bad, of English clerics bowing to covetousness in imitation of him, of lax and complacent clergy living off their endowments rather than bestirring themselves to "finish" the cloth that baptism has made or to spread Christianity at least to those who already believe in the one true God—all these forcefully indict contemporary churchmen. Langland's indignant cry that lords should reclaim the church's landed endowments closely resembles that of Wyclif, tempered only by the condition that follows: "*if* temporal endowments be poison and make them imperfect, it *would be* charity to dispossess them, for Holy Church's sake" (564–67). Although Langland's voice, once again, seems to come to the fore here,[52] Anima perfectly represents the interests on behalf of which the poet speaks: the soul is beneficiary or victim of what clerics do, its good the purpose of their ministry, its fate much dependent upon their lives and actions. Anima speaks on behalf of Haukyn and of the "good will of people here," rising powerfully to characterize universally and to condemn those defects that the doctor had just exhibited at Conscience's palace.

Of all Langland's poem, this passus seems most likely to impress modern readers as tedious, especially Anima's long last speech (198–613). The many striking individual touches the passus contains[53] only partially mitigate that impression. We may actually wish for more abstraction than Langland provides, for he proceeds from one concrete image, example, or analogy to the next rather than explicitly setting out topics, and following the train of thought demands attention and reflection. Nowhere else, I think, do we become so aware of Langland's associative logic. Any attempt to abstract "treatise headings" from the text leaves behind significance as well as resonance.

Anima's description of charity (149–346), embedded in this critique as an antiphonal theme, deserves special attention. The transition to the topic incidentally illustrates how the passus typically develops. Langland plants the word *charity* at the very end of Anima's criticism of avaricious clerics. By typical contrastive juxtaposition (144–47), he moves from the greedy, whose death no one laments, to the generous, whom all mourn "in perfect charity" (148). Will seizes on the word *charity* and asks Anima to define it. In a series of images, Anima incrementally describes a charity powerfully antithetical to the selfish, acquisitive clerical behavior depicted throughout the episode. First, Charity is childlike without childishness, a free and generous will (149–50, cf. Matt. 18:3–6). Second, Charity does not deal for profit or contend or crave, is easily satisfied, rejoices with the glad, shares whatever it has, never curses or scorns, and endures all injuries patiently (165–75, cf. 1 Cor. 13:4–7). Third, Charity seeks its friends not among the rich and the powerful but among the poor and imprisoned and then spends its spare time in penitence (177–94).[54] Fourth, Charity is a well-behaved child, lighthearted, loving, and companionable (216–19, cf. Matt. 6:16–17). Finally, Charity urges mild speech, gentle looks, lack of concern for earthly goods, and forbearance in the realization that whatever one might suffer, God has suffered more (251–62).

Responding to the first of these descriptions, Will exclaims he has never experienced anything so generous. Everyone acts selfishly; charity cannot be the competition for possession or the business quid pro quo (164) with which he feels himself surrounded. Clerics may say that Christ is everywhere, but Will has seen Christ reflected in their lives no more clearly than he has seen himself "through a glass, in a dark manner" (162–62a, 1 Cor. 13:12). In response to Anima's third description, Will cries, "By Christ, I wish I knew him!" (195). Anima's rejoinder echoes Will's earlier remark that charity exists now only in badly disfigured embodiments: one will never see this creature without help of Piers Plowman. That is, one will see Charity clearly only in a person who lives charity to the full.

Will's next query, do clerks "know him [Charity]?" (197), allows Anima to extend both the critique of clerics and the description of the virtue. Anima recognizes the twofold nature of the question: Are clerics Charity's familiars—is charity known among them? And can clerics recognize charity when they see it? As to the first, Anima says that charity consists not in appearance or estate (e.g., acting like a penitent, or being a cleric, cf. 209) but in the disposition of the will. Therefore, as to the second, no earthly creature can definitively know whether a fellow human has charity. Only perfect Charity (Piers realized in God, Christ, 199–200a, 212) can read the human will.

Anima's fourth description of charity follows immediately and completes an authoritative description of the virtue. He describes an inner disposition that generates external acts and behavior. The Clergie of passus 13 had said that Piers had rendered worthless all "science" except love, that to see Dowel was to await Piers. To know surely that a free, liberal will exists in a particular human being remains the province of Christ alone. Nevertheless the clergy, who profess most closely to follow Christ and have the most responsibility to manifest and so to teach charity, seem to have failed wretchedly. Anima does allow that charity *can* exist in most walks of life (220 –51). But these instances of charity perceived "in a mirror" pale before all those in which it cannot be recognized at all. To the great cost of the Haukyns, Wills, and all souls in this world, Charity remains a promise rather than a reality.

Chapter Eight

"What One Does, All Do": Will Reconnected (Passus 16 –18)

Any reader following the present analysis of the poem over the course of passus 11 to 15 would be justified in thinking I have presented Langland as almost intolerably bleak. Will's third dream had stripped him down, the inner dream of passus 11 completing the process, leaving him bare in his basic tendencies, radically isolated, the center of culpability. Passus 12 reasserted lessons his new disposition permitted him to accept, but these correctives did little in themselves to diminish his isolation. His fourth dream, in passus 13 and 14, dramatized in Patience and Haukyn the conditions of, and the need for, penitential amendment. Beginning his fifth dream in passus 15, Will encountered little relief. Although Anima represented all Christian souls and added vividly to the image of charity for whose realization Will so longs, that longing only emphasizes the absence of this climactic Christian virtue, and Anima's survey of the leaders of the Christian community left Will as he had been: largely unaided and solitary.

But now, beginning in passus 16, Langland sets out to remove this isolation. Having dramatized Will's "negative way" (the stripping of pretense and resistance, the actual undertaking of penitential reform), the poet offers him a "positive way," emphasizing Will's reintegration into a shared recovery of grace and of community. Will discovers himself participating in a common process as all humanity strives toward salvation. Langland develops this reintegration of Will through a powerfully effective combination of traditions.[1]

First, let us recall that Langland regarded human beings as special images of God, not just designed by God and given unique freedom of will but so closely participating in the lineaments of the divine exemplar that the Trinity "dwells within" them and will go to any lengths to preserve its *imago*. Human beings exist in this state, this constitutes their common *kynde*, and consequently their shared condition might be thought to constitute an "ontological community."[2] Langland dramatizes it, beginning in the "tree of charity" episode.

Langland connects this ontological community with another, the community of humans that, during the long course of salvation history, longed for God's intervention under the Old Law, then for the fulfillment of the Old Law in the New Law and for the victory of Christ that would finally free humanity from the devil's power. Countless shared in this collective longing, and Will thus finds fellowship in that impressive series of biblical figures who awaited the coming of Christ just as Will now waits to experience Christ's charity in deed. Thus we encounter, in passus 16 and 17, Abraham, Moses, and the Samaritan; the process reaches its lyrical climax as passus 18 recounts Christ's death and harrowing of hell and then in the next dream extends forward into Christian time.

Also associated with this shared ontology and with the communal experience of salvation history is another community in which both of these unite, the liturgical community of Langland's own day that publicly commemorated and ritually reenacted the events of salvation history in the course of every liturgical year.[3] This communal commemoration offered Christians the annual opportunity of celebrating and contemplating their relationship with salvation history. It allowed them to renew their own participation in it, collective and individual, by renewing their commitment to respond to the grace offered them: thus to fast during Lent, to imitate Christ's death by "death to self" and to sin, and to "rise with him" restored to grace and amendment.[4] Ideally, such an annual "renovation" might produce not a circle futilely recurring in place but an upward spiral of growth and development. Langland now presents Will's quest as united with, and supported by, all these communities.

"A Very Choice Tree": The Fruit Charity

As passus 16 opens, Will exclaims to Anima, "For the sake of Haukyn the Active Man, I shall always love you . . ." (16.1–2). Will has recognized his moral likeness in the individual Christian struggling with the life of patient penitence. His reiterated request to understand Charity serves to trigger the ensuing episodes. Charity, a virtue Christians must practice, is here presented as a shared benefit, extended through and to the community of Christians and manifested fully in time by the incarnation of Love.

In response to Will's perplexity about Charity, Anima describes "a very excellent tree" (16.4–9). Its root is God's mercy, its trunk contrition, its leaves law-conforming words, its blossoms humble speech and loving concern. The entire tree can be called "sufferance" and detached simplicity of heart, and from all of this, finally, the "fruit" Charity results. This tree models an inherently communal and organic process: all the members must cooperate to produce the fruit. Thus Anima's image succinctly restates what Will's guides have been saying about charity in a way that maximizes the virtue's communal aspects.

When he responds to Will's question about where this wonderful tree grows, Anima reminds us that in Langland's hands, allegory rarely remains a static picture from which significances can mechanically be "read off."[5] Rather, allegory becomes an extraordinarily supple vehicle for discovering and illustrating complementary aspects of truth. Anima presents another view of the tree, one that shifts our attention from the community of all Christians to the ontology that every Christian shares (16.13–17): the tree is a planting from the stock of humanity that has been set to grow in the human heart;[6] free will has the land on lease to till and care for under the direction of Piers Plowman. We can understand how "free will" has the land "on lease": it is free will whose choices lead the soul to virtue or to vice, and the "lease" expires when the Creator calls the soul home. But before we follow Will into the second inner dream, this reference to Piers Plowman requires us to pause over that figure's range of meanings.

Who Is Piers the Plowman?

Piers Plowman is apparently Langland's own invention. Despite disagreement over precisely how to capture Piers in words, critics substantially agree on his central meaning, and he clearly finds his ultimate expression in the person of Christ.[7] Nevertheless, equating Piers with Christ, even in these passus retelling the Redemption, would miss a significant aspect of Langland's poetic strategy.

I suggested earlier that we think of Piers as "human nature at its best"—human nature that is "true" in the sense of Lady Holy Church's speech. Langland presents this best with different emphases in different contexts. Thus, in passus 5 to 7, Piers labors honestly at his "pilgrimage" on the half acre and accepts Truth's terms when the pardon is granted him. This faithful Christian workman is the Piers referred to in the priest's prayer at 13.237: human nature in human society viewed primarily in the context of winning and using temporal goods. In the latter parts of the poem, emphasis falls on spiritual goods: salvation, penitence, grace, and the need for Christian community. Thus, beginning with Clergie's definition of Dowel in passus 13, Piers has come increasingly to be associated with, and to evoke, an expression of truth that emphasizes the love adumbrated by Clergie and the charity so engagingly described by Anima: childlike, selfless, supportive of others, to be encountered only when Piers comes (13.124–30, 133; 15.196). This new realization of Piers ultimately points to Christ, the apotheosis of human nature—the only totally clear manifestation of selfless love in human form. But even then Piers is not Christ. As God, Christ is ready to vanquish the devil the instant he is born; but "Piers Plowman perceived the fulness of time" (16.103): human nature urges Christ to tarry in it for the years of Christ's life on earth, to abide long enough to "learn" by experience its frailty and suffering. Later Christ appears "somewhat like" Piers (18.10) to joust in Piers's "battle clothing" (18.22, cf. 18.25, 19.12). Piers here means the best of human nature as assumed by Christ and perfectly realized in him: Christ is God's idea of what a human being should be. But Piers remains the best of *human* nature, beckoning to be realized by each Christian. Thus after Christ's Ascension, when the new church is being "sown" and "tilled," Piers Plowman is Peter, the apostles, and their successors tilling new soil and establishing the church. By the end of the poem, where Piers can be found has become an anxious question. Returning to Anima's announcement of Piers's name, at which Will swoons, we find "human nature at its best" in a somewhat different context: what I have called its ontological relationship with its Creator and exemplar, both "now" and as salvation history began.

"A Love-Dream": The Second Inner Dream (16.19–166)

The second inner dream balances the first in passus 11. The first one completed Will's radical isolation as a culpable individual; the second initiates his sense of reintegration with humanity and its Creator. The tree Will sees, whose fruit Piers struggles to protect, exists in the "now" of Christian time, after the Fall and the Redemption, for it suffers temptation and enjoys the support of Christ's passion (16.37) and of Christian grace (16.51). The scene bristles with activity: the winds of the three temptations assail the tree's attempts to bear fruit, and familiar sins (covetousness, fleshly desire, unkindness of neighbors) attack it. But Will notices first the three "props" that support the tree and that Piers uses against its foes. Integral to the garden, ready to help the tree, the Persons of the Trinity stand always near to cooperate with Piers. They do not function simply on their own: for example, free will must choose to resist the devil and must seize on the grace the Holy Spirit offers. But in the human heart, always accessible to the capacity of human nature to do its best, the Trinity stands close by its *imago*.

Piers describes the tree's fruit (16.67–72) as three grades of chastity: fidelity in marriage, sexual abstinence after one's spouse has died, and total celibacy. Christianity associated controlling sexual desire with over-coming selfishness and the disposition to sin and with turning the mind and heart toward God (contrast the "lord who lived according to lust" in passus 20). The tree remains communal, producing the "charity" of dif-ferent "lives" (marriage, widowhood, virginity).[8] And because they grow on this tree protected by the Trinity, we should notice that Abraham will soon elaborate an analogy between these three states and the three Per-sons of the Trinity.

Lines 73 to 85 recall the Fall of Adam and Eve in the Garden of Eden. Will wants to taste the fruit (16.73–74), and at his prompting Piers disturbs the tree. Immediately the fruits of charity just described all experience the Fall's effects (16.75–77). At the top, virginity cries out (because maintaining it is so difficult), widowhood weeps (because death enters human experience), and marriage makes a foul noise when disturbed (because fierce passion accompanies sexual intercourse). And all the fruit, all good humans subject to death and so to falling from the tree, find themselves carried off to hell by the devil.[9]

But, one may object, if Piers represents "human nature at its best," how can Langland here portray him participating in the Fall? Because that is exactly what happened. Human nature at its best, newly created by God and living in God's presence in Eden, free of uncontrolled pas-sion and free in will, chose to taste the forbidden fruit and so fell:[10] for Christians, a terrible mystery (as Langland has said before), but one whose happy outcome they could choose to celebrate. For the Fall demonstrated God's commitment to humanity and occasioned Christ's appearance among them. In the words of the Easter Vigil's exultant song, "O blessed fault, O necessary sin of Adam!" (see 5.583a).

Thus the vision of the tree and garden in the inner dream begins with the ongoing moral conflict of Will's present—humanity's struggle to produce charity from a tree that grows in the human heart (cf. 5.605–9). Temptations and threats press on it, as they have in Will's own experience (and in Haukyn's). But this vision emphasizes how Piers attends and protects and how the very Persons of the Trinity closely support the endeavor. And when the Fall occurs—the Fall in which all share—Langland portrays the remarkable aftermath: Piers seizes the prop of the Son, with the cooperation of Father and Holy Spirit, and sets out to despoil the despoiler (16.86–89). Does this say that human nature's potential to be true could compel God the Son? Not quite. But in a theology where God knows all from all eternity, the Trinity knows that its favorite creature and *imago* will fall, creates it nevertheless, and, intent on recovering and restoring its *imago*, on salvaging the best in human nature, has been eternally committed to the Redemption. The bonds in this community are profound indeed.

No attentive reader can miss the abrupt shift in tone and mode that now occurs. With "and then the Holy Spirit spoke in Gabriel's mouth" (16.90), we pass from allegorical tableau to biblical narrative, to the Annunciation and Incarnation. Within 10 lines we read about Christ's birth, in another 20 about his public life of wondrous healing and the raising of Lazarus (a portent of Christian resurrection). Christ's conflicts with the Jewish leaders who reject his miracles and misuse God's temple and his prediction of its destruction and restoration lead quickly to their accusations, his betrayal and arrest, his "joust" in Jerusalem, and his death and promised resurrection. And with that, the inner dream concludes, and Langland launches into his most sweeping commemoration of salvation history: the Fall (already evoked); Abraham, Moses, and the Samaritan all straining impatiently, with Will, toward the "joust" in Jerusalem; and the harrowing, vividly presented in passus 18. But why has Langland already retold Christ's life here in the inner dream?[11]

One might answer, first, that as the central events of Christian faith, the Incarnation and Redemption are a fundamental theme, never far below the surface of this poem; they have, in fact, been rehearsed at some length previously and will be again (e.g., 1.148–75, 5.477–505, 19.40–198). Second, Langland never pretends they have not already happened, that they are not history (thus in the inner dream he recounts them in the past, not the future, tense). Third, Langland must have intended Will and the audience to reencounter this familiar story in different contexts and under different emphases so as to come away with different reactions. In the inner dream, Langland emphasizes Christ's intimate relationship with Piers, with Christ's learning firsthand about human suffering, his skill in healing human misery, and his own experience of rejection and suffering. The intimate companionship with humanity here portrayed begins immediately after the Fall and ends

with Christ's triumph on humanity's behalf: "He died, and destroyed
death, and made night into day" (16.166). Thus the inner dream has
taken Will from allegorically portrayed ontology into literal history: the
shared "now" of defending the tree with Piers; the shared Fall, which
precipitates us into history; the association of God the Son with Piers,
sharing human experience. Reunited with the human community in all
these ways, Will wakes, wiping his eyes, and seeks to rejoin Piers.[12]

"A Midlenten Sunday": Abraham, Moses, Samaritan (16.172–17)

As Will searches on, Langland continues to envelop him in communal
processes. The poem first clearly evokes the liturgy with its reference to
"a midlenten Sunday" (16.172) and further dramatizes the community
of salvation history by the figures Will meets. This history emerges so
vividly because Langland makes us imagine all these actors simultaneously alive: the past of Christ's life becomes a moment toward which
Abraham and Moses are brought forward, Will brought back. Thus, for
example, Abraham has just heard of Christ's baptism (16.249–50), the
Samaritan speaks of the babe born in Bethlehem (17.125), and in the
end they all hasten toward the joust in Jerusalem (17.81–88, 355). This
sort of imaginative simultaneity, this "omnitemporalness," creates
exactly the kind of overlaid experiences for which the liturgy strives as it
reenacts biblical events (both Old Testament "figures" and their New
Testament fulfillments) and applies them to current time.

Langland had excellent reasons for choosing Abraham, Moses, and
the Samaritan and for associating them with Faith, Hope, and Charity.
God called Abraham as first patriarch of the chosen people, promised
"land and lordship" to him and his innumerable offspring, entered into
the covenant of circumcision with him, and first revealed himself as
Trinity to him. Abraham, for his part, persevered for years in the faith
that God would finally send him the offspring promised and then
endured God's test when asked to sacrifice Isaac, his only son (Gen.
12–22). Thus Abraham fitly represents all the chosen whom God has
promised to save; in his willingness to sacrifice his only son, moreover,
he was regarded as a "figure," an analogue, of God the Father. For all
these reasons, Piers's fruit, the just who must wait in hell until Christ
reopens heaven, abide in the bosom of this keeper of the promise.

As Abraham was foremost patriarch of the chosen "before the law,"
so Moses was first in the age of the Old Law, the one to whom God gave

the Ten Commandments[13] and whom God chose to lead his people out of Egypt toward the promised land.[14] As leader of the Exodus, Moses was considered a figure of God the Son, who would finally lead humanity from the Egypt of Original Sin to the promised land of grace, from *limbo inferni* to heaven. Postponing for a moment consideration of the Samaritan, let us recall that Faith, Hope, and Charity are the three fundamental theological virtues of Christianity;[15] the dynamic of their interrelationship and their fruition in charity, analogous to the "procession" of the Holy Spirit from Father and Son, constitutes another analogue in these overlapping communities.[16] To this section of the poem that began with the participation of the Trinity in protecting the tree of charity, then, Langland adds two more trinities: we might have expected them to be Abraham, Moses, and Christ paralleled with Faith, Hope, and Charity. Instead we find Abraham, Moses, and *the Samaritan* beside Faith, Hope, and *the Samaritan*. Can we see any purpose in this?

First, Langland obviously wishes to evoke analogies between Father, Son, and Holy Spirit that discover and express the community binding humanity to deity. The analogies between Abraham and the Father and between Moses and Christ the Son had long been established by biblical commentary. The poet therefore needed an analogue in salvation history for the Holy Spirit, and as we shall see shortly, he discovered a brilliantly effective one in the Samaritan. Second, the Samaritan functions as surrogate. He exists, after all, in a parable Christ told in answer to the question "Who is my neighbor?" (Luke 10:30–35). The Samaritan is not Christ: he defers to the babe born in Bethlehem, whose blood will finally heal (17.96–100, 122–126); even as he performs his selfless deed, he refers to Christ's dying on the cross (17.112); finally he rushes like Abraham, Moses, and Will toward Jerusalem to witness Christ's joust.[17] Nor is he, fully, Charity; rather he is the *potential* for charity that becomes fully efficacious only through Christ's sacrifice (cf. 17.121–26). Thus in the Samaritan we not only find another type of actor (a character from a parable) made to walk the same stage as the poet's Will and salvation history's Abraham and Moses but also encounter one more promise, one more postponing anticipation, of Piers fully realized in the Charity that is Christ.

"As We Went, Speaking Together": Truth in Trinities

Will, joined by this accumulating group of figures traveling expectantly toward fulfillment, shares in the experience of each as they go. Abraham emphasizes faith in the Trinity because this central truth about the Christian God, revealed first to him, remains the most fundamental tenet of the faith. But his speech stresses not static dogma but dynamic and productive interactions of the divine persons among themselves (e.g., 16.186, 193)[18] and of these persons with humanity. Thus, for example, the Father sends the Son to "generate issue" on "mother church," an issue that in its turn is three-in-one.[19] Humanity, in its own activities, replicates the Trinity: thus Father, Son, and Holy Spirit find their analogues in man, woman, and issue, in marriage, widowhood, and virginity. Far from being a distant and arid abstraction, Abraham's Trinity lives, interacting with and continually manifested in human lives. However, the Trinity's full impact can be achieved, its original *imago* restored, only with the completion of God's redemptive plan.

Moses speaks as recipient of the Law. Strikingly, the stone tablets of Sinai and the enormous elaboration of Old Testament law and ritual become just two injunctions with a single gloss (17.11–16): the "two great commandments" given by Christ, which sum up all the law and the prophets (Matt. 22:36 – 40); as Christ said, he came not to dissolve the Old Law but to fulfill it (Matt. 5:17). This love has saved many, as both Moses and Abraham attest. But Moses straightway identifies himself as *Spes,* "hope" (17.1). Until the Redemption, Moses' charity remains only hope, for until Christ fulfills the law with the Charity of his self-sacrifice, those who lived such love remain, like Abraham's faithful, with the rest of Piers's fruit in *limbo inferni*. At the same time, Langland probably intended another effect of making "love" the law of "hope": he implies that those who want any hope of salvation must love, as the Samaritan will later insist.

Will's attempt to choose between Abraham's faith and Moses' hopeful love (17.26 – 49) reintroduces the perspective of a Christian seeking to separate Dowel from Dobet and Dobest: it is easier to believe in three lovely persons than to love a wretch! (17.45 – 46). The narrative reenactment of Christ's parable of the Samaritan that follows clearly counters Will's attempt to separate them, for both in the events (55–82) and in the Samaritan's gloss on them (93–126), all three virtues prove necessary.[20] Meanwhile Will, impressed by the Samaritan's compassion, pursues him and offers to be his servant (17.86 –88). And then Langland uses Will's all too human question as entry point for the Samaritan's lesson: should one choose faith or love? (17.127–33). The answer fulfills Clergie's earlier surmise (13.128 –30) and binds the three virtues in love, in imitation of Trinity.

Embrace both belief and love, says the Samaritan, and if tempted to think otherwise, look at your hand (134–38). But the immediately following lines on "God as hand" say nothing that explicitly addresses faith versus hopeful love or even the two together. Rather, given that faith is the Father and hopeful love the Son (as we have noted, the traditional analogies for Abraham and Moses), the hand image shifts our attention to the Third Person of the Trinity, the Holy Spirit, for the Samaritan's exploitation of this image compels our attention to the overwhelming importance of the "palm" (Holy Spirit) in the "hand's" activities. It concludes that whoever sins "against the Holy Spirit" risks losing all grace and absolution. Asked "Faith/Abraham/Father, or Hopeful Love/Moses/Son?" the Samaritan has answered "Grace/Holy Spirit." The last word of this speech, "quench" (17.205), carries us on to the argument's resolution in the image of the torch.[21]

This new Trinitarian metaphor compares Father, Son, and Holy Spirit to the wax, wick, and light of a candle. But the image actually has four terms, not three; the fourth is the blaze that this torch can kindle. For the torch of the Trinity to have effect, it must be allowed to set people afire (209 –13). In this blaze, "love and belief" become one, as indistinguishable as "flame and lovely fire" (17.213, 210). Humanity can choose to blow this blaze out or to blow it into vital flame. *Unkyndness*, unnatural nonlove, selfishly destroys love and life and blows the flame out; then the spark of the Holy Spirit, though still alight within the Trinity, nevertheless remains "grace without mercy" (17.218), its effects for humanity nullified. Faithful love, on the other hand, blows the spark into flame, producing grace with forgiveness as the blaze of love melts Father and Son into mercy like icicles melted by the sun (17.215–34). Christ the Son finally made grace available through his death on the cross, but Langland once again describes how the entire Trinity cooperated in the Redemption and invokes the tradition whereby the Holy Spirit, the love that "issues" between Father and Son, dispenses the grace Christ won.

Christians cannot, of course, do without faith or hope any more than the Trinity can consist of Father without Son: God remains three in one just as faith and hope blaze indistinguishably in the fire of people's faithful love. Langland's imagination nevertheless plays with the idea of wax without wick and wick without wax for the sake of emphasizing that each can burn in itself, mercifully responding to the blaze of human penitence (17.235– 47). But the Samaritan will not allow Will to imagine that the Trinity's candle can have any efficacy without the "tinder" of a cooperative human disposition (17.248–61). This tinder, this potential for self-giving love, ready to burst into flame when touched with the grace that the Redemption supplies, is precisely what the Samaritan represents. The capacity for charity is the *kyndnes* defined by the quotation from 1 Cor. 13 (17.261a). *Unkyndnes* will not catch fire in response to the Trinity's light, and for such a disposition, the Samaritan repeats, the Holy Spirit remains merely "grace without mercy" (17.252).

The speech's conclusion sets out *unkyndnes* in very practical terms, anchored on the Gospel story of the rich man *Dives* who, through sheer, heedless selfishness, allowed the poor Lazarus to starve (17.267–69, cf. Luke 16:19–31). Such unnatural behavior, tantamount to that of thieves who kill fellow humans for mere "things," destroys the Trinity's "taper," the light of life and love in human beings; people who annihilate that light should expect no mercy for themselves (17.262–98).

Will's final question to the Samaritan voices a concern that might have occurred at this point to many in Langland's audience: can one who has lived an *unkynd* life repent and confess, even at the end? Put more crudely, can one persist in unloving sin and snatch absolving grace at the last moment? The Samaritan's answer, given through similes, discourages anyone from clinging to such a hope. Notably, he suggests that the human psyche is fundamentally too sound to tolerate such unreasonable expectations. If people live badly, their inherent sense of justice will more likely generate despair than hope for grace (17.303–20, esp. 313–14). And just as a smoky fire most surely drives one from his own dwelling, so *unkyndnes* drives out grace; it is totally against reason not to love, not to be generous, not to wish others well here and hereafter (17.351–54). These are, of course, the sentiments of the Samaritan. But he speaks for the Trinity and for Christ.

"And Lay Low Terrible Death Forever": Dream 6 (Passus 18)

The combination of the Samaritan's rushing off, Will's waking, and the ensuing interlude (18.1–6) breaks any simple sequence from the "mid-lenten Sunday" of passus 16 to the events that passus 18 next describes. The interlude even suggests that Will toils on for a very long while ("all my life time," 18.3), an effect that mirrors the patient endurance of humanity awaiting the climax of salvation history.[22] Once again, the interlude attests no "perfection" in Will. But his condition can be read as that of one persevering in the quest for Piers: a life without physical comfort, detached from worldly goods and joys, worthless in the eyes of the world (1–3). Because these lines emphasize hardship, the consolations offered by the coming dream—the climactic reunion of all Piers's fruit with Christ—will stand out all the more compellingly, and the mood of the interlude following this new dream will emphasize its impact on Will.

The sixth dream returns Will to the last week of Lent.[23] It begins on Palm Sunday, which commemorates Christ's triumphal entry into Jerusalem, which quickly precipitated the events of his Passion.[24] In the opening lines (7–35), Langland establishes the mode he will use throughout the dream. The verse, striking and often lyrical, combines strains from contemporary life, Gospel story, the liturgy, and the figurative characters already established to generate a rich texture of meaning and resonance. Reflecting contemporary life, a young knight rides spurless into a city where he will be dubbed and joust in his first tournament; a herald of arms sees and announces his arrival from an upperstory window. His mount is not a charger but the ass (11) of the Gospels. The children and *gloria laus* (7), *Osanna* (8), *fili David* (15), and "Blessed is he who comes in the name of the Lord!" (17a) all evoke both the Gospel accounts and the liturgical commemorations of them.[25] Samaritan, Piers Plowman, and Faith resume figurative personalities from the previous dream, while Old Jews (17) captures the people of the Old Testament, perhaps even the "old man" (*vetus homo*, cf. Rom. 6:6) awaiting Redemption. The stratagem luring death and the devil to the tournament, the redeeming guile that will entrap Satan the beguiler, finds eloquent expression in Jesus' jousting in Piers's arms so that Christ not be recognized (22, 24). Then the herald Faith explains Jesus' "challenge" in artful language that focuses on the outcome of the battle (28–35). Christ's trial, scourging, mocking, crucifixion, and death are told in just two dozen lines (36–59). Into these Langland seamlessly weaves Latin tags from the Gospels (e.g., 39, 46, 47, 50), thus evoking both Scripture and liturgy,[26] and he ends the account with two wonderfully effective lines (58–59).

Having so deftly evoked the events of Holy Week through Good Friday, Langland then devotes the rest of this dream to the effects, to the aftermath, of the Crucifixion. He builds toward the final demonstration of Christ's victory and heightens the sense of glorious hope that victory generates by maintaining a sense of opposition and suspense until the climax. Thus the sun grows dark, the wall of the temple splits,[27] and tombs gape open and the dead come forth to ask how this battle between life and death will end (cf. Matt. 27:52–53). Langland then takes up that question in two stages. Has the New Law replaced the Old Law? Has Christ conquered death and the devil?

The first stage concerns the death of Christ and the end of the Old Law (71–109). To ensure that those crucified had indeed died, executioners broke the victims' legs; that Christ's were not broken fulfilled a prophecy.[28] Instead his side was pierced, the last of his blood running out (John 15:34). Langland turns this "proof" of death into an expression of Christ's first victory in his joust: Longinus, traditionally a Roman soldier, appears as a blind Jewish knight representing the Old Law in judicial combat, striking the dead Christ at the instigation of his superiors in a parody of prowess (94–97). Paradoxically, the victor loses, falls to his knees before the vanquished in submission, renounces the Old Law, and accepts the New. Longinus regains his sight at the same instant he converts to Christianity.[29] Langland then has Faith, both as herald of arms and as patriarch Abraham, keeper of the Old Covenant, pronounce Christ's victory in this tournament, declaring the Old Law superseded by the New.[30]

But Will has not yet witnessed the victory that Faith declares. Christ's ultimate goal is not to die on the cross but to conquer death and the devil, to reclaim Piers's fruit from the prison of hell and then to reemerge among humanity. Thus the real climax is to be the harrowing of hell and the Resurrection, and until these events have occurred, the issue remains in doubt. Consequently the dreamer, still fearful, "withdrew in that darkness to 'he descended into hell' " where he witnesses the harrowing " 'according to the scriptures' " (111–12). The two Latin quotations, both well-known creedal phrases, portend what is to come.[31] Langland's retelling of these events further heightens their drama and exults in the victory they proclaim: he situates the harrowing within a traditional discussion of whether Redemption is even thinkable, the debate of the "four daughters of God." This tradition is based on Ps. 84:11, quoted at 421a: "Mercy and Truth have met on the way; Justice and Peace have kissed" (see further Pearsall, 324, 116).

God's decree justly condemned Adam and Eve to death (and hell) for having violated his precept in the garden. Can Piers's fruit possibly be saved through God's Mercy and Peace without violating his Truth and Justice? This question was the subject of the traditional "debate" between the four virtues, and Langland uses it to frame the events (112–260, 408–23). He takes the issues seriously, and he (like the medieval theologians) has certainly paid attention to making Christ's victory consonant with Reason and the law.[32] But the inclusion of the debate here serves not to prove the Redemption possible but rather to celebrate its marvelous triumph, its proffer of universal hope. And so the debate concludes not just with the kiss of the psalm verse but with exultant songs that come to merge with the choirs and bells celebrating Easter morning.

The virtues' debate fits smoothly into the unfolding drama: Mercy and Truth encounter each other as they arrive to marvel at the events unfolding just outside hell: the din and darkness and dawning day, the light and blaze before hell's gates (123–24). Beneath the verse's fluid surface lies a tight structure. The virtues appear in pairs, as in the psalm verse (Mercy and Truth, then Peace and Justice). In each pair, the benign member recognizes what is about to transpire, the severe one exclaims that it cannot be, then the benign one counters with an argument that Redemption can indeed reach completion. Mercy sets out the rationale for like antidotes (venom against venom, death against death, grace's guile against the devil's, 150 – 62). Peace argues that consigning Adam, Eve, and the rest of the just to hell for a finite length of time has served God's purpose because it has taught them the real meaning of joy (203–29). Finally, a character with "two eyes set wide apart" named Book (apparently representing Scripture)[33] adds his testimony to that of Mercy and Peace: all the elements (as Scripture reports them) have acknowledged Jesus to be Christ; unless Christ rises to comfort his people and undo those who would reject him, Book itself becomes meaningless and so would willingly be burned.[34]

This debate encloses the events of the harrowing. Langland makes Truth the one to say "Let's wait, I see and hear" what now goes forward (261– 65). Associated with the harrowing from the earliest times were the last four verses of Psalm 23, which voiced a twice-repeated challenge and response: "Lift up your gates [*Attolite portas*], O ye princes, and be ye lifted up, O eternal gates; and the king of glory will enter in. Who is this king of Glory? The Lord who is strong and mighty: the Lord mighty in battle."[35] Medieval tradition developed the drama inherent in the psalm into the confrontation between Christ and devils. After Truth reports the first challenge, the devils debate their course of action, exposing in the process both their futility and the "legality" of Christ's raiding their stronghold. Then (316 –20) Lucifer and Christ speak the second pair of psalm verses, and at Christ's words, hell bursts open, and the just greet the Victor with joyful song (321–27). Christ addresses Satan, then binds "all the rout" of devils (403– 4) and leads the just to heaven (406–7). These acts constitute the triumph, and the proof, of the Redemption for Piers and for all of humanity.

In presenting Christ's long address to Satan (327–403), Langland has done everything possible to hold out the hope of forgiveness and salvation to all of humankind. That address not only asserts the possibility and "legality" of salvation (esp. 340–57, 400–403) but also seems to suggest its universality. Two kinds of sin must be overcome: original and actual. The souls Christ removes from hell at the harrowing are the just, condemned for their share in Original Sin (330–68), and only the "worthy" depart with Christ now (328). But after an ingenious play on drinks of death,[36] the speech turns to the Last Judgment (371–99) and those in hell because of actual sin, insisting that Christ can save not only all Christians (his "whole brethren," 377) but also other human beings (his "half brethren," 393). They may have to suffer the punishments of hell (that is, of purgatory, 392) until that time, but in the end, Christ can have all humanity in heaven (397).[37] The possibility of universal salvation dominates here, at the poem's most elevated commemoration of the Redemption, and that possibility drives its exultant tone. Conditions and limitations practically disappear: for example, the penitential requirements of restitution and satisfaction become muted to mere whispers.[38] To this eloquently celebrated possibility I believe Langland hoped his every reader would respond.

Will certainly does. For once not solitary, he rouses "wife" and "daughter"[39] to come reverence the cross, the jewel that brings remedy and banishes every threatening spirit (424–31). As the interlude continues into the start of passus 19, we see him dressed in handsome clothes, for a change, in church at Easter morning mass. For the moment, he seems optimistic and once again part of society.

Chapter Nine
"Paying Piers's Pardon, *redde quod debes*" (Passus 19–20)

At the beginning of passus 19, on the verge of his seventh and next-to-last dream, Will seems animated by the vision of Piers triumphant, by the hope that Langland so eloquently sought to evoke. This dream will continue the celebration, but in an increasingly somber tone, one through which Langland returns Will, and the audience, to life still to be lived and to moral responsibility.

"Conscience on Christ and the Cross": Easter Morning

Passus 18 represents the harrowing of hell as occurring some time after Christ's death on the cross but before his Resurrection in the body on Easter Sunday morning. Passus 19 resumes the narrative of Christ's triumph as one of its topics, for what Will dreams when he falls asleep at Easter mass continues salvation history from the harrowing through Pentecost. The brisk review of Christ's life soon reaches the events of Holy Week (19.138–39). After the briefest mention of Christ's capture, trial, and crucifixion (140–42), the account emphasizes the events of that first Easter morning, the Resurrection, and Christ's subsequent appearances to his disciples, as told in the Gospels. Thus Langland describes the guarding of the tomb (143–48, Matt. 27:62–66), the appearance of the angels to the guards and the Resurrection (149–53, Matt. 28:1–4), the subsequent attempt to silence the guards (154–56, Matt. 28:11–15), Christ's appearance to Mary Magdalen (157–62, John 20:1–2, 11–18), and the visit by Peter and others to the empty tomb (163–65, John 20:3–10, cf. Luke 24:12). Tradition associated all these episodes with the original Easter morning. Next Langland recounts Christ's two appearances to the assembled apostles, first in "doubting" Thomas's absence, then with him present (165–81, John 20:19–29, cf. Luke 24:36–43).

In the Gospel accounts, what follows is Christ's "commissioning" apostles and church: "Going therefore, teach ye all nations; baptizing them in the name of the Father, and of the Son, and of the Holy Ghost."[1] Langland substituted for this an earlier passage in which Christ declares Peter the rock upon which he will establish the church and gives to him the "power of the keys" (182–90, Matt. 16:18–19). Christ's Ascension follows (191–92),[2] and here Langland interrupts his sequential narrative with a reference to the Second Coming and Last Judgment (192–98). Why the substituted commissioning and the pause here on Judgment? Both are, I think, essential to the poet's strategy in this passus, to which we shall turn in a moment. For now let us simply note that the creeds regularly listed Second Coming and Judgment immediately after the Ascension. Having thus closed the life of Christ, Langland goes on to describe the launching of the church, traditionally associated with Pentecost, when the Paraclete, the Holy Spirit, descended upon the fearful and sequestered apostles in the form of tongues of fire (201– 6, Acts 2:1– 4).[3] From this point, as it recounts the "planting" and "tilling" of the church, the passus leaves historical narrative for allegory.

In the two previous dreams, Langland explicitly evoked the liturgy; does he do so here? This passus contains two unmistakable references to liturgical commemoration. The first, obviously, is the mass that Will attends (3–5). The second is the *Veni Creator Spiritus* ("Come, Creator, Spirit," 210), a hymn especially associated with Pentecost. Other events this dream recounts were, of course, the subject of liturgical readings and liturgical song: Christ's appearance to Mary, Peter's visit to the tomb, and the announcing angels were all recalled on Easter Sunday; Christ's appearance to doubting Thomas was the Gospel reading for the Sunday after Easter. But, in fact, the events from Palm Sunday through Pentecost had been interpretatively mapped onto precise days of the week and then exactly imitated in the liturgical calendar, so that during this part of the year original event and ritual reenactment were inseparable. Langland's retelling, effectively evoking both Gospels and liturgy, once again generates the effect of simultaneity in which past and present revitalize each other in the audience's imagination.

Langland aimed, then, at carrying through the celebration of the Resurrection in this dream. But he also sought to lead Will to another perspective, one not simply celebratory: What God has done demands something in return. Will fell asleep "when men went to the offering" (4)[4] and dreamed that Piers/Jesus came before the congregation, all bloody and bearing a cross (4–8). Some particular detail of the Easter liturgy in Langland's day might have suggested this sequence of events.[5] But the offertory and the paradoxes traditionally associated with Christ and his cross allow us to surmise Langland's associations. On the cross, the author of life suffered death, death died, and through that death came life for all. Two well-known hymns by the seventh-century bishop Venantius Fortunatus, the *Pange Lingua* ("Declare, O tongue") and the *Vexilla Regis* ("The battle standard of the King"), illustrate the traditional associations.[6] Both hymns present the cross as instrument of torture on the one hand and as trophy of victory, a gleaming battle ensign of the conquering king, on the other. Both hymns juxtapose the suffering humanity of Jesus with the omnipotence of Christ-God triumphant, the blood of the passion with the royal purple of Christ's imperial rule. The cross, then, especially on Easter morning, inevitably evokes both suffering human victim and triumphant divine victor, Jesus and Christ.

At the offertory of the mass, moreover, bread and wine are prepared to be offered to God as a reenactment of Christ's sacrifice on the cross.[7] A late-medieval meditation suggests what a Christian should be thinking at this moment:

> At the offertory when the priest takes the chalice and holds it up and makes the offering: meditate on how Our Lord the Savior of all humankind most willingly offered himself to his eternal father to be sacrifice and oblation for humanity's Redemption and offer yourself to him again, both body and soul, which he so dearly bought. (*Lay Folks' Mass Book*, 233)

Why should Will turn, at this moment, to Conscience as his guide? Because both crucifix and offertory should remind Will that Christ died for his sins and now demands moral choice of him. Will must seize the cross as his "weapon" and offer in his turn the suffering he will experience in resisting sin and undertaking penitence (63–68).

As Conscience embarks on his review of Christ's life, he uses terms appropriate to this theme. He replaces Will's "Jesus," the young jouster who assumed Piers's garments, with "Christ" the conqueror. By invoking a triad, three degrees each more desirable than the one before (knight, king, conqueror, 27–31), Conscience establishes a new scale for appreciating the stages of Christ's life, his Dowel, Dobet, and Dobest. Christ embodies all three, but he emerges finally as conqueror and judge, and as such he will exalt his faithful followers as surely as he will lay low those

140 WILLIAM LANGLAND REVISITED

who oppose him and reject his laws (32– 62). As "Jesus," he was already sovereign over all, knight, incarnate but not yet "grown," and his Dowel consisted in revealing his powers, at his mother's request, in his first public miracle at the wedding feast at Cana: he turned water into wine and simultaneously heralded the new law of love (69 –123). But then, grown to manhood, he left his mother, becoming famous for his healing and nourishing; and so he did better and was proclaimed worthy to be king (124–39). The latter precipitated his capture, trial, and death, and from the time he conquered on the cross and arose from the dead, he became "Christ," conqueror (140 –81).[8] He did best, finally, when he made the effects of his conquest available, establishing the dispensation of grace, of baptism and penance (182–90). But as king and conqueror, able to establish and enforce his laws, he requires some compliance from humanity, some cooperation, *redde quod debes,* "pay what you owe" (187). As Conscience's narrative pauses on the reference to the Last Judgment, his morally demanding perspective on Christ's triumph comes to rest at this sobering conclusion.

"Piers the Plowman's Pardon, *redde quod debes*"[9] essentially repeats the pardon of passus 7: Christ's law requires human reaction, the poem insists. Specifically, Christians must make restitution for temporal goods unjustly gotten and must offer satisfaction (penance and amendment) to God for their sins. At the same time, powerful overtones of the Latin that Langland has chosen indicate that he does not speak of harsh justice. The injunction comes from a parable Christ told about forgiveness, in which a king agrees to ignore a huge debt owed him by one of his servants. But the forgiven servant then goes to a fellow and demands immediate payment of a much smaller debt, declaring to him, "Redde quod debes" (Matt. 18:28). The king, learning of this, retracts his mercy and gives the unforgiving servant over to the torturers.

Later in this passus, Conscience will say that forgiving one another can pass for *redde quod debes:* "Or let each person forgive another, and that is what the *Our Father* urges: *And forgive us our debts {as we forgive our debtors},* and so be absolved" (19.394–95). Augustine's Sermon 83 on this parable emphasized that it has two lessons: "Forgive and be forgiven" and "Give and it shall be given unto you."[10] Earlier the Samaritan urged that only "smoky" unnaturalness drives away God's mercy, that wishing others well and extending them goodwill should be within the power of every human being (17.347–53). *Redde* does not make impossibly harsh demands.

I think Langland strives for the rhetorical middle way. We next see Piers cultivating "truth" in the new church by sowing the seeds of the very practical cardinal virtues. Langland wants social justice to prevail, and he will continue to lambaste selfish and unjust use of temporal goods, most especially when combined with the travesty of spiritual ones. He passionately wants, in short, humanity's response to the Redemption to drive social reform on earth. But he does not want to frighten sinners away. The Dobest of this conquering king consists of his establishing an economy of forgiveness; if people will at least strive to forgive one another, to "love their enemies" in this everyday sense, they can hope for forgiveness from Christ. But Christ's mercy, as we have seen, can damn as well as save. *Redde quod debes,* in its full implications, allows Conscience to demand response while still keeping alive hope in that mercy.

"Grace Set Out with Piers": The Idea of the Church

After Pentecost, as Grace sets out with Piers to summon Conscience and the people (213), Langland may be generalizing on the immediate aftermath of the Spirit's descent (Acts 2:6 – 47). But lines 213 to 261 also present us with another of Langland's moral paradigms, this one of the specifically Christian society, the church.

Why does Langland immediately voice the threat to that society (213–26)? The notion of Antichrist appears in Christian tradition from the outset: "Who is a liar, but he who denieth that Jesus is the Christ? This is Antichrist, who denieth the truth of the Son" (1 John 2:22; cf. 4:1, 2 John 1:5). Part of the paradigm of the City of God is the lasting opposition it faces from the City of Man.[11] Langland will soon dramatize this conflict in two complementary scenes, one archetypal and general, the other historical.

Langland bases his account of the weapons and treasures that Grace distributes to the church on Paul's first letter to the Corinthians (1 Cor. 12:4, quoted at 228a). Like Paul, Langland stresses that although people perform many different ministries, God operates through all. But the gifts Paul describes are spiritual only: wisdom, knowledge, faith, healing, prophecy, discernment, tongues, and interpretation (1 Cor. 12:5–11). Langland begins with gifts of teaching and knowledge and ends with the monastic, or eremetic, vocation, but the intervening list includes the human "skills" of all estates. The last gift, "longing to be hence" (248 – 49), reminds all of society's ultimate destination, yet as always Langland visualizes the concrete effects in this world of Christian life well lived.

Paul concluded his division of gifts with the "mystical body" metaphor: one whole body, collectively that "of Christ," made up of many different members (feet, hands, ears, eyes), each with its necessary function. Some may be more "honorable" or more "comely" than others (1 Cor. 12:23–24, cf. line 252), but all make up one whole that must cooperate without rift, and Paul proceeds directly to account all such gifts as worthless in comparison with charity (1 Cor. 13:1). Langland follows him, insisting that Grace taught everyone to be *lele,* "law abiding," and urging all to love in harmony (250 –55). Let rational conduct rule the world (256 –57, cf. Pr.112–22). But this is society precisely as redeemed, as subject to Christ, king and conqueror; so Piers (Christ's vicar in Peter and his successors) should be overseer and treasurer, his task to lead humanity in "tilling truth" (258 – 61).

As Langland develops this new agrarian scenario, he recasts the half acre of passus 6. Now it is human souls that come under cultivation, and the crop consists in virtuous behavior. A plow team of the four Evangelists opens the "ground," which is further loosened and kept free of weeds by the teaching of the great church Fathers who "harrow" it with Old and New Testaments. To appreciate Langland's complex metaphor, we must resist the temptation to read this passus as a single and simple picture allegory. For example, people are both the tilled earth and the beneficiaries of its fruit: Piers sows his seed in human souls, and those souls should eat the grain produced (275–78). Far from being inconsistent nonsense, the image implies how, in human society, virtuous behavior begets more virtuous behavior.

Critics have found it surprising that Piers sows the cardinal virtues (274–308); here in Christian time should he not be sowing the theological ones?[12] But the Evangelists and the doctor-exegetes have already prepared the soil with the theological virtues: the revelation that they represent instills the faith, hope, and charity that direct humanity toward God. Now the cardinal, moral virtues must follow.[13] Furthermore, Piers does not sow merely natural virtue. Grace has given him these seeds, and Langland carefully names them—not prudence, temperance, justice, and fortitude, but the *spiritus,* the "spirit," of each virtue. This clearly indicates that Piers sows the "infused," or "instilled," virtues specific to Christianity, God-given gifts implanted in the soul that dispose it toward virtuous behavior, shares in divine goodness.[14]

Not at all independent of the theological virtues, these infused virtues take their orientation from the charity that directs humanity to a supernatural end, love of God and neighbor.[15] Given that end, they seek a higher standard than mere natural virtues: thus, for example, temperance in Christians seeks not just to use food in a healthful way but to "chastise the body and bring it into subjection."[16] Finally, given the effects of the Fall on human nature, humans could not hope to achieve consistent virtue without God's grace. In the face of the many impulses of the sensual appetites, even a human whose mind had accepted God as goal would, without grace, be unlikely to avoid all sin, and those who have fallen into serious sin would inevitably sin again unless they availed themselves of grace's help.[17]

Langland concludes this paradigm of Christian society with a brief account of the "barn," "Unity, Holy Church" (317–34).[18] The materials from which it is made are Christ's passion and mercy along with God's revelation. Contrition and confession bring Christians into it, and priesthood is the guard and keeper. The image recapitulates grace's origins (revelation and Redemption), its instruments (the sacraments, especially penance, met by corresponding human disposition), and its ministers.

Having sketched his paradigm of the church, which served also to commemorate its original establishment, Langland now describes it under attack. Pride, here a type of Antichrist (Emmerson, 196–97), sees the flourishing endeavor and summons his hosts to savage Piers's crop (335–54). Arrogance and nonlove (Spill-Love, Speak-Evil-Behind) make the advance party, with plans so to confuse Conscience by sophistry as to leave Christians uncertain about right and wrong. Then Pride, along with lust of the flesh and of the world, can try to prevail (352–54). Despite all of Grace's gifts, the outcome is in doubt. Grace cannot compel virtue, merely assist it in the willing Christian.

Resistance begins well. People respond to Conscience's summons to Unity, and natural understanding apparently rids Conscience of whatever sophistic confusions Pride's spies had tried to foment (347–50). Christians cooperate in fortifying Unity through their repentance and penance, their tears of contrition and clean living—cooperation that, in this ideal instance, extends even to the lives of the clergy. Conscience declares victory and invites all to partake of a nourishing reward, the Eucharist (385). The people should eat it as often as they have need—as long as they have paid *redde quod debes* to Piers the Plowman's pardon (389–90).

Why do the people suddenly cry out in surprise (391–92)? I think Langland chose this moment to make the transition from allegorical paradigm to more recognizable historical "reality." Conscience's own words have just suggested extension into time ("once a month or as often as necessary," 388–89). We should recall the people's frustration after being shriven at the end of passus 5, Haukyn's lament about how hard it is to live and keep committing sins (14.323–25), and even Will's long and lonely struggles as depicted in the interludes. Responding to the pardon demands continual reaction. How many will accomplish it? What support will they give one another? How will Piers and the clergy help? Conscience and the cardinal virtues urge them, in effect, to persevere in the difficult life of virtue, in penance—or at least in forgiving one another. And by the responses he now depicts, Langland returns us from the idea of the church to the world of his own experience.

A brewer (396 – 402) intends to water his beer and reject both Conscience and the spirit of justice. A lord (459 – 64) will make might his right and so make a travesty of fortitude. A king—one recalls what the glutton of words said in the prologue—will do as he sees fit, for he is the very source of "law" and will judge "justice" as his needs require (465–76).[19] But the most distressing response of all comes from the "ignorant vicar" (409 –58). This poorly trained clerical stand-in would have occupied a rung very near the bottom of the medieval ecclesiastical ladder.[20] From this perspective, he delivers yet another devastating assessment of what has become of Piers's successors. The vicar speaks not necessarily as one who himself scorns virtue but as an observer of how far actuality has departed from founding norm. His speech presents another dense cluster of those contrastive juxtapositions so typical of Langland's writing, tightly interweaving idealization and satire.

Responding to Conscience's injunction that Christians live by the cardinal virtues or be lost (407–8), the vicar exclaims: In that case, very many are lost! For there is no one to teach the cardinal virtues or to commend Conscience, and things are worst at the summit of the church—with the successors of Piers and the apostles. By their actions, pope and cardinals (cf. Pr.100 –110) teach flagrant rapacity for temporal goods; let them stay at Avignon or Rome! (413–23). Would that Conscience ruled the King, Grace all clergy, and a worthy vicar of Christ all the world, according to the Scriptures (424–27). Instead, one sees a pope hiring mercenaries to slay Christians in petty territorial squabbles (428 –29, 442– 48). All best wishes to a Piers who would model himself on God, raining down good upon all, concerned to save the wretched and sinful as well as the grand and the good. May such a Piers put the papacy right! (430 – 42). And may Christ save the cardinals, as well, turning their selfish intellects to true wisdom and setting their sights on spiritual wealth. For the people already incline to make "prudence" into guile in the service of their cupidity and to dress such behavior up as virtue.

Among the cardinal virtues, prudence played the most crucial role: it functioned to understand ends and means and so to direct people in the fulfillment of the other virtues.[21] Given the state of the church, who now teaches prudence? If, as the vicar says, cardinals and pope seek only wealth and power, who directs Christians to spiritual ends and goods? Ignorant priests at the bottom of the ladder could hardly be expected to stem such a tide. Nor could the people on their own, in the face of such overwhelming bad example. In the paradigm, when Pride assailed the church, the clean living of the clergy played a crucial role in successful resistance. In its pristine age, led by Peter and those zealous apostles who converted nearly all the world (cf. 15.438–51), the church came near to embodying an ideal Christian society led by Piers, vicar of Christ the King. Now no Piers the Plowman can be found. No wonder the "body" fragments into its selfish members, brewers and lords, kings and commons, each bent on his own misguided ends.

"I Met with Need": The Final Interlude

We cannot be surprised to find Will, waking from that scene of incipient dissolution, sad and miserable in heart (20.2). The speaker once again appears as a poor pilgrim, away from home, for he specifically says he knew not where to eat nor in what house.[22] In this condition, as the time of the day's main meal draws near, he is confronted by Need.[23]

Before discussing the figure of Need, let us recall that the last time Will experienced a lengthy encounter outside his dreams, he met friars (8.8). The mendicant (begging) friars claimed to accept a kind of professional "need" as their way of life, yet as the poem closes, we face calamity caused by the friars' cupidity. In Need, then, Langland personifies a condition capable of arousing a wide range of responses.

Although a journeying Will could well find himself physically hungry, when he mentions "eating," we might not think simply of literal food. The last "dining" mentioned in the poem occurred when Conscience summoned the folk in Unity to the Eucharist (19.383). "Nourishment," moreover, has connoted moral instruction and penitential action at least since Conscience's dinner; given the moral vacuity of Friar Jurdan (13.84), of the clergy in general, even (as the vicar has just said) of cardinals and pope, Christendom languishes in starvation for the example of virtue and good lives. When Christ stopped wearing Piers's vesture on earth, Piers lived on in Peter and the other zealous founders of the church. Where can Piers now be found among churchmen? And when Conscience called the people of Unity to communion, to the nourishment of grace, their sense of having failed in restitution and satisfaction, of their unresponsiveness to Christ's laws, expressed itself in rejection of the sacrament, then in the incipient travesties of virtue with which passus 19 ended.

Christian society, in its current state, feels desperate spiritual need. But Need, of course, should also measure the use of temporal goods, specifically natural goods (food, drink, clothing). Lady Holy Church had remarked this when, at the beginning of her first speech, she criticized the behavior of the folk of the prologue. As the last dream unfolds, people's response to need determines whose side they will take in the conflict that arises. Need's speech displays again a range of attitudes toward goods, temporal and spiritual, beginning with temporal, natural ones.

Medieval theology (and law) held that under most circumstances, individuals who through no fault of their own faced death for want of natural goods had the right to take what preserving life required. But what guidelines measure need and sufficiency? Need explicitly suggests that Will model his "temperance" upon those selfish redefinitions of virtue by "the king and others" (6) at the end of passus 19; in comparing temperance with those virtues, he pictures each of them at its worst: fortitude becomes oppression of others, justice the plaything of political compromise, prudence mere surmise (23–33). "Temperance" remains undefined.[24] As for Conscience, Need simply sets it aside (21). Because he so humbles those who experience him, Need places himself next to God (35–50); however, in the final dream, though it may make Will meek, need certainly fails to humble the friars. Then Need shifts senses, becoming the renunciation of wealth and ease (38–39), detachment from artificial goods, adopted by those who would be philosophers. No philosophers appear in the final dream. One will not find good teachers in want, but rather the want of good teachers.

Finally Need speaks of Christ (40–50) who willingly laid aside his divinity to experience and suffer all the wants and griefs of humanity. But in following the tradition that made Christ's words about having no place to lay his head into his dying words on the cross, Langland forcibly reminds his audience that Christ not only endured need but succumbed to it. At any point in his life, he could, literally, have declared victory and returned to the "weal" of heaven. With one word, he could have halted the Crucifixion, stopped his suffering. Yet, because of humanity's need, he endured his own to the bitter end—embracing death rather than "taking" relief. And so need can transcend the necessities of physical life, subordinating them to the needs of the spirit. Need concludes: "Therefore, do not be ashamed to endure and be needy" (48). The friars will shamelessly nourish their cupidity at the cost of perverting spiritual goods; Will accepts the detachment from worldly necessities the poem has all along urged and follows the path of love.

"Antichrist Came Then": Dream as Nightmare

The instant Will falls into his eighth and final dream, Antichrist appears, wrecking the crop of Truth sown by a flourishing Church in passus 19.[25] We find ourselves once again in the field of folk, at Westminster under siege by Meed, on the half acre threatened by ruffians and idlers. But now the setting is all Christianity and the institution at risk is the church—or rather an ideal church in real time. Pride's earlier attack (19.335) dramatized moral paradigms: the nature of the assault and the means of successful resistance. That paradigm remains relevant. But at the end of passus 19, Langland moved us from paradigm toward history, from ideal toward reality, and this attack is surely meant to evoke the one Christians expected near the close of salvation history, in which Antichrist would appear as precursor to Christ's Second Coming and the Last Judgment. Antimendicant literature had forcefully portrayed the friars as Antichrist's agents in this attack, and lines 52 to 71 unmistakably employ apocalyptic images describing the last days.[26] Langland uses this tradition to create a dream—a fiction that characterizes the church in recent times as plagued by corruption so dreadful that it merits consideration as, at least, the beginning of the end.

We should notice how this "historical" attack compares with the earlier paradigmatic one. In the earlier attack (19.342–50), Pride's spies threatened to destroy the cardinal virtues, demolish Piers's barn, entice those within Unity out, corrupt confession and contrition, and leave Conscience unsure about right and wrong. No sooner did these spies appear than Conscience summoned all within Unity, Kynde Wit (natural knowledge) came to instruct Conscience, and all Christians cooperated in prayers and penance—including the clergy (19.360–80); thus when Pride and "the Lord who lives according to bodily lust" actually attacked (19.352), the defenders of Unity repulsed them.

i

In the second attack, Antichrist wins over most of a weakened Christendom at the outset (52–71), leaving only a few "fools" (61, 74, 77).[27] Friars and religious (58– 60) immediately join him, and as the battle rages Avarice assails pope and prelates (127–28), worldly priests join the attack (218–27), and when Conscience cries out to Clergie for help (228), only the Friars (already with Antichrist) respond. Finally, hypocrisy and unkind speech wound such "wise teachers" as may remain (299 –303). The communal cooperation of the paradigm, notably that of the clergy, fails utterly, and the Kynde Wit of that paradigm does not appear here. Rather, Conscience must call upon an equally natural but much less subtle instructor: Kynde as natural but extraordinary instrument of divine warning and retribution (80 –89, 95–105)[28] and reminder of the natural course of human life, through Elde (old age) to death (165– 68, 175–77).

As he describes the siege of Unity, Langland draws on a rich tradition of vices battling virtues[29] as well as on apocalyptic and antimendicant literature. In the first part of this conflict (52–183), Langland's focus shifts between the defensive struggles by Kynde on Conscience's behalf and a collective figure, Life. We first see this figure as "a lord who lives according to bodily pleasures," who joins Pride in carrying Antichrist's banner.[30] Life appears again as "the lord who lived according to lust" (90), then simply as "Life" (143, 169 –82). Paradoxically, he comes to represent the "life" that death obliterates. In the melee of Kynde's first assault, he calls to Comfort for aid, shouting "Every one for himself!" (92). When Kynde eases his attack, Langland describes how the survivors perversely follow Fortune and the three temptations: lust of the flesh, lust of the eyes (Covetousness, Avarice), and "pride of life" (110 –55). Life (143), with his "arrogance of heart" (153), embodies humanity heedlessly dedicated to earth's possessions and pleasures (cf. 11.12–15) and sums up those attitudes that destroy Conscience and the cardinal virtues. When Elde and death pursue Life (169 –83), he resorts first to physicians, then to revelry, though we know (witness the fate of the physician) that Elde and death will prevail.

As Elde pursues Life, he incidentally passes so close over Will's head that Will becomes bald (183–85). In the humorously cast scene that follows, Elde so beats Will as to leave him deaf, toothless, lame, and impotent. Unlike Life, Will reacts to "need" by asking Kynde for remedy (203). Obediently, Will accepts Kynde's advice to learn love as his occupation, to trust in God for his sustenance, and so passes through contrition and confession into Unity. Some have suggested that only here does Will "convert," accept the faith, or "enter the church." But to the extent that Will has a consistent "biography" within the poem's dreams, he has always been a Christian (see 1.76 –78). He has undergone the self-confrontation of passus 11 to 12, has spent time with Conscience and Patience, and, as the interludes suggest, has struggled on, however imperfectly. This cannot be his first act of faith, his first entry into the church, his first confession. But then why has Will not already responded to Conscience's call to enter Unity? First of all, because he has served as Langland's observer outside the besieged fortress, as hereafter he will serve from within. But more important, I think Langland wished to dramatize Will's choice to enter. In contrast to Life, who ignored both Conscience and Nature, Will, whatever his past sins, leaves all quest for worldly goods, renews his coat of Christendom through penance, and becomes part of Unity through love—the poem's consistent demand. We must return to him at the end of the dream.

As for the friars, Langland has left little to our imagination. Since the prologue, the poem has depicted them as shameless hucksters who with horrifying cynicism pervert the economy of grace. Even in describing why Conscience will not "wage" them (give them regular employment), Langland manages to compare them to ghouls who strip corpses on the battlefield (262– 63). In castigating the friars' ambition for "learning," their envy of the endowed clergy, and their greedy desire for the right to hear confessions, Langland follows a swelling chorus of contemporary antimendicant satire.[31]

This tradition, as we have seen, imagined friars precisely as Antichrist's agents. Their guide in the dream is Envy (273, 294) who leads them to usurp the prestige of university teachers and the incomes and functions of parish clergy. Langland intervenes, in the first person, to counter their lying cupidity (277–93), defending the sharper penances that parish priests administer and that Conscience will later permit "wounded" Christians to abandon. The suggestion that friars enter Unity to heal teachers wounded by hypocrisy (300 –305) contains a stinging irony because contemporaries accused friars particularly of that vice. The friar-confessor in whose person Langland distills his consummate disgust bears not only the name "Flatterer" (315) but also the crowning epithet *Sire Penetrans Domos* (Sir Creeping-into-Houses, 340): trenchant in itself, Peace spells it out plainly (341– 47).[32] About the friars, then, Langland intended no suspense and no surprises—save perhaps on Conscience's part.

But before we consider Conscience, what does Unity represent? Can we simply equate Unity Holy Church with the church, in either of its

obvious institutional senses: all baptized Christians, or the visible hierarchy of ecclesiastical officials from pope to humblest cleric? Unity might
have embraced the entire Christian world; in the paradigm of passus 19,
it very nearly did. In the division of gifts, all Christians are taught loyal
love for one another (19.250, 254–55): "unity" was the Holy Spirit's
idea of the church. Then Unity Holy Church appeared as the barn hous-
ing Piers's harvest: the community of Christians in the state of grace
(19.319–32). When that paradigm came under attack, all Christians
(save a few wretches) followed Conscience into Unity, fortified it with
repentance (362), and by their good lives made it stand in holiness
(380). Unity thus represents not just clerical hierarchy or all baptized
Christians but Christians cooperating in love and penitence so as to form
a moral community above and beyond any merely formal one.

By the end of passus 19, the ignorant vicar characterized pope and
cardinals (and by implication much of the clergy) as being outside any
such moral community: we might take this as Langland's caricature of
the curia in the late 1370s. With the beginning of the Great Schism in
1378, antipopes vied for recognition and even formal "unity" was
threatened. We already noted that when Antichrist begins his attack in
passus 20, "hundreds" of Christians, including friars, monks, and nuns,
flock to his banner, while only "fools" follow Conscience into Unity.
Among those apparently outside the besieged fortress who survived
Kynde's assaults, Avarice and Simony "exerted pressure on the pope and
created prelates who sided with Antichrist" (127–28). Yet I think we
would take the allegorical vehicle of besiegers and besieged too wood-
enly were we to exclude the *idea* of the papacy from the Unity within
the fortress, at least until the very end of the poem. For Langland apparently portrays this "historical" devolution of Unity as occurring in the
thirteenth century and resulting from the papacy's decisions.

Conscience represents, in this episode, the collective moral judgment
of the church, originally formed in Piers/Peter and the other apostles by
Christ's life and teaching, subsequently confirmed by the Holy Spirit at
Pentecost, and supported by the cardinal virtues. Langland calls Conscience "custodian and guide over *kynde* [natural, loving] Christians"
(72–73) as well as "warden" of Unity (214). In the ideal paradigm of
Unity's resistance, Conscience, taught by Kynde Wit, judged well and
Christians responded. Now Conscience seems less influential, a somewhat vestigial force, present only among a moral remnant: too few people cultivate it; it receives too little help. Because Conscience (whether
individual or collective) involves practical moral judgment, it needs for-

mation, instruction, example, and the support of the virtues in order to
flourish in the community and to function effectively in difficult cases.[33]
Here it never loses sight of ultimate right and wrong. But, especially
because institutional prudence is wanting (as the ignorant vicar has suggested), Langland portrays Conscience as making some dreadful choices
about means to ends.

Conscience did not err in imploring that Kynde ease its assaults to see
whether people might reform (106 –9).[34] But Conscience's behavior
with respect to the friars surely reflects Langland's critique of decisions
made by the church (especially pope and curia) during a turbulent century in which friars gained official admittance to the ecclesiastical establishment[35] and subsequently to the "cure of souls": the rights to preach,
hear confessions, and bury the dead in their churches and cemeteries.[36]

Desperate for Clergie, Conscience ignores Need's stern advice and
welcomes the friars to Unity, albeit with a long caution (244–72): they
should be content to follow the rule of their founders and not covet
advancement or the status of beneficed clergy—there are too many of
them for that. Ironically, Need now echoes the attitude of bishops and
parish priests who objected to the friars' ministry.[37] Yet Unity's situation
grows increasingly desperate. Even wise teachers fall wounded by sin,
and when Conscience calls confessor-physicians who prescribe painful
penitential remedies, such is the general moral environment that "some
of the people" (309 –11) seek gentler care. A surgeon, one Friar Flatterer, stands ready to provide it (315). A weakened Contrition begs
Conscience to admit him; Conscience, imprudently solicitous for Contrition's "health," agrees. The nonexpression of grammatical disjunction
(the absence of a word like "but" or "nevertheless") between lines 322
and 323 is striking. It suggests either Conscience's befuddlement or his
totally unwarranted confidence that even so descriptively named a practitioner should enter without displacing the physicians already present.[38]
Making a final error, Conscience greets Friar Flatterer sympathetically,
trusting Contrition to the surgeon's devious ministrations, and the
patient ends in a drugged stupor (377). Conscience, anxious to save
Contrition, has killed it. The church, even that moral remnant that
struggles for Dowel and Truth, has made a grievous error and has been
betrayed.

Conscience sets out on his pilgrimage (380), expressing the hope that
Piers, when found, might provide a *fyndyng,* a permanent endowment,
for the friars (383) to obviate their wretched abuses. Taking this suggestion at face value, as most readers of the poem do, seems to overlook

Conscience's earlier arguments: how can one "wage" a class of religious who teem without "number"? Apart from that, taken literally, this solution—the single institutional change Langland suggests for his shattered society—seems ludicrously inadequate. Given the friars' depiction as creatures of the Antichrist driven by cupidity and envy, providing them with a regular endowment seems an extraordinarily naive solution.[39] Just conceivably, Langland wishes us now to set aside his caricature of the mendicants and contemplate this suggestion seriously. More likely, Conscience has some more ironic remedy in mind.[40]

"He Cried Out for Grace": Nightmare's End

As this dream ends, what of Unity, Conscience, and Will? As for Unity, given Langland's portrayal of his world, and especially of the clergy, we could hardly have expected him to close with a picture of Holy Church flourishing in love and unity. Langland ends on the exclamation that Christian community has become so morally devastated that no unity remains, no hope of easily finding Piers, its appropriate moral leader.

Therefore Conscience—that is, those who attempt to preserve conscience and the cardinal virtues—has no nurturing community upon which to depend. It must indeed call to God for luck and grace and seek a new Piers Plowman. In the apocalyptic fiction Langland has created, that Piers will finally be Christ returning. In the moral world of Langland's age, anyone who loves and cares must seek out Truth and True Humanity by individual effort, with God's grace, and must strive earnestly for a renovation of clergy and papacy, that these might more nearly resemble the Piers upon whom the church was founded.

Will had been told by Kynde to wait in Unity until sent for (205). If, however, we are to imagine Will persevering in this struggle, we must imagine him setting out once again with Conscience. What would Conscience have him do? Avoid the friars! Whether layman or clergyman, practice the cardinal virtues. Persevere in the penitential quest for Truth. Seek Piers in himself and in others.

Conclusions

The poem thus ends just as restlessly as it began. Yet how else could it end? Langland is no escapist: to present us with a church viewed through rose-colored glasses would defeat the poem's entire purpose, which is to indict the moral corruption of his world and to plead for restoration of moral order. Will and Langland's audience can be "safe" only so long as they might persevere, with God's grace, in love and penance, in heeding Kynde and Conscience.

How bleak is the poem's conclusion? Readers' responses have differed widely.[41] Is Langland near despair, anticipating the end of the world? A poet who expected the world's end in his lifetime would hardly have spent two decades of it writing and rewriting this poem. Even as the dire action of the final dream unfolds, his energy and humor remain insuppressible.[42] I agree with Frank that "the climactic battle with the sins and Antichrist has produced splendid Beethovian thunder, but . . . the drama of salvation continues as long as mankind exists. . . ." (Frank, *Salvation,* 118). Langland devoted all but the last passus of his poem to reawakening in his audience an acknowledgment, and an acceptance, of each individual's moral responsibility in the remaking of village, court, and church. The poem's conclusion is not meant to eradicate all that, nor the *ideal* of unity portrayed by the paradigm of passus 19, nor the invisible communities so vividly evoked by passus 16 to 18. But these are beliefs and hopes to fire the longing and resolve of those who must, finally, persevere in the actual world of daily experience. Although the nightmare ending jars, even here Langland plays the moralist *provocateur,* wielding caricature and hyperbole in an effort to arouse and to stir, to clear a path through which his audience might recollect and desire the ideal and the promise.

Notes and References

Chapter One

1. B 12.16 –17. I cite the poem by version, section, and line number from the edition by George Kane and E. Talbot Donaldson, *Piers Plowman: the B Version*, rev. ed. (London: Athlone; Berkeley: University of California Press, 1988); hereafter cited in text as Kane and Donaldson. In quotations, thorn and yogh have been modernized. Editions are further discussed at the end of this chapter. Unless otherwise noted, all translations in this book are my own.

2. MS 212, Trinity College, Dublin; the note dates from about 1412. For the Latin text see George Kane, *Piers Plowman: The Evidence for Authorship* (London: Athlone, 1965), 26, with facsimile facing p. 32; hereafter cited in text as Kane, *Authorship*. Kane's book gathered all the known external evidence about the author. A recent discussion with supplementary bibliography is Ralph Hanna III, *William Langland*, Authors of the Middle Ages 3: English Writers of the Late Middle Ages (Brookfield, Vt.: Variorum, 1993), whose appendices (25 –36) conveniently reproduce the documents; hereafter cited in text.

3. Lister M. Matheson, review of *William Langland,* by Ralph Hanna III, *Yearbook of Langland Studies* 8 (1994): 193; hereafter cited as *YLS.*

4. For manuscripts and texts see George Kane, "The Text," in *Companion to Piers Plowman*, ed. John A. Alford (Berkeley: University of California Press, 1988), 175 –200, and Hanna, 37 – 44.

5. Langland's authorship of all three versions is generally accepted. In 1983 it was proposed that a version earlier than A survived, the "Z text": A. G. Rigg and Charlotte Brewer, eds., *William Langland, Piers Plowman: The Z Version* (Toronto: Pontifical Institute, 1983). Their proposal has had a mixed reception: see Kane, "The Text," 182, and Hanna, 37–38. Recently Jill Mann suggested that B was written before A: "The Power of the Alphabet: A Reassessment of the Relation between the A and the B Versions of *Piers Plowman,*" *YLS* 8 (1994): 21–50. I will speak of three versions, composed in the order A, B, C.

6. We cannot establish absolute dates. Langland could have finished A well after the latest datable event to which A refers and could have begun B before the earliest datable event to which B refers.

7. See Kane, "The Text," 184–86, and Hanna, 6 –17. Kane believes Langland had died by 1387; Hanna argues he lived until at least 1388 (10).

8. A work called *The Pricke* (stimulus) *of Conscience* exists in 115 copies, Chaucer's *Canterbury Tales* in 64, and an 80-line poem by John Lydgate on good

diet in 55. By contrast, works we regard as masterpieces survive in fewer manuscripts (Chaucer's *Troilus* in 17) or in a unique copy (*Gawain* and *Pearl*).

9.   John Burrow, "The Audience of Piers Plowman," *Anglia* 75 (1957):
373–84.

10.   Anne Middleton, "The Audience and Public of 'Piers Plowman,' "
in *Middle English Alliterative Poetry and Its Literary Background: Seven Essays*, ed.
David Lawton (Cambridge: Brewer, 1982), 101–23; hereafter cited in text.

11.   George Kane has suggested that the alliterative line offered the only
medium for serious poetry at the time Langland wrote: "Music 'Neither
Unpleasant nor Monotonous,' " in *Medieval Studies for J. A. W. Bennett*, ed. P. L.
Heyworth (Oxford: Clarendon, 1981), 43. On Langland's versification see also
the articles by Hoyt N. Duggan and David A. Lawton listed in the bibliography.

12.   In *Pearl* the dreamer sees the New Jerusalem; in Chaucer's *House of
Fame* an eagle flies "Chaucer" into the heavens. In *Piers* the dreamer meets personified abstractions such as Conscience and converses with long-dead characters such as Abraham and Moses.

13.   Chaucer, for instance, in *House of Fame,* 1– 65; *Piers Plowman* at B
7.154–73. All references to Chaucer are to *The Riverside Chaucer*, ed. Larry D.
Benson (Boston: Houghton Mifflin, 1987).

14.   The awkward and dull-witted "Chaucer" of the dream visions is an
instructive example. On the relationship between dreamer, poet, and audience,
see especially George Kane, *The Autobiographical Fallacy in Chaucer and Langland
Studies,* Chambers Memorial Lecture (London: University College, 1965),
10 –17; hereafter cited in text as Kane, *Fallacy*.

15.   On "signatures" of this kind in medieval poetry and on Will's self-
naming see Kane, *Authorship*, 52–70.

16.   E. Talbot Donaldson, *Piers Plowman: The C Text and Its Poet* (New
Haven: Yale University Press, 1949), 199 –226; hereafter cited in text as Donaldson, *C Text*.

17.   The fullest exploration of dreamer as human will is John M. Bowers, *The Crisis of Will in Piers Plowman* (Washington, D.C.: Catholic University
of America Press, 1986).

18.   For a dramatic illustration of the difference between poetry and versified information, compare *Piers* with *The Pricke of Conscience* (see n. 8), which
covers many of the same topics.

19.   For various arguments about the extent of Langland's education see
Hanna, 20. Schmidt pointed out ("Langland and Scholastic Philosophy,"
Medium Aevum 38 [1969]: 144) that many encyclopedias and treatises, not
technical university texts, synthesized Platonic, Aristotelian, and patristic
authors (for me, the point Schmidt makes most convincingly about Langland's
sources). Langland's understanding of human psychology, for example, is not
the Aristotelian one that predominated in the universities but one based on the
traditional synthesis represented in works such as the encyclopedia of Bartholomaeus Anglicus, translated into English in the late fourteenth century: *On the*

Properties of Things: John Trevisa's Translation of Bartholomaeus Anglicus De Proprietatibus Rerum, A Critical Edition, ed. M. C. Seymour et al., 3 vols. (Oxford: Clarendon, 1975–88).

20. Langland twice uses technical grammatical concepts (B 13.128–30, C 3.332–405); for discussions see Hanna, 20 n. 65. An excellent general guide to the intellectual life of the period is William J. Courtenay, *Schools and Scholars in Fourteenth-Century England* (Princeton: Princeton University Press, 1987); on universities and their curricula see 20–55, on higher education outside Oxford and Cambridge see 88–117, and on the relationship between intellectual life and late-fourteenth-century literature see especially 368–80; hereafter cited in text.

21. Its first episode begins there (B Pr.5) and makes passing reference to the mist on the hills (B Pr.215); a subsequent episode ends there (B 7.147).

22. Morton W. Bloomfield suggested this (*Piers Plowman as a Fourteenth-Century Apocalypse* [New Brunswick: Rutgers University Press, 1962], 68–97), but inconclusively, because the characteristics Bloomfield pointed to as monastic are typical of traditional, synthetic philosophy and theology, and divisions between monks, secular clergy, and friars on these grounds are misleading. For example, Bartholomaeus Anglicus, the encyclopedist very much in this tradition, was a Franciscan friar.

23. Although by far the largest city in England, London in the last quarter of the century had an estimated total population of 30,000; see Alan R. H. Baker, "Changes in the Later Middle Ages," in *A New Historical Geography of England before 1600,* ed. H. C. Darby (Cambridge: Cambridge University Press, 1976), 192.

24. *Piers* is the Anglo-French form of *Peter.*

25. The authenticity of a 12th passus, found in some manuscripts, is uncertain.

26. For Kane and Donaldson, see n. 1. E. Talbot Donaldson, *Piers Plowman: An Alliterative Verse Translation,* edited, introduced, and annotated by Elizabeth D. Kirk and Judith H. Anderson (New York: Norton, 1990).

27. A. V. C. Schmidt, *The Vision of Piers Plowman: A Critical Edition of the B-Text,* 2d ed. (Rutland, Vt.: Tuttle, 1996). The slight discrepancy in line numbering arises chiefly because of different policies for numbering or not numbering lines of Latin quoted in the text. Schmidt's literary and historical notes are extremely useful.

28. These are listed in the bibliography. Besides Schmidt, note especially the editions by Skeat, Bennett, and Pearsall. In the editions by Skeat and Bennett, line numbering can differ noticeably from that in Kane and Donaldson and Schmidt because Skeat and Bennett based their texts on different manuscripts in which text had been added, omitted, or rearranged. Pearsall's edition of C contains very useful notes; readers can locate corresponding passages in the various versions by using one of the parallel editions (see bibliography) that print the versions side by side.

Chapter Two

1. R. E. Kaske, "Holy Church's Speech and the Structure of *Piers Plowman*," in *Chaucer and Middle English Studies in Honor of Rossell Hope Robbins,* ed. Beryl Rowland (London: Allen and Unwin, 1974), 320.

2. Literally, "to do (perform, behave, work, live) well, better, best." The "three do's" are introduced by Thought at 8.78.

3. See Robert Adams, "Langland's *Ordinatio:* The *Visio* and the *Vita* Once More," *YLS* 8 (1994): 51–84.

4. *Piers* is, of course, an allegorical poem featuring personified abstractions and employing familiar events to explore abstract ideas (here *marry* suggests "enter into an exclusive, officially sanctioned, and permanent relationship with").

5. The three figures represent crucial stages in salvation history, the crucial events in the relationship of God with humanity beginning with the Creation and Fall and extending through the Redemption to the Second Coming and Last Judgment. Faith, hope, and charity are the three *theological* virtues, so called because they originate in God's revelation about himself and about salvation history.

6. Prudence, temperance, justice, and fortitude are the four cardinal (most important) *natural* virtues.

7. See Anne Hudson, "*Piers Plowman* and the Peasants' Revolt: A Problem Revisited," *YLS* 8 (1994): 85–106.

8. On Langland's lack of Lollard sympathies, see, e.g., Middleton, "Audience," 107–8. Wendy Scase, *Piers Plowman and the New Anticlericalism* (Cambridge: Cambridge University Press, 1989) provides an illuminating context for Langland's various criticisms of clerical abuses.

9. See, e.g., James Simpson, "Spirituality and Economics in Passus 1–7 of the B Text," *YLS* 1 (1987): 83–103.

10. In the poem, the term *grace* generally has this technical sense. Cf. "Grace," in *The Oxford Dictionary of the Christian Church*, 2d ed., ed. F. L. Cross and E. A. Livingstone (Oxford: Oxford University Press, 1973); hereafter cited as *ODCC*. *ODCC* contains brief, useful definitions of theological terms (e.g., *grace, sacrament, church*). For extended discussions see *The Catholic Encyclopedia*, 15 vols. (New York: Appleton, 1907–1912). See also Robert Adams, "Langland's Theology," in *Companion*, 87–114.

11. The sacraments were rituals whereby, through a form of words and actions, the church was understood to have the power to impart God's grace to Christians. The most important sacraments for Langland were baptism, penance, and the Eucharist.

12. Langland expresses this "alas" through the character Haukyn, 14.323–24.

13. Langland speaks often of *dedly synne* (e.g., 1.144, 5.20); he speaks once of *venial* sin as deadly sin rendered forgivable through contrition (14.84, 93).

14.   Today's term is "the Sacrament of Reconciliation."

15.   Passus 5.75 through 5.460 depict personified sins going through various steps of confessing.

16.   These ideas, so clearly set out in Chaucer's *Parson's Tale*, also permeate *Piers*: see, e.g., Conscience's admonition to Haukyn in 14.16 – 28. The idea that Christians "owe" something in response to the Redemption and should "pay what they owe" sounds repeatedly in the last two passus.

17.   In the poem, friars often allow this sort of empty, formulaic confession in exchange for money. Langland regarded this practice as a terrible menace to humanity's well-being: see, e.g., 3.35 – 46, 11.54, and 20.362.

18.   Lack of sorrow and failure to do penance lead ultimately to a kind of spiritual sloth and finally to *wanhope* (despair): e.g., 13.406 –20, 17.303–20, 20.156 – 60.

19.   Theoretically one might, even after a life of sin and without a priest, be saved at death by making a "perfect act of contrition" (being sorry for one's sins not because one feared hell but solely because one had offended God). Langland cautions against counting on this at 17.299 –320.

20.   Baptism could be received only once. Penance and the Eucharist could be received as often as piety directed, but the Fourth Lateran Council (1215) obliged every Christian to receive them at least once a year.

21.   Langland dramatizes the situation at 19.383–92.

22.   Ymaginatif will tell the dreamer that "grace does not grow until good will gives rain" (12.60); the Samaritan gives Langland's definitive position (17.206 –53).

23.   The phrase *a pena & a culpa,* "from punishment and from guilt," first occurs in the poem at 7.3 when Truth sends the "Pardon."

24.   Langland refers to it as "the strongbox of Christ's treasure" (12.109).

25.   Sins that deprived another (e.g., of property or reputation) also incurred a debt that had to be repaid to the injured party through "restitution."

26.   Because Christ died to deliver humanity from the guilt of its mortal sins as well as from Original Sin, and because even one mortal sin would theoretically have required Redemption, one could logically argue that every single mortal sin crucified Christ.

27.   The church's ability to dispense grace in this way was traced to the Gospel passage (Matt. 19:16) in which Christ gave Peter the "power of the keys."

28.   On purgatory as a place of punishment and cleansing see, e.g., 6.44, 10.375, 11.133, 18.392; on true behavior or earthly suffering obviating it, 7.11, 106; on the dreamer's desire to avoid it, 10.427, 469.

29.   The most striking instance is the "good thief" to whom Christ on the cross promised heaven. The good thief is a source of hope for Robert the Robber (5.465), justification of blissful ignorance for a still recalcitrant dreamer (10.426), and an instance to be regarded cautiously for Ymaginatif (12.192).

30.   Ecclus. 1:16 and Ps.110:10; Wit quotes the verse at 9.96. Cf. Ecclus. 1:17, Ecclus. 25:16. See further Joseph S. Wittig, "Piers Plowman B, Passus IX–XII: Elements in the Design of the Inward Journey," *Traditio* 28 (1972): 219–20. All quotations of the Bible are from the Douay-Rheims translation: *The Holy Bible Translated from the Latin Vulgate* (Baltimore: Murphy, 1899; reprint, Rockford, Ill.: Tan, 1989).

Chapter Three

1.   Chapter 1 spoke of the poem as combining features of *chanson d'aventure* and dream vision, but it incorporates features of other genres as well; see Stephen A. Barney, "Allegorical Visions," in *Companion*, 117–33.

2.   E.g., the encounter with the Green Knight in *Gawain* or the transformation of the old hag in Chaucer's *Wife of Bath's Tale*.

3.   On the conventions of medieval dream poetry see Kane, *Fallacy,* and A. C. Spearing, *Medieval Dream Poetry* (Cambridge: Cambridge University Press, 1978), 1–47. On the "authority" of dreams, cf. chapter 1 of this book and Barney, "Allegorical Visions," esp. 123. Chaucer's dream narrator is often troubled, humorously dense, and little improved by his dream experience; the narrator of *Pearl* is anguished as well as recalcitrant.

4.   On the poem as satire see especially John A. Yunck, "Satire," in *Companion*, 135–54; for an introduction to estates satire see Jill Mann, *Chaucer and Medieval Estates Satire* (Cambridge: Cambridge University Press, 1973), 1–10. On the structure of society see further Anna P. Baldwin, "The Historical Context," in *Companion*, 67–86; hereafter cited in text as Baldwin, "The Historical Context."

5.   Technically, the rite of tonsure made men clerics; it included symbolic cutting of the recipient's hair while he recited Ps. 15:5, *Dominus pars hereditatis meae*, "The Lord is the portion of my inheritance." A cleric was subject to ecclesiastical, rather than secular, law: cf. 12.189–91. Women entered the ranks of the "religious" by associating themselves with a monastery or convent with the intention of taking vows.

6.   Critics disagree about whether the inadequacy of the estates model disturbed Langland: See e.g. David Aers, *Chaucer, Langland and the Creative Imagination* (London: Routledge, 1980), 1–37, and Alan J. Fletcher, "The Social Trinity of *Piers Plowman*," *Review of English Studies* 44 (1993): 343–49. I think Langland used the estates convention merely as a convenient, general classification of basic functions.

7.   See 3.257–58. For evil merchants who practice trickery, cf. esp. 7.18–22. On Langland's portrayal of minstrels and the association between minstrels and friars, "God's jesters," see Penn R. Szittya, *The Antifraternal Tradition in Medieval Literature* (Princeton: Princeton University Press, 1986), 251–57; hereafter cited in text.

8.   Chaucer makes a joke of not having got such people in order in the "General Prologue," *Canterbury Tales,* fragment 1, lines 744–46.

9.   For Langland's quotations in general see John Alford, *Piers Plowman: A Guide to the Quotations* (Binghamton, N.Y.: Medieval and Renaissance Texts and Studies, 1992); cited in text as Alford, *Guide to the Quotations.* Also see A. V. C. Schmidt, *The Clerkly Maker: Langland's Poetic Art* (Cambridge: Brewer, 1987), 81–107. For this passage cf. Eph. 5:3–4 and Col. 3:8. Alford (*Guide to the Quotations,* 33) notes relevant adaptations by Peter Lombard and John Bromyard that associate these passages with Langland's term *turpiloquium.*

10.   Donaldson translates *bidderes* as "beadsmen" (cf. *bedemen,* 15.205), those who undertake the obligation of praying for benefactors. But *bidde(n)* can mean both "ask for" and "pray (for)"; for the sense of "ask persistently, importune," see 7.84, 15.227.

11.   Langland repeatedly condemns those who beg when they could work and those who assume handicaps in order to become "professional" beggars (e.g., 5.440, 6.194, 6.213, 7.84, 7.89–99). But he also insists that Christians have an obligation to care for the truly needy (e.g., 11.198, 9.92–94, 10.83–85, 10.361–67, 13.439).

12.   On abuses of pilgrimage see, e.g., Muriel Bowden, *A Commentary on the General Prologue to the Canterbury Tales,* 2d ed. (New York: Macmillan, 1967), 19–43. For a contrasting description of how pilgrimage was originally conceived, see Jonathan Sumption, *Pilgrimage: An Image of Medieval Religion* (London: Faber, 1975), 168–75.

13.   *Middle English Dictionary* (hereafter cited as *MED*), s.v. "cope n.," 2 and 3.

14.   See, e.g., John Moorman, *A History of the Franciscan Order* (Oxford: Oxford University Press, 1968; reprint, Chicago: Franciscan Herald, 1988), 14–18. For an introduction to the relationship between the friars and the outcome of the Fourth Lateran Council of 1215, see Yunck, "Satire," 141–43.

15.   Only three alliterating syllables are required, here *syngen, symonie,* and *siluer.*

16.   E.g., 51–52, 64–65, 74–75, 86, 99.

17.   The likelihood of topical references is discussed later in this chapter. On the papacy in this period see Bernhard Schimmelpfennig, *The Papacy,* trans. James Sievert (New York: Columbia University Press, 1992); the Avignon Captivity is discussed on pages 198–218, the Great Schism on 219–36.

18.   *Commons* at this date probably meant "common people, community," not "House of Commons"; see Donaldson, *Translation,* 251, and *MED.*

19.   John Alford, *Piers Plowman: A Glossary of Legal Diction* (Cambridge: Brewer, 1988), 92–93, s.v. "LUNATIK."

20.   For sources and translations of these and the following lines see Alford, *Guide to the Quotations,* 33, and J. A. W. Bennett, ed., *Piers Plowman: The Prologue and Passus I–VII of the B Text as Found in Bodleian MS. Laud 581, Edited*

with Notes and Glossary (Oxford: Clarendon, 1972), 98, note to line 128. Notes from this edition are hereafter cited in the text as Bennett, page, line.

21.   Missing from the Latin lines is a key term etymologically related to *regere* indicating "justice." See the parallels quoted in Alford, *Guide to the Quotations*, 33–34: *recte* (justly), *rege te* (rule thyself), and *corrigere* (correct). Here no such qualifier occurs. The second line means "He has the name without the fact unless he strives to keep *iura*," but *iura* not only is etymologically independent of *regere*, but need mean no more than "laws, privileges."

22.   See Alford, *Guide to the Quotations*, 34, and A. V. C. Schmidt, *B-Text*, 413, note to line 145. Hereafter cited in the text as Schmidt, *B-Text*, page, line.

23.   Donaldson, *Translation*, 6, suggests the former; Bennett, 101, 161–62, the latter.

24.   See J. A. W. Bennett, "The Date of the B-Text of *Piers Plowman*," *Medium Ævum* 12 (1943): 55–64. Of modern editors, Bennett's notes pursue topical references in most detail. See also Donaldson, *C-Text*, 115, and Kane, "The Text," 184–86.

25.   Against overdoing topical references, see Donaldson, *C-Text*, 115, and Schmidt, *B-Text*, 413, 146. For Langland's treatment of kingship in historical context, see Anna P. Baldwin, *The Theme of Government in Piers Plowman* (Cambridge: Brewer, 1981).

26.   For Langland's use of biblical sources, see Alford, "Introduction," in *Guide to the Quotations*, 16–22. The poet names the early, authoritative interpreters of Scripture (Ambrose, Jerome, Augustine, and Gregory the Great) at 19.267–73. For an overview of biblical commentary, see R. E. Kaske, "Biblical Exegesis," in *Medieval Christian Literary Imagery: A Guide to Interpretation* (Toronto: University of Toronto Press, 1988), 3–52.

Chapter Four

1.   Translated from the basic theological textbook of the later Middle Ages, the *Sentences* of Peter Lombard, book II, distinction 1, cap. 4.1 (*Sententiae in IV Libris Distinctae*, Spicilegium Bonaventurianaum IV [Rome: College of St. Bonaventure, 1971]). For the Middle English equivalent (which cites this passage of Lombard as its source), see Thomas Frederick Simmons and Henry Edward Nolloth, eds., *The Lay Folks' Catechism*, Early English Text Society (hereafter EETS), o.s., 118 (London: Paul, Trench, Trübner, 1901), lines 5–15. The formula survives into the twentieth century: the "Baltimore Catechism," reprinted as *This We Believe* (Patterson, N.J.: St. Anthony Guild, 1957), 2–4.

2.   To the extent that he induces the audience to identify with the dreamer in his confrontation with authority figures, the poet exploits another dimension of response.

3.   See *ODCC*, "Church"; *Lay Folks' Catechism*, 18, lines 316–18.

4.   For Reason, see Guillaume de Lorris and Jean de Meun, *Roman de la Rose,* trans. Charles Dahlberg (Princeton: Princeton University Press, 1971), lines 4221–7229. For Nature, see *Roman,* lines 16249–19410, Alan of Lille's *Complaint of Nature,* and Chaucer's *Parliament of Fowles.* For Lady Philosophy, see *Consolation of Philosophy,* book 1, prose 1.

5.   First clearly set out by T. P. Dunning, *Piers Plowman: An Interpretation of the A-Text* (Dublin: Talbot, 1937); 2d ed. rev. by T. P. Dolan (Oxford: Clarendon, 1980).

6.   *Love* in this context means not (necessarily) feelings of affection but a disposition that leads to fulfilling one's obligations to others and to God.

7.   R. E. Kaske, "Holy Church's Speech and the Structure of *Piers Plowman,*" in *Chaucer and Middle English Studies in Honor of Rossell Hope Robbins,* ed. Beryl Rowland (London: Allen and Unwin, 1974), 320 –27. See also Dunning, *Interpretation,* 19 –71, and his "The Structure of the B-Text of *Piers Plowman,*" *Review of English Studies,* n.s., 7 (1956): 225 –37; hereafter cited in text as Dunning, "Structure."

8.   Kaske ("Holy Church's Speech and the Structure of *Piers Plowman,*" 324–25) suggests that this change occurs in the section referred to as "Patience's Riddle," 13.135 –71.

9.   Bennett, 106, 33, points out that the results of this union, "children who were wretches" (line 33), in turn begot the Moabites and Ammonites, constant enemies of Israel (Genesis 19:37–38).

10.   Langland echoes the traditional three temptations of 1 John 2:16, "the world, the flesh, and the devil." See Derek Pearsall, ed., *Piers Plowman by William Langland: An Edition of the C-text* (London: Arnold, 1978; reprint, Exeter: University of Exeter Press, 1994), 44, note to lines 37–38. Hereafter cited as Pearsall, page, line.

11.   That the speech is deliberately so structured was suggested by both Dunning and Kaske.

12.   Natural law and the old law required one to love one's friends and neighbors; Langland will emphasize that Christianity requires one to love one's enemies as well.

13.   Siegfried Wenzel, "Medieval Sermons," in *Companion,* 155–72, offers a very useful discussion of the passage (165– 67).

14.   "Saint Luke's words" probably refer to Luke 6:35.

15.   On David as a "type" (a forerunner) of Christ, see Thomas D. Hill, "Davidic Typology and the Characterization of Christ: *Piers Plowman* B. XIX.95 –103," *Notes and Queries* 20 (1976): 291–94.

16.   Cf. Schmidt, *B-Text,* 414, 85. Alford argues (along somewhat different lines) that the passus "represents Langland's basic attempt to broaden the conceptual framework of truth" ("The Design of the Poem," in *Companion,* 34). Alford's essay is a fine overview of the poem as a whole and includes an excellent selected bibliography.

17.   Alfred L. Kellogg, "Langland and Two Scriptural Texts," *Traditio* 14 (1958): 387–89.

18.   Augustine explores such triads as memory, intellect, and will; mind, knowledge, and love; and lover, beloved, and the love between them. See Henry Chadwick, *Augustine*, Past Masters (Oxford and New York: Oxford University Press, 1986), 90 –95, and Lawrence M. Clopper, "Langland's Trinitarian Analogies as Key to Meaning and Structure," *Medievalia et Humanistica* 9 (1979): 87–90.

19.   The wording in John's Gospel may be more familiar: "For God so loved the world that he gave his only begotten Son, that those who believe in him may not perish, but may have life everlasting" (John 3:16).

20.   Love of neighbor as a crucial expression of love of God is a constant theme of the epistle: e.g., 3:16 –17, 4:7–8, 11, 20.

21.   For the "two great commandments" see Matt. 22:36 – 40, Mark 12:29 –31, and Luke 10:27.

22.   *Kynde knowyng* recurs at 1.142, 165, 8.57, 113, 12.135; *knowe(n) kyndely* at 1.163, 5.538, 10.151, 223, 15.2, 18.221.

23.   See Mary Clemente Davlin, "*Kynde Knowyng* as a Middle English Equivalent for 'Wisdom' in *Piers Plowman*," *Medium Ævum* 50 (1981): 11 and 13–14; hereafter cited in text as Davlin, "*Kynde Knowyng*." As Davlin points out, it is nearly impossible to translate the phrase adequately, because significant connotations are normally present.

24.   *MED*, s.v. "kind(e) adj.," 4 and 5.

25.   *MED*, s.v. "knoue(n) v.," esp. 3a, 3b, and 7.

26.   Or to repugnance and dislike, where that response is appropriate. Thus when the dreamer asks Lady Holy Church to teach him "to know the false" (2.4), she responds by showing him Meed and her entourage, a picture calculated finally to provoke distaste.

27.   Holy Church calls the dreamer a dull fool (140), but because "truth" turns out to be "love," she does not speak simply of his failing to "understand" some idea; perhaps the Latin she accuses him of not "knowing" is *Deus caritas* (86).

28.   See Bennett, 112, 146, and P. M. Kean, "Langland on the Incarnation," *Review of English Studies* 16 (1965): 349 – 63.

29.   Kane and Donaldson emend the end of line 154 to *of the erthe yeten hitselue*, "until it had *cast itself in an earthly mold*." Other editions keep *eten his fylle*, "until it had eaten its fill of earth." Kean, "Incarnation," endeavors to justify the latter in traditional imagery.

30.   Contrast the *lettere of loue* (69), the "hinderer of love" who is Satan. The most famous depiction of Christ as wooer of the stubborn soul occurs in *Ancrene Wisse*; for text with facing translation, see *Medieval English Prose for Women*, ed. Bella Millett and Jocelyn Wogan-Browne (Oxford: Clarendon, 1990), 112–17. For other allusions in Langland's lines, cf. Bennett, 114, 154–58.

31.   Father/*might* and Son/*meke* are quite clear. The Holy Spirit as *mercy* is less obvious, but cf. 170 –71: "Meekly, with his mouth, he [the Son] asked mercy [the Holy Spirit] / to have pity on that people." Lines 172–74 are susceptible of similar interpretation: "Here you can see examples right in himself [the Godhead] / That He was powerful [Father] and meek [Son] and granted mercy [Holy Spirit] / To those who hanged him [the Son, but in him the deity] aloft and pierced his heart."

32.   Langland makes a neat transition: God's mercy toward humanity provides an analogical example for the relationship between rich and poor.

33.   On Langland's wordplay, see Mary Clemente Davlin, *A Game of Heuene: Word Play and the Meaning of "Piers Plowman B"* (Cambridge: Brewer, 1989).

Chapter Five

1.   The meaning of "Meed" will emerge as the narrative unfolds. On this episode see Alford, "Design of the Poem," 36 –39; Simpson, *Introduction*, 39 – 60; and M. Teresa Tavormina, *Kindly Similitude: Marriage and Family in "Piers Plowman"* (Woodbridge, Suffolk: Brewer, 1995), 1– 47; hereafter cited in text.

2.   Marriage came under the jurisdiction of the ecclesiastical courts. *Simony* meant exchanging ecclesiastical positions for money; *Civil* is Roman law as practiced in ecclesiastical courts. Cf. Alford, *Glossary of Legal Diction*.

3.   Although Conscience rejects "measureless hire," God grants it to humans, who could never merit salvation on their own. Langland is certainly aware of this contrast between heavenly and earthly reward; it has even been suggested that he portrays Meed as a perverse parody of Christ's generosity: see David Benson, "The Function of Lady Meed in *Piers Plowman*," *English Studies* 61 (1980): 193–205.

4.   *Allegory* derives from a Greek word meaning "to say another thing," and one classic definition of it was "to say one thing and mean another."

5.   *Leaute* had a wide spectrum of meaning; its fundamental sense is conformity with law, obligation, duty.

6.   Robert Worth Frank Jr., "The Art of Reading Medieval Personification-Allegory," *ELH* 20 (1953): 242; hereafter cited in text.

7.   David Aers, *Piers Plowman and Christian Allegory* (London: Arnold, 1975), 13, 47–51, 60 – 63.

8.   Chaucer uses this well-known figure, ironically, toward the end of *The Nuns' Priest's Tale*: "Taketh the fruyt, and lat the chaf be stille" (fragment 7, line 3443).

9.   For literally consistent images and deadly dull allegorical writing, cf. the French poems discussed by Eloise R. Grathwohl, " 'Piers Plowman' and Old French Religious Allegory, 1150 –1400" (Ph.D. diss., University of North Carolina–Chapel Hill, 1992).

10.   This sense predominates, for instance, in Augustine and in Peter Lombard's *Sentences*.

11.   See, e.g., Thomas Aquinas, *Summa Theologiae*, ed. Peter Caramell, 3 vols. (Rome: Marietti, 1952), I, Q. 79, a. 13. The edition by the English Black-friars has introductions, facing-page translation, and notes (60 vols. [London: Eyre and Spottiswoode; New York: McGraw Hill, 1964]). Timothy McDer-mott, *Summa Theologiae: A Concise Translation* (Westminster, Md.: Christian Classics, 1989) gives a readable English paraphrase; for Q. 79, a. 13, see McDermott, 124.

12.   In Peace, who comes to Parliament bloodied and distressed, Lang-land presents a poignantly named set of qualities absent but desired: amity, peaceableness, freedom from molestation or disturbance, lack of civil disorder, the "king's peace." See *MED*, s.v. "pes n.," esp. 1, 2, 4, 6.

13.   John Alford, "The Idea of Reason in *Piers Plowman*," in *Medieval English Studies Presented to George Kane*, ed. Edward Donald Kennedy, Ronald Waldron, and Joseph S. Wittig (Woodbridge, Suffolk: Brewer, 1988), 199–215.

14.   On this episode cf.: Alford, "Design of the Poem," 41; John Burrow, "The Action of Langland's Second Vision," *Essays in Criticism* 15 (1965): 247–68; Simpson, *Introduction*, 67–71.

15.   Langland thus provides a Piers figure for the world of temporal, natural goods and a series of figures for the realm of spiritual goods (most notably Christ and Peter), but none directly associated with the realm of tem-poral artificial goods (passus 2–4).

16.   The knight does not attempt to compel wasters by force but threat-ens them with law; the lack of resolution here perhaps echoes the plight of law dramatized in the Meed episode.

17.   The peas (and "pease porridge"), beans, and bran referred to here are all regarded as the diet of animals (hogs, horses), which will sustain human life but is neither appetizing nor easily digestible.

18.   *Hunger* is thus a synecdoche standing for hunger, thirst, and naked-ness.

19.   For gluttony, swearing, and gambling as the "tavern sins," cf. the beginning of Chaucer's *Pardoner's Tale*.

20.   Repentance represents both an encouraging confessor and the dispo-sition within a sinner to repent. On the role of Repentance, see John Alford, "The Figure of Repentance in *Piers Plowman*," in *Suche Werkis to Werche: Essays on Piers Plowman in Honor of David C. Fowler*, ed. Miceal F. Vaughan (East Lansing, Mich.: Colleagues Press, 1993), 3–28; hereafter cited in text as Alford, "Repentance."

21.   Cf. Gen. 4:5–6. On the association of friars with Cain, see Szittya, *Antifraternal Tradition*, 163–64 and 220–30. Cain was "the first and most treacherous *frater* [brother]" (229): first brother, first murderer, first fratricide.

22.   Siegfried Wenzel, *The Sin of Sloth: Acedia in Medieval Thought and Literature* (Chapel Hill: University of North Carolina Press, 1967), 139; here-after cited in text as Wenzel, *Sloth*.

23.   E.g., Siegfried Wenzel, ed. and trans., *Fasciculus Morum: A Fourteenth-Century Preacher's Handbook* (University Park: Pennsylvania State University Press, 1989).

24.   These included tangible goods (taken by theft, cheating, sharp practice) as well as intangible (e.g., another's good name).

25.   On "Robert the Robber" see Wenzel, *Sloth*, 144–47, and Alford, "The Figure of Repentance," 17–21. I agree with Wenzel that Langland draws an analogy between restitution and satisfaction.

26.   This is implicit in the Pardon scene and explicit later in the poem: *redde quod debes* (19.187, 19.259, 19.390, 20.308).

27.   The seven penitential psalms (in the Vulgate numbering 6, 31, 37, 50, 101, 129, and 142) were associated with private prayers of penance and prominently included, e.g., in the liturgy for Lent.

28.   *MED*, s.v. "rennen v.," 16–18.

29.   For the possibility that wafer makers (*waferer*, 632) might have been as unsavory as pickpockets and ape keepers, see chapter 7.

Chapter Six

1.   The truly infirm or helpless not only may beg but hardly need a pardon, for they have suffered their purgatory on earth (100 –106). Langland criticizes false beggars but cautions the fortunate not to withhold alms just because some beggars are thieves (72–78): Christian love (Gregory) goes beyond pagan wisdom (Cato).

2.   The full Latin text can be found in Henry Denziger, *Enchiridion Symbolorum* (Handbook of Creeds), ed. Karl Rahner, 31st ed. (Rome: Herder, 1957), 17–18; cf. John F. Clarkson, et al., *The Church Teaches: Documents of the Church in English Translation* (Saint Louis: Herder, 1960), 4–6.

3.   The creeds (Apostles', Nicene, Athanasian) close with Resurrection, Ascension, Second Coming, and Last Judgment (e.g., "He will return in glory to judge the living and the dead," Nicene Creed). The Pardon occurs in the Athanasian creed's statement about Second Coming and Last Judgment; cf. Alford, *Guide to the Quotations,* 57.

4.   See Robert W. Frank Jr., *Piers Plowman and the Scheme of Salvation: An Interpretation of Dowel, Dobet and Dobest* (New Haven: Yale University Press, 1957), 28–31. The meaning of the scene has been much debated (Alford, "Design of the Poem," 42), and Langland removed the confrontation between priest and Piers from the C version.

5.   Piers quotes Ps. 41:4, "My tears have been my bread day and night. . . ." Scripture provides other penitential "food" at 13.46 –56.

6.   "The just man falls seven times a day" (8.20a).

7.   Cf. *kynde knowyng* (chapter 4). Dowel will at last be rendered concrete and "naturally" knowable in the person of Christ.

8.   Given the widespread antimendicant satire of the time, the friar's claim must have produced derision in much of Langland's audience.

9.   *Champion* suggests one who fights on another's behalf: see *MED,* s.v. "champioun n.," 1–3, and Alford, *Glossary of Legal Diction,* 24.

10.   See Alford, "Design of the Poem," 45–46; Wittig, "Elements"; Gillian Rudd, *Managing Language in "Piers Plowman"* (Cambridge: Brewer, 1994).

11.   *Clergy* embraces a spectrum of meanings: learning; "the clergy," within whose sphere literacy and learning typically resided; the Christian faith as taught by the clergy; Christian liturgical and sacramental functions, carried out in Latin, the "learned" language. Langland's text sometimes requires the last sense, only implicit in the *MED,* s.v. "clergie n.," 3a, 3c.

12.   The "seven years" (75) and "three days" (117) probably denote "a long time" and "for a while."

13.   See *MED,* s.v. "thought n.," 1a, 1d, 1f, 2b, 4a, 5a. *Cogitatio* (thought) was often used of the mind's fundamental operations: see, e.g., Augustine, *The Trinity,* trans. Stephen McKenna (Washington: Catholic University of America Press, 1963), bk. 15, chap. 9, p. 472.

14.   They appear throughout Thought's speech and in the following passus (9–12), in a transitional sense in passus 13.98–138, and thereafter rarely (14.18–22, 19.116–82).

15.   See Adams, "Theology," 90–95; Alford, "Design of the Poem," 45–56; Rudd, *Managing Language,* 135–51. A classic essay is S. S. Hussey, "Langland, Hilton and the Three Lives," *Review of English Studies,* n.s., 7 (1956): 132–50.

16.   Ascending excellence recurs in subsequent definitions, as does the idea of Dobest imposing ultimate spiritual discipline (correcting, teaching) only after "doing well" itself (e.g., 10.264–66).

17.   Dobet is not simply "clergy." It begins as generosity added to justice (85–90) and only then adds "running to religion." Extending love from the disposition of temporal goods to the sharing of spiritual goods (91–92) also underlies the transition.

18.   Wit prominently supplements his exposition with Genesis, I think, because he describes both how human nature was originally constituted and how it subsequently fell.

19.   On passus 9, see Wittig, "Elements," 211–29, and, for an excellent detailed discussion, M. Teresa Tavormina, *Kindly Similitude,* 48–109.

20.   For the Latin tradition, cf. 15.22–39 and Wittig, "Elements," 213 and n. 9. This psychology appears in John Trevisa's Middle English translation of Bartholomeus's *Properties of Things,* bk. 3 (ed. M. S. Seymour et al., 2:90–128).

21.   See *MED,* s.v. "inwit n.," 1a, 3a. The medieval Latin equivalent is *ratio* (reason), a word that risks confusion with the more objective sense of Reason discussed earlier. Medieval writers often reserved *intellectus* for mental activ-

ity that endeavored to apprehend God and the transcendent. Some critics translate *Inwit* as "conscience," but conscience has a more specific sense (an act of practical moral judgment).

22.   "And just as in man and woman there is one flesh of two, so the one nature of the mind embraces our intellect and action, or our council and execution, or our reason and reasonable appetite, or whatever other more significant terms there may be for expressing them, so that as it was said of those: 'they shall be two in one flesh' [Gen. 2:24], so it can be said of these: 'Two in one mind' " (Augustine, *The Trinity*, bk. 12, chap. 3; McKenna, 345).

23.   On the Fall of the interior "couple," see Augustine, *The Trinity*, bk. 12, chaps. 8–10 and 12 (McKenna 355–57 and 359). According to Augustine, this disruption within the soul not only images the Fall and is reenacted by subsequent sins but actually constituted the Original Sin of Adam and of Eve.

24.   Sight and sound are explicit in See-well and Hear-well; taste is transmuted to speech (Say-well), touch to the hand at work (Work-well-with-thy-hand). Perhaps smell becomes locomotion (Go-well) because it has no direct moral ramifications.

25.   For Augustine, the principal image of God in the soul consisted in memory, understanding, and will, which he related to Father, Son, and Holy Spirit, respectively (e.g., *The Trinity* 14.9). Triads in Langland (work, word, wit, 44; work, workmanship, life, 46) do not obviously correspond to Father, Son, and Holy Spirit. Christ was universally regarded as the "word" expressing the Father's "wisdom" (cf. John 1:1–5), but terms expressing general attributes (power, wisdom, life) pertained to the "essence" of God, not just to one of the Three Persons (*The Trinity*, bk. 7, chaps. 1–3).

26.   Human intelligence and speech are likened to God's fiddle and God's songster (104, 105), which should help direct Anima toward God rather than beguile or mislead it.

27.   Married couples were called upon to abstain from sexual intercourse at times (e.g., solemn fasting days or feast days) (Tavormina, 100–101). The bad marriages that produced the race of monsters were interpreted as humanity's succumbing to selfish lust and earthly desires—what Langland might well have termed *wikked wille* (Tavormina, 84–87, Wittig, "Elements," 226–28).

28.   Pride was considered the cause of the Fall. E.g., Augustine, *The Trinity*, bk. 12, chap. 9: the soul, disregarding "the whole" of nature's plan and seduced by bodily desires, fell to "that apostatizing pride, which is called 'the beginnings of sin' [Ecclus. 10:15]" (trans. McKenna, 356).

29.   *Study* signifies not only acquisition of knowledge but any "Zealous and diligent effort . . . labor, industry . . . a pursuit" (*MED*, s.v. "studie n.," 1 and 2).

30.   Intellect plus study lead to learning; Will's informants progress from intellect through application to *clergie*.

31.   The seven arts consisted of the *trivium* (grammar, rhetoric, and logic) plus the *quadrivium* (arithmetic, geometry, astronomy, and music). The

higher sciences were law, medicine, philosophy and—at the summit—theology. On the rationale of the liberal arts (especially logic and the quadrivium), see Henry Chadwick, *Boethius: The Consolations of Music, Logic, Theology and Philosophy* (Oxford: Clarendon, 1981), chaps. 2–3; on higher education in fourteenth-century England, see Courtenay, *Schools and Scholars,* esp. chap. 1.

32.   Human learning, though not thought to have originated Holy Scripture, was necessary for recording and subsequently interpreting it. Other learning and writing offered valuable moral truth and helped interpret Scripture.

33.   With 194–209 compare the opposition between Cato and Gregory (7.72–78).

34.   "For mercy's sake, see that you perform in act, to the extent of your power, what your 'word' manifests" (259 – 60).

35.   Monks, nuns, and cathedral canons (324) all lived on permanent endowments, theoretically modeled on the Donation of Constantine, which the threatened new king will revoke.

36.   *Dominus,* (lordship), can refer to any position of authority, from husband or head of household to kingship.

37.   *Poule preveth* (341) probably refers to 1 Tim. 6:10: *Radix malorum est cupiditas,* "the desire of money is the root of all evils; which some coveting have erred from the faith. . . ." Chaucer's Pardoner uses this verse as his theme.

38.   10.346 is the first of many explicit linkings of patience and poverty in the poem. The Bible joins them most explicitly in Ps. 9:19: "For the poor man shall not be forgotten to the end: the patience of the poor shall not perish for ever."

39.   "In Christ there is neither Gentile nor Jew, circumcision nor uncircumcision, Barbarian or Scythian, bond nor free"—that is, work to extend Redemption in Christ to all humanity.

40.   Those who love "do well" (James 2:8), but those who offend in any way [e.g., those who "believe" but do not love] are guilty of breaking the whole law (2:10). The verse about the same God forbidding both adultery and murder follows immediately (2:11).

41.   In C he reassigned the speech to Recklessness; cf. Pearsall, 201, 163 and 203, 196.

42.   Implicit in the critique of teachers here, Anima states it explicitly in passus 15.

43.   "Many people know many things, and they do not know themselves"; for the source of this text and its tradition, see Wittig, "Elements," 212–15.

44.   The three temptations appeared in passus 1. "Land of longing" suggests both "land where one longs" and "land where one is a long way from home"; for this and other details of this episode see Wittig, "Elements," 231–38.

45.   Because *Fortune* means "mutability," Will's folly is obvious, and line 26 is heavily ironic. The tradition of Fortune's whimsically revolving wheel raising peasant to king and flinging king low underlies the pun on "crown" in line

36. This notion of Fortune is based on Boethius, *Consolation of Philosophy,* bk. 2, pr. 2, trans. S. J. Tester, Loeb Classical Library vol. 74 (Cambridge: Harvard University Press, 1973), 180 –83.

46. Received doctrine taught that *in extremis* (on the point of death, with no confessor available), an act of perfect contrition could save (cf. 12.174–78). The dreamer invokes the letter of this teaching because he seems, at this point, incapable of the interior dispositions required for such contrition: cf. 17.299 –320.

47. Line 96 affirms that it is morally permissible for someone like Will to accuse the friars; lines 101–2 justify Langland's versified condemnation of notorious wrongs. The poet seems aware that he personally harbored some of the faults he dramatized in Will.

48. Scripture adds a condition Will seems to have missed, *and Mekenesse hir folwe,* "provided that humility [here recognition of guilt and appropriate repentance] accompany her" (138).

49. The "Legends of Saints," (11.161, 220), also called *Legenda Aurea* (Golden Legend), was composed by Jacob of Voragine c. 1255–1266 and achieved enormous popularity. On Trajan see Wittig, "Elements," 249 – 63, and Adams, "Theology," 97–98; hereafter cited in text as Adams, "Theology."

50. The opposition is not strictly between works and grace, for all need grace for salvation; but grace came to Trajan (149) not because of Pope Gregory's priestly prayers and masses (just what the dreamer has been counting on from the friars) but because of Trajan's own behavior.

51. Kane and Donaldson assign only 140 –53 and 171 to Trajan, while Schmidt, *B-Text,* 451, 140 assigns all of 140 –318 to Trajan. The passage is much revised in C (C 12.73–13.99), and Pearsall 215, 87 tentatively assigns what corresponds to B 11.154–319 to Recklessness (named at C 13.128). I think Langland's own voice dominates 154–319.

52. Lev. 19:18 as modified by Matt. 5:43– 44; the dreamer has just quoted Lev. 19:17 to justify his rebuke of the friars.

53. Contrast the narcissistic banqueting Study condemned in passus 10 with the feast described here (190 –96).

54. The prostitute of the Gospel story (Luke 7:37–50) who washed Christ's feet with her tears, dried them with her hair, and anointed them with oil was interpreted as a model of contrition and repentance. Only after these actions did Christ say to her, "Thy faith hath made thee safe" (Luke 7:50).

55. A title in this sense (11.290, 292) was a certificate of preferment to a *benefice*—a situation of priestly responsibility that provided a regular living. Both ecclesiastical and secular magnates had such benefices in their gift, the latter (along with the country gentry) typically in order to provide parish priests for churches on their lands. See W. A. Pantin, *The English Church in the Fourteenth Century* (South Bend: University of Notre Dame Press, 1963), 30 – 46.

56. Reason is again that objective *Ratio* representing the rationale of behavior based on the nature of things.

57. See, e.g., Boethius, *Consolation of Philosophy,* bk. 2, pr. 5, trans. Tester, 202–3.

58. Tavormina (183) points out that *kynde* at 11.403 probably refers to specifically sexual nature; whereas sex before the Fall was "without corruption," after the Fall passion in the act of procreation passed on the Fall's effects.

Chapter Seven

1. On the tradition of intellective and affective faculties, see Wittig, "Elements," 220 –22, on the reluctant *affectus* 229 –30. A defect of that article was my making "spiritual ascent" sound like an esoteric cognitive exercise rather than the entry point for the process of reforming one's life.

2. On Ymaginatif see Alford, "Design of the Poem," 47– 48, Wittig, "Elements," 264–70, and Alastair J. Minnis, "Langland's Ymaginatif and Late-Medieval Theories of Imagination," *Comparative Criticism* 3 (1981): 71–77.

3. E.g., Ernest N. Kaulbach, *Imaginative Prophecy in the B-Text of "Piers Plowman"* (Woodbridge, Suffolk: Brewer, 1993).

4. See Wittig, "Elements," 270 –73. The Latin *imaginativa* (understood as modifying "power" or "cell" in the brain) does sometimes appear by itself in Latin and in English *(imaginatif)* referring to the imagination.

5. Chief among them: all baptized are saved (10.349 –51, repeated in 11); predestination makes Dowel meaningless (377–83); men famous for learning are damned (384); grace saves (395– 402); the good thief and other sinners recall predestination and make Dowel nonsense (420 –31); God will provide (448 –55); the ignorant are more likely to reach heaven (458 –71). Pearsall, 238, 90 –91 has remarked the "burr-like quality of Ymaginatif's argument by association"; the speech indeed unfolds associatively but covers all these topics without digressions.

6. See T. P. Dunning, "Langland and the Salvation of the Heathen," *Medium Ævum* 12 (1943): 46, and Wittig, "Elements," n. 135.

7. Trajan has served to make a point, and Ymaginatif does not go beyond the affirmation of the *Legenda Aurea.* Trajan, because he lived in Christian times, is a somewhat different case than the righteous who lived before Christ.

8. "Of water" (sacramental baptism), "of blood" (martyrdom suffered by those who, though not yet baptized, believed in Christ), and "of fire" (or "of desire," for those who so lived that one judges they would have become Christians had they heard God's word). For further discussion, see, e.g., Dunning, "Langland and the Salvation of the Heathen."

9. The Latin anagram of 293a spells DEUS (God) from the words D*ans* E*ternam* U*itam* S*uis,* "giving eternal life [to] his own," then glosses "own" with *hoc est fidelibus,* "that is, to the faithful." Ymaginatif's use of the phrase implies that "faithful" equals "truthful, loyal to the truth they knew."

10. "It is an ordinary life, to believe in Holy Church . . . faithfully" (Clergy, 10.238–40); "If Dowel pleases you, see that you love faithfully" (Study, 10.192); "Dowel is to do as law teaches" (Wit, 9.202).

11. Only two states (marriage and virginity) are represented here, for religious were unmarried and (apart from those who might have taken vows after the death of a spouse) putatively virgins. Perhaps under "virginity" Langland is thinking of the lay unmarried; whatever the cause of their state (e.g., lack of means to marry), they could do well by living in chaste charity (cf. 1.188, 194), dedicating their virginity to God.

12. For the biblical texts see Deuteronomy 22:23–4 and John 8:1–11.

13. Based on Jerome, *Dialogus adversus Pelagianos*, ed. C. Moreschini, Corpus Christianorum Series Latina (hereafter CCSL) 80 (Turnholt: Brepols, 1990), bk. 2, par. 17, line 20.

14. When all the accusers slink away, Christ says to the woman, "Neither will I condemn thee. Go, and now sin no more" (John 8:11).

15. See, e.g., *In Iohannis evangelium tractatus*, ed. D. R. Willems, CCSL 36 (Turnholt: Brepols, 1954), tractatus 33, esp. par. 5.

16. Glosses on Luke 2:8 stated that shepherds lived simple lives, in the tradition of the Old Testament patriarchs, far from the "wisdom of this world"; cf. Wittig, "Elements," 276.

17. The probable source of *Quare placuit? quia voluit* is Exod. 33:19 (*miserebor cui voluero et clemens ero in quem mihi placuerit*, "And I will have mercy on whom I will, and I will be merciful to whom it shall please me").

18. Cf. Britton J. Harwood, "Imaginative in *Piers Plowman*," *Medium Ævum* 44 (1975): 254, and Minnis, "Langland's Ymaginatif," 87–92.

19. *MED*, s.v. "poet n.," (d) "any ancient writer"; Pearsall, 239, 92.

20. For this famous passage, discussed briefly in chapter 1, see Alford, "Design of the Poem," 48, and A. V. C. Schmidt, *Clerkly Maker*, 5–20.

21. I agree with those who regard the poem as a controlled rhetorical performance in which one must distinguish persona from poet (cf. Minnis, "Langland's Ymaginatif," 91). Even so, in the process of constructing it, the poet must have discovered for himself many of the striking associations and juxtapositions his verse came to express.

22. Many have thought these lines refer to the last episode of the inner dream. But they more likely refer to Ymaginatif's restatement of it in 12.214–29. As Minnis remarked ("Langland's Ymaginatif," p. 71, n. 4) *Ymaginatif*'s resolution of Will's problems holds up for the rest of the poem.

23. I think that from this point on the interludes suggest the state of a protagonist with *potential* for moral progress.

24. On this dream see especially Alford, "Design of the Poem," 48–51.

25. See, e.g., *ODCC*, "Conscience," and Thomas Aquinas, *Summa Theologiae*, I, Q. 79, a. 13; and I-II, Q. 19, a. 3–6 (McDermott, 124, 196–97).

26.   He is called *maister* ("master," 25, 33, 40), then *doctour* (61–172), terms that roughly correspond to our M.A. and Ph.D. degrees and here indicate a university-trained teacher of theology. He also seems to be a friar (70, 74, 95, 109).

27.   Compare Patience's observation (86 –93) that by using his dialectical skills on apparently spurious texts, the doctor could "prove" that meat and dishes made with meat or fish are "neither fish nor flesh" but fit fare for penitents (who were often required to abstain from such foods).

28.   "Eating people's sins" (the Latin quoted at 45) is based on Hosea 4:8, a verse regularly interpreted as describing priests who failed to correct the faults of their charges and accepted a share of the unjustly obtained money rather than demanding restitution and penance.

29.   The noun comes from the Latin verb *patior*, "suffer," and that root meaning dominates here.

30.   The texts that Scripture "feeds" Patience come principally from penitential psalms 31 and 50.

31.   Patience is called "pilgrim" and "hermit" (30). The latter did not simply mean "one who leads an ascetic life" but suggested a life lived in relative solitude (see *MED*, s.v. "heremit n.").

32.   Patience shares Will's opinion of the doctor (86 –98); fault lies not in recognizing hypocrisy or other bad behavior but in wrongfully (e.g., hypocritically) proclaiming it aloud.

33.   Kane and Donaldson's punctuation of 131–35 suggests that Clergy issues the invitation to Patience.

34.   Merely hinted at here, this Piers begins to be fleshed out by Anima in passus 15.

35.   Anne Middleton ("Two Infinites: Grammatical Metaphor in *Piers Plowman*," *ELH* 39 [1972]: 169 –88) is certainly correct in arguing that these do's represent "something intelligible only in its completed form" (173), but I do not think she successfully demonstrates that *Infinites* is a grammatical term.

36.   See especially R. E. Kaske, " 'Ex vi transitionis' and Its Passage in *Piers Plowman*," *Journal of English and Germanic Studies* 62 (1963), 32– 60; Edward C. Schweitzer, " 'Half a Laumpe Lyne in Latyne' and Patience's Riddle in *Piers Plowman*," *Journal of English and Germanic Studies* 73 (1974): 313–27. Recently Andrew Galloway has suggested a context in which to understand the riddling passages in the poem: "The Rhetoric of Riddling in Late Medieval England: The 'Oxford' Riddles, the *Secretum Philosophorum*, and the Riddles in *Piers Plowman*," *Speculum* 70 (1995): 68 –105. Although Galloway does not (to my mind) solve this riddle, the kinds of solutions he illustrates seem promising.

37.   On this all proffered solutions agree, guided by what Patience says clearly (140 – 47, 158 – 63) and by the relevant scriptural contexts (esp. 1 John 4, alluded to at 163, and 1 Cor. 13).

38.   One of the ways conscience can be applied is to judge and accuse concerning deeds done: cf. Thomas Aquinas, *Summa Theologiae*, I, Q. 79, a. 13 (McDermott, 124).

39.   See especially Stella Maguire, "The Significance of Haukyn, *Activa Vita*, in *Piers Plowman*," *Review of English Studies* 25 (1949): 97–109.

40.   For the sense "servant, functionary," see *MED*, s.v. "minstrel n.," 2, a meaning not widely attested. He does not seem particularly to fit among "God's minstrels" described at the end of passus 13.

41.   Cf. the *waferer* of 5.632 and Bennett, 196, 641 (his edition reads *wafestre* at 5.541). *OED*, "waferer," suggests wafer makers acted as go-betweens in amatory affairs; Chaucer's *Pardoner's Tale* puts them in taverns among "the devil's officers" (fragment 6, lines 479–80) and Absolon of the *Miller's Tale* woos Alison with "wafers" (fragment 1, line 3379). Cf. Malcolm Godden, "Plowmen and Hermits in Langland's *Piers Plowman*," *Review of English Studies*, n.s., 35 (1984): 138–41. A pun, "way-farer," seems highly unlikely, because "way," *wey*, had a quite different pronunciation than *wa-* in this word.

42.   See *MED*, s.v. "hauking ger. 2" (also spelled "haukin"), "hukker n." (in names through the fourteenth century), and cf. "hukkerye" (5.225).

43.   Opposed to the "active" life, engaged in the business of making a living or governing society, was the "contemplative" life, free to dedicate itself to thought and prayer. Both were perfectly acceptable for Christians; see Hussey.

44.   E.g., those of a landholder in 370, those of a merchant in 391.

45.   The verse quoted at 3a is one of the many excuses given by "guests" invited to a feast in the parable (Luke 14).

46.   Schmidt, *B-Text,* 463, 1–15 follows Skeat in understanding the coat as "carnal nature"; Alford accepts that sense but thinks the image's meaning is "not constant but multifarious and shifting": see "Haukyn's Coat: Some Observations on *Piers Plowman* B.XIV, 22–7," *Medium Ævum* 43 (1974): 136.

47.   If Haukyn confessed only once a year, as required by the Fourth Lateran Council, a life such as he led would present him with countless opportunities to soil his coat between confessions. But even if he confessed more frequently, his examination of conscience and contrition might be too distracted, too superficial, for the coat to be cleansed thoroughly from the sins he has actually committed.

48.   See Derek Pearsall, "Poverty and Poor People in *Piers Plowman*," in *Medieval English Studies Presented to George Kane*, ed. Edward D. Kennedy, Ronald Waldron, and Joseph S. Wittig (Woodbridge, Suffolk: Boydell and Brewer, 1988), 167–85.

49.   See *MED*, s.v. "charite n.," 2.

50.   That charity is God's "chamberlain" (101, the official who manages a sovereign's intimate household) suggests God's own presence in the souls of those so disposed (cf. 1 John 4:16 and passus 5.605–8).

51.   The Middle English meaning ranged from "not quite fully engaged in the serious quest for spiritual perfection" to "sinful, immoral, not complete, rudimentary" (*MED*, s.v. "imparfit adj."). Will, even if seriously embarked on a journey of penance and amendment, would remain inclined to sin. Perfection would mean that he had so purged his sinful tendencies that he fell no more—a state achieved, e.g., only at the summit of Dante's Mount Purgatory.

52.   Although almost everything said is perfectly appropriate for Anima, a few gestures (e.g., 414) suggest the poet assuming a pose (he *does* speak despite his alleged fear).

53.   E.g., the wonderful irony of the friars' "generosity" (328–30); the way line 429 imports a proverb ("Salt preserves goods!") only to turn it on its head; the interaction of wordplay and imagery in the coin passages (349–53, 539–45); the pun on *fullyng* (baptizing, finishing cloth) expanded into simile (451–55).

54.   Line 194 quotes from the fourth penitential psalm (Ps. 50:19).

Chapter Eight

1.   Cf. Elizabeth Kirk, *The Dream Thought of Piers Plowman* (New Haven: Yale University Press, 1972), esp. 183–89.

2.   By "ontological" I mean to suggest a community based upon the very "being" of its members as distinct from a "historical" community based on shared experience through time.

3.   The poem's connection with the liturgy has sometimes been exaggerated, as Robert Adams points out in "Langland and the Liturgy Revisited," *Studies in Philology* 73 (1976): 266–84. Nevertheless, passus 16–19 often explicitly invoke the liturgical year.

4.   Cf. Raymond St-Jacques, "Conscience's Final Pilgrimage in *Piers Plowman* and the Cyclical Structure of the Liturgy," *Revue de l'Université d'Ottawa* 40 (1970): 219–23.

5.   On the tree of Charity see: Alford, "Design of the Poem," 53; Aers, *Christian Allegory*, 79–109; Peter Dronke, "Arbor Caritatis," in *Medieval Studies for J. A. W. Bennett*, ed. P. L. Heyworth (Oxford: Clarendon, 1981), 207–53.

6.   The C text (18.1–172) has been much revised; garden, props, and tree are simplified, and the fruit is elaborated. The tree *imago Dei* is an *ymp* (grafted plant) set in the heart of man by the Trinity. B 16.14 also suggests that the "tree" Charity results from a graft, an implantation of the Trinity (or of God the Son) onto the stalk of humanity.

7.   Alford suggests he "symbolizes the perfect conformity of wills that unites God and man" ("Design of the Poem," 55; see further his discussion 54–56). Margaret E. Goldsmith calls him "an example and pattern of righteousness," "the *forma justitiae* which is nothing less than man bearing the Image of God" (*The Figure of Piers Plowman: The Image on the Coin* [Cambridge: Brewer,

1981], 16, 20). Cf. Samuel A. Overstreet, "Langland's Elusive Plowman," *Traditio* 45 (1989 –90): 257– 61 and *passim*.

8.   On the fruit, see Tavormina, *Kindly Similitude*, 116 –18 and, for the much expanded C version, 118 – 40. For the same three "lives" cf. 12.33 –39. C 18.76 –80 adds the notion of "active" and "contemplative" lives, the former associated with marriage, the later with sexual continence.

9.   Because of Original Sin, even the souls of the just cannot be admitted to heaven until after the Redemption: their release is described in passus 18.

10.   Will's persistent curiosity, for which he has been so often chided and which only a sour look from Piers had managed to contain (16.64– 65), thus has an archetypal model in the wills of Adam and Eve.

11.   In the C text, Langland halts this retelling with Christ's arrest (18.179), thus enhancing the sense of narrative resumed later.

12.   We must infer the cause of Will's tears: Proximate, for Christ's suffering? More universal, for the Fall and the state of Piers's "fruit"? In C, Will wakes at the clamor accompanying Christ's arrest (18.179).

13.   Moses not only received the Ten Commandments on Mount Sinai (Exod. 20) but was regarded as recipient and codifier of all the Jewish laws set out in the last three "books of Moses" (Numbers, Leviticus, and Deuteronomy).

14.   Moses never entered that promised land (cf. Num. 20:12) and is therefore an especially apt representative of hope still awaiting fulfillment.

15.   Ymaginatif (quoting 1 Cor. 13:13) listed them at 12.29 –31. "The greatest of these is charity" (1 Cor. 13:13), the perfection of the virtues: see, e.g., Aquinas, *Summa Theologiae,* II-II, Q. 23, a. 7–8 (McDermott, 351).

16.   Augustine analogizes the Holy Spirit as the love that arises between Father and Son contemplating one another, and he explicitly associates the Spirit with charity: see *The Trinity*, bk. 15, chaps. 17–18 (McKenna, 491–97).

17.   The Samaritan is, however, a "figure," or analogue, of Christ; see Raymond St-Jacques, "The Liturgical Associations of Langland's Samaritan," *Traditio* 25 (1969): 217–30.

18.   Doctrine about the Trinity stressed the persons' eternal, dynamic interaction: the Son is "eternally [and continually] begotten of " the Father; the Spirit "proceeds" eternally and continually from Father and Son.

19.   On the church as spouse of Christ, see Eph. 5:24–32 and 1 Cor. 11:2. On Christians as Christ's body, see esp. 1 Cor. 12:14–27. Line 198 expresses three manifestations (before the law, Old Law, New Law) of God's one chosen people; 199 with its triple repetition of "Christ(-)" articulates another (Christ, Christendom, Christians). On Abraham's speech, see further Tavormina, *Kindly Similitude*, 140 – 63.

20.   Obviously argued by the whole, this point finds explicit expression: e.g., Faith and Hope pass safely through the wilderness because the devil sees the Samaritan following them (109 –11); after the Redemption, Faith, Hope, and the Samaritan will cooperate in helping people through the "forest" (112–24).

21. On the hand image see Clopper, "Trinitarian Analogies," 89–91, and Frederick M. Biggs, "For God Is after an Hand: *Piers Plowman* B.17. 138–205," *YLS* 5 (1991): 17–30. On the torch see Clopper, 91–94.

22. Langland was not portraying one consecutive liturgical year. The Samaritan's words have already suggested that his act of charity took place simultaneously with the Crucifixion: see 17.112–13.

23. I translate 18.4–9 as follows: "Until I grew weary of the world and wanted to sleep again. And I gave myself over to a Lent and slept for a long time; I rested myself there and slept hard till Palm Sunday. I dreamed much of children and of *gloria laus* and of how old people sang *Hosanna* to musical accompaniment, and of Christ's passion and suffering, which carried off the people."

24. See Matt. 21:7–11, Mark 11:7–11, Luke 19:35–38, and John 12:12–13. Here and throughout the passus, as Schmidt notes (*B-Text,* 478, 4), the Latin tags serve to evoke not only the Gospel accounts but also the songs and readings of the Holy Week liturgy.

25. The Hebrew children were among those who celebrated Christ's entry into the city; *Gloria laus, Hosanna, Fili David,* and *Benedictus qui venit in nomine Domini* all were among the greetings shouted in the Gospels and were woven into liturgical songs commemorating the event.

26. The Passion is retold in all four Gospels (Matt. 26–27, Mark 14–15, Luke 22–23, and John 18–19). These accounts were read at subsequent masses during Holy Week, beginning on Palm Sunday, and were often performed in a quasi-dramatic fashion; the Latin phrases Langland quotes come almost exclusively from those assigned to "the people" and spoken by them or their clerical representatives.

27. In the Gospels it is the "curtain" shielding the holy of holies that is rent (Matt. 27:51, Mark 15:38, Luke 23:45); this was interpreted as a sign of the passing of the Old Law.

28. John 19:36, invoking the Passover ritual from Exod. 12:46.

29. He has in fact been baptized in the blood of the babe: cf. 17.97.

30. Cf. Pearsall, 323, 96. Lines 102–9 undoubtedly contain anti-Semitism describing the Jews as a homeless and propertyless people doomed to usury. But Langland indulges not in ethnic or economic but in theological stereotyping: the chosen people to whom God gave "land and lordship" (16.240) lose it when they reject Christ, sent to fulfill the Old Law in the New.

31. "He descended into hell" comes from the Apostles' Creed, which every Christian was supposed to know by heart. The second phrase, which brings with it the entire clause from which it is drawn ("on the third day he arose from the dead, according to the scriptures"), occurs in the Nicene Creed recited at mass. The earliest extended account of the harrowing is the *Gospel of Nicodemus*: see *New Testament Apocrypha*, rev. ed. Wilhelm Schneemelcher, trans. R. McL. Wilson (Westminster: John Knox, 1991), 1:501–36, esp. 522–25. On liturgical commemorations of the harrowing, see Karl Young, *The Drama of the*

Medieval Church (Oxford, Clarendon, 1933), 1:149 –77, esp. 167–77. Full dramatic presentation occurred in the mystery plays (York 37, Townely 25, Chester 17). The Apostles' Creed puts harrowing before Resurrection; tradition assumed Christ's triumphant spirit (here described as a blazing light) raided hell then resumed its body and emerged from the tomb. The Resurrection and Christ's subsequent appearances are not really described until 19.134–81.

32.   On Langland's concern for legal accuracy, see Alford, "Design of the Poem," 57.

33.   The two "eyes" suggest something like the two Testaments, or the literal and spiritual understanding of the Bible, or even (given what Book says) the "book" of Nature as reported in the "book" of revelation; see R. E. Kaske, "The Speech of 'Book' in *Piers Plowman*," *Anglia* 77 (1959): 117– 44.

34.   Thus Book's posture both heightens the assumed suspense (will the Bible be burned?) and argues for the Resurrection (it remains unburnt).

35.   Ps. 23:7–8; verses 9 –10 repeat 7–8 with minor variations.

36.   Lines 363–70 imaginatively recombine the "cup of death" that all humanity must drink because of Original Sin, the cup that could not pass away (Matt. 26:39) and that Christ subsequently drank, his thirst on the cross, and the vintage of the grapes of wrath at the Last Judgment.

37.   See Thomas D. Hill, "Universal Salvation and Its Literary Context in *Piers Plowman* B.18," *YLS* 5 (1991): 65–76.

38.   "If the effrontery of their sins is made up for *to any degree*, I can be merciful . . ." (388 –89, emphasis added). Contrast the emphasis on paying what one owes in passus 19 and 20 and Conscience's words at 19.195–98.

39.   Their names, "Kytte" and "Calote" (426), are entirely conventional, both in themselves and in combination with one another (Pearsall, 341, 472). Langland, then, may be inventing an ad hoc "family" for Will to dramatize a sense of kinship with humanity newly awakened by his response to this dream of the Redemption.

Chapter Nine

1.   Matt. 28:16 –20, Mark 16:15–18; cf. John 21:1–23, Luke 24:44– 49.

2.   Mark 16:19 –20, Luke 24:50 –53, Acts 1:9 –12.

3.   The Apostles' and Nicene Creed reflect the same tight sequence.

4.   I see no reason to think the speaker slothful here, as Bowers suggests (*Crisis of Will*, 155–58). Dream visions require dreams, and George D. Economou has argued that this dream in particular is anything but slothful: see "The Vision's Aftermath in *Piers Plowman*: The Poetics of the Middle English Dream-Vision," *Genre* 18 (1985): 313–21.

5.   There would have been an offertory procession on Easter, according to Joseph S. Jungmann, *The Mass of the Roman Rite: Its Origins and Development* (New York: Benziger, 1955), 2:22, but no evidence indicates that a ceremonial

crucifix would lead the procession. A large crucifix would have hung over the altar or stood close by it and so would have been visible to the congregation. Will's noticing the body "all bloody" could conceivably be stimulated by the custom of removing, on Easter Sunday, the coverings that had veiled the figure on the cross during the last days of Lent.

6. These are printed as numbers 54 and 55 in F. J. R. Raby, *The Oxford Book of Medieval Latin Verse* (Oxford: Clarendon, 1959). Both were used in the Holy Week liturgy, and Langland quotes *Pange Lingua* at 18.162a.

7. For an English translation of words prayed by the priest at the offertory, see, e.g., the York Use as printed in *Lay Folks' Mass Book*, 98–102; hereafter cited in text.

8. Langland has been quite deliberate with the names. *Jesus* dominates until the moment of the Resurrection (lines 70–151), then *Christ* replaces it (152–200). The few exceptions occur for good reasons: e.g., line 117 wittily uses *Christ* to subordinate it to *Jesus;* Peter, James, and John seek *Jesus* as they knew him (164).

9. Introduced at 19.187, the line is repeated at 19.390 and closely echoed at 20.308; *redde* occurs again at 19.259. On the Latin see Alford, *Guide to the Quotations,* 114, and John A. Yunck, "Satire," in *Companion,* 149–50.

10. *Patrologia Latina* 38, cols. 514–15.

11. Recall the opposing citadels of Pr.13–16. On the development of the Antichrist tradition, see Richard Kenneth Emmerson, *Antichrist in the Middle Ages* (Seattle: University of Washington Press, 1981); hereafter cited in text.

12. See, e.g., Bloomfield, *Apocalypse,* 134. For useful background concerning the cardinal virtues see Frank, *Salvation,* 104–5.

13. Theological treatises regularly considered the theological virtues followed by the cardinal virtues: e.g., Peter Lombard's *Sentences,* Thomas Aquinas's *Summa Theologiae.* The same order was reflected in more popular works, e.g., *The Lay Folks' Catechism* (see 80–87).

14. On instilled virtues see, e.g., Aquinas, *Summa Theologiae,* I-II, Q. 110, a. 2 (McDermott, 313).

15. *Summa Theologiae,* I-II, Q. 65, a. 2 (McDermott, 243).

16. 1 Cor. 9:27, quoted by Aquinas in his discussion of this point in *Summa Theologiae,* I-II, Q. 63, a. 4 (McDermott, 241). Langland's description of temperance does not explicitly demand bodily mortification but stresses a demanding level of detachment: cf. Patience on poverty in passus 14.

17. Aquinas, *Summa Theologiae,* I-II, Q. 109, a. 8 (McDermott, 311).

18. The word means a building in which to store farm produce, rather than a shelter for animals or equipment: see *MED*, s.v. "bern n. (2)."

19. The heart of Conscience's reply lies in the Latin of 479a: the king has power to defend the goods of others, not to appropriate them to himself, and he must shape his laws accordingly. We are left to imagine how the king might respond.

20. A vicar undertook the priestly obligations owed by another. Some-one who had obtained a benefice (an ecclesiastical income) could sublet it to a vicar, typically for a fraction of its full value, thus becoming free to live else-where while enjoying the balance. Under the circumstances, the benefice holder had little incentive to find a vicar more than minimally qualified. See W. A. Pantin, *English Church*, 35–36.

21. See, e.g., Aquinas, *Summa Theologiae*, I-II, Q. 66, a. 1–2 (McDer-mott, 244).

22. *Place* likely means "house, establishment" (*MED*, s.v. "place n." 6). Cf. 1 Cor. 4:11, "Even unto this hour we both hunger and thirst, and are naked, and are buffeted, and have no fixed abode."

23. On Need in this episode, see especially Szittya, *Antifraternal Tradi-tion*, 267–76, and Robert Adams, "The Nature of Need in 'Piers Plowman' XX," *Traditio* 34 (1978): 273–301.

24. The behavior of the "needy" friar confessor offering to absolve Lady Meed in exchange for a gift of stained glass (3.48–50) illustrates how easily temperance can be similarly caricatured.

25. On this last dream see especially Alford, "Design of the Poem," 60 – 61; Frank, *Salvation*, 109–18; Szittya, *Antifraternal Tradition*, 247–87; Emmerson, *Antichrist*, 197–203.

26. Adams, "Need" (293–301), thinks Langland expected Doomsday in his own lifetime; Emmerson (197, 201) tends to agree. Szittya regards the dream as an "omen" of the end, without indication of how imminent it might be. Frank speaks of the dream as a "symbolic expression" meant to indict cor-rupt clergy (*Salvation,* 111). We must distinguish between the events evoked (the "historical" prelude to the end of the world) and Langland's fictive use of them here.

27. That is, God's wise who are fools in the eyes of this world; e.g., 1 Cor. 4:10, "We are fools for Christ's sake. . . ."

28. Compare Reason's explanation of natural disasters at 5.13–15.

29. Cf. Wenzel, *Sloth*, p. 37 and n. 20.

30. Lines 70 –72 are closely paralleled in the paradigm at 19.351–52.

31. See Frank, *Salvation*, 114–16, who summarizes the main conclu-sions of Archbishop Richard Fitzralph, the most influential antimendicant voice of Langland's time. Moorman, *History*, provides a succinct overview of "The Fri-ars and Their Critics," 339 – 49, and Szittya an extended discussion of Fitzralph in *Antifraternal Tradition*, 123–51. For a Middle English translation of Fitzralph's famous sermon defending parish clergy against the friars (the *Defen-sio Curatorum*), see Aaron J. Perry, ed., *Trevisa's Dialogues*, EETS, o.s., 167 (Lon-don: Oxford University Press, 1925), 39 –93. Scase, *New Anticlericalism*, reviews the entire debate in the context of late-fourteenth-century polemic.

32. To appreciate the full, sharp flavor of the phrase, one must read it in the context from which it is drawn: 2 Tim. 3:1– 6.

33. It is crucial to remember Conscience's fallibility. Without instruction, clear teaching, and example, Conscience can err. Witness the threats of Pride's spies at 19.344–50 and how, earlier, the Samaritan had offered Will the image of God as hand in case his conscience ever resisted his pursuing both faith and hopeful love (17.138).

34. In an age that theoretically privileged spiritual over material well-being, Christians were known to call down natural disasters upon their fellows in hopes that moral perspective might be restored. Such catastrophes were thought to convey God's displeasure at human behavior as well as to remind them of the transitory nature of life on earth. Charity would surely have such horrors cease the instant they achieved their effect. Recall how Piers asked Hunger to desist in passus 6.199.

35. Francis had his first rule accepted by Pope Innocent III in 1209; a revised form was approved by Honorius III in 1223. The Dominicans received papal approval from Innocent III in 1215 and 1216.

36. The series of papal decrees granting the friars cure of souls extended from 1231 through 1312. The last, a reinstatement of a bull called *Super cathedram* issued after the Council of Vienne in 1312, was in force in Langland's day and is what Fitzralph attacked. Despite many efforts by "secular" clergy (bishops and parish priests) to prevent such encroachments on their responsibilities (and incomes), the papacy steadfastly upheld the friars' privileges, though requiring them to get permission from the bishops. See Moorman, *History*, esp. 121–22, 181–84, 363–65.

37. Secular clergy opposed the friars' increasing role on the grounds that the friars were unnecessary and motivated by greed. The popes and their advisors countered that the friars were actually better-trained and more effective spiritual guides, "the only healthy limb in the body of Christ" (Moorman, *History*, 184; cf. 178, 202–3). Langland, copious in his criticism of the secular clergy, must be aware of the irony; perhaps he shares that sense of promise betrayed so prominent in fourteenth-century antifraternal satire.

38. Schmidt, *B-Text*, 492, 311 suggests that Conscience has already been swayed by the glib speech posing as "courtesy" (*hende speche*, 348, 354) associated with the friars. Or perhaps Conscience gives way to a mistaken impulse to be courteous and lets down his guard.

39. If not as rich as their detractors claimed, the friars were not as a group poor, although they did continually have to solicit donations and fees. See Moorman, *History*, 350–68.

40. As Szittya remarks (286), *Clergie* had earlier prophesied that unless religious reformed, the friars should get hold of their endowments (10.328–330). This solution could be read as "a pox on both their houses."

41. See Alford, "Design of the Poem," 61.

42. E.g., *Elde* smiting the physician (175–79), Peace's vigorous gloss on *Sire Penetrans domos* (341–47), Will's description of his wife's reaction to (and participation in) his impotence (194–98, cf. the antimatrimonial vein found in Chaucer's *Wife of Bath's Prologue*).

Selected Bibliography

Note: For more detailed bibliography on particular topics, consult the notes to the pertinent chapters.

BIBLIOGRAPHIES

Pearsall, Derek. *An Annotated Critical Bibliography of Langland*. Ann Arbor: University of Michigan Press, 1990. For previous bibliographies see items 1–10.

YLS: The Yearbook of Langland Studies. East Lansing, Mich.: Colleagues Press, vol. 1– (1987–). Articles, notes, reviews, and an annotated annual bibliography for 1985 and following.

EDITIONS AND TRANSLATIONS

Standard Scholarly Editions of the Versions

Kane, George, ed. *Piers Plowman: The A Version*. Rev. ed. London: Athlone; Berkeley: University of California Press, 1988.

Kane, George, and E. Talbot Donaldson, eds. *Piers Plowman: The B Version*. Rev. ed. London: Athlone; Berkeley: University of California Press, 1988.

Rigg, A. G., and Charlotte Brewer, eds. *William Langland, Piers Plowman: The Z Version*. Toronto: Pontifical Institute, 1983.

Russell, George, and George Kane, eds. *Piers Plowman: The C Version*. London: Athlone; Berkeley: University of California Press, 1997.

Editions with Glosses and Explanatory Notes

Bennett, J. A. W., ed. *Piers Plowman: The Prologue and Passus I–VII of the B Text as Found in Bodleian MS. Laud 581, Edited with Notes and Glossary*. Oxford: Clarendon, 1972.

Pearsall, Derek, ed. *Piers Plowman by William Langland: An Edition of the C-Text*. London: Arnold, 1978; reprint, Exeter: University of Exeter Press, 1994.

Schmidt, A. V. C., ed. *The Vision of Piers Plowman: A Critical Edition of the B-Text Based on Trinity College Cambridge MS B.15.17*. 2d ed. London: Dent; Rutland, Vt.: Tuttle, 1995.

Skeat, Walter W., ed. *The Vision of William concerning Piers the Plowman in Three Parallel Texts*. 2 vols. Oxford: Oxford University Press, 1886.

Parallel-Text Editions

Schmidt, A. V. C., ed. *Piers Plowman: A Parallel-Text Edition of the A, B, C and Z Versions*. Vol. 1. Text. London: Longman, 1995. Vol. 2 is to contain introduction, commentary, and glossary.
Skeat (see previous section).

Langland's Versification

Duggan, Hoyt N. "Notes toward a Theory of Langland's Meter." *YLS* 1 (1987): 41–70. The form of the poet's verse.
Kane, George. "Music 'Neither Unpleasant nor Monotonous.' " In *Medieval Studies for J. A. W. Bennett*, edited by P. L. Heyworth. Oxford: Clarendon, 1981. The variety and flexibility with which the poet manipulates his verse form.
Lawton, David A. "Alliterative Style." In *A Companion to Piers Plowman*, edited by John A. Alford. Berkeley: University of California Press, 1988. How verse form combines with other features of language in Langland's style.

Translations

Donaldson, E. Talbot. *Piers Plowman: An Alliterative Verse Translation*. Edited by Elizabeth D. Kirk and Judith H. Anderson. New York: Norton, 1990. B version, based on Kane and Donaldson text.
Economou, George. *William Langland's Piers Plowman: The C Version. A Verse Translation*. Middle Ages Series. Philadelphia: University of Pennsylvania Press, 1996. Based on Pearsall's edition.
Goodridge, J. F. *Piers the Plowman: Translated into Modern English with an Introduction*. Rev. ed. Harmondsworth: Penguin, 1966. Prose translation of the B version based on Skeat's text, but still very useful.
Schmidt, A. V. C. *William Langland: Piers Plowman*. Oxford: Oxford University Press, 1992. Prose translation of the B version based on Schmidt's text; see the review by George Kane, *YLS* 7.

REFERENCE AND BACKGROUND

Alford, John A. *Piers Plowman: A Glossary of Legal Diction*. Woodbridge, Suffolk: Boydell and Brewer, 1988.
————. *Piers Plowman: A Guide to the Quotations*. Binghamton, N.Y.: Medieval and Renaissance Texts and Studies, 1992.
Aquinas, Thomas. *Summa Theologiae: A Concise Translation*. Edited by Timothy McDermott. Westminster, Md.: Christian Classics, 1989. An accurate and readable English paraphrase of this accessible theological compendium.

Catholic Encyclopedia. 15 vols. New York: Appleton, 1907–1912. More useful
than the new edition for medieval matters.

Courtenay, William J. *Schools and Scholars in Fourteenth-Century England.* Princeton, N.J.: Princeton University Press, 1987.

Fasciculus Morum: A Fourteenth-Century Preacher's Handbook. Edited and translated by Siegfried Wenzel. University Park: Pennsylvania State University Press, 1989. Illustrates penitential tradition and seven deadly sins.

Lay Folks' Catechism. Edited by Thomas Frederick Simmons and Henry Edward
Nolloth. Early English Text Society, o.s., 118. London: Paul, Trench,
Trübner, 1901. Illustrates basic prayers and religious teaching.

Mann, Jill. *Chaucer and Medieval Estates Satire.* Cambridge: Cambridge University Press, 1973.

McKisack, May. *The Fourteenth Century: 1307–1399.* Oxford: Clarendon Press,
1959. Standard handbook for history of the period.

MED: Middle English Dictionary. Edited by Hans Kurath, Sherman M. Kuhn,
Robert E. Lewis, John Reidy, et al. Ann Arbor: University of Michigan
Press, 1954– (published through the letter *t*).

Moorman, John. *A History of the Franciscan Order from Its Origins to the Year 1517.*
Oxford: Oxford University Press, 1968; reprint, Chicago: Franciscan
Herald Press, 1988.

ODCC: Oxford Dictionary of the Christian Church. Edited by F. L. Cross and E. A.
Livingstone. 2d ed. Oxford: Oxford University Press, 1974. Excellent
brief articles.

Pantin, W. A. *The English Church in the Fourteenth Century.* South Bend, Ind.:
University of Notre Dame Press, 1963.

Trevisa, John. *On the Properties of Things: John Trevisa's Translation of Bartholomaeus
Anglicus De Proprietatibus Rerum, A Critical Edition.* Edited by M. C. Seymour et al. 3 vols. Oxford: Clarendon, 1975–1988. A late-fourteenth-
century translation.

(Forthcoming from Athlone are a glossary to the three versions by George Kane
and, in conjunction with it, a glossarial concordance to the Athlone editions by Joseph S. Wittig.)

INTRODUCTIONS TO THE POEM

Alford, John A., ed. *A Companion to Piers Plowman.* Berkeley: University of California Press, 1988. Excellent introductory articles by major scholars.

Frank, Robert W., Jr. *Piers Plowman and the Scheme of Salvation: An Interpretation
of Dowel, Dobet and Dobest.* Yale Studies in English 136. New Haven: Yale
University Press, 1957. Remains a valuable overview of the poem in its
context.

Simpson, James. *Piers Plowman: An Introduction to the B-Text*. London: Longman, 1990. A lucid introduction that sees Langland as being critical of conventional thought and institutions.

STUDIES OF *PIERS PLOWMAN* AND RELATED WORKS

Adams, Robert. "Langland and the Liturgy Revisited." *Studies in Philology* 73 (1976): 266–84.

———. "The Nature of Need in 'Piers Plowman' XX." *Traditio* 34 (1978): 273–301.

———. "Langland's Theology." In Alford, *Companion*.

Aers, David. *Piers Plowman and Christian Allegory*. London: Arnold, 1975. Langland's relationship to different models of allegory.

———. *Chaucer, Langland and the Creative Imagination*. London: Routledge, 1980. Langland's implicit dialectic with social and ecclesiastical ideologies.

Alford, John A. "The Design of the Poem." In Alford, *Companion*.

———. "The Idea of Reason in *Piers Plowman*." In *Medieval English Studies Presented to George Kane*, edited by Edward D. Kennedy, Ronald Waldron, and Joseph S. Wittig. Woodbridge, Suffolk: Boydell and Brewer, 1988.

———. "The Figure of Repentance in *Piers Plowman*." In *Suche Werkis to Werche: Essays on Piers Plowman in Honor of David C. Fowler*, edited by Miceal F. Vaughan. East Lansing, Mich.: Colleagues Press, 1993.

Baldwin, Anna P. *The Theme of Government in Piers Plowman*. Woodbridge, Suffolk: Boydell and Brewer, 1981.

———. "The Historical Context." In Alford, *Companion*.

Barney, Stephen A. "Allegorical Visions." In Alford, *Companion*.

Barr, Helen, ed. *The Piers Plowman Tradition: A Critical Edition of Pierce the Ploughman's Crede, Richard the Redeless, Mum and the Sothsegger and The Crowned King*. Everyman's Library. London: Dent and Rutland; Vermont: Tuttle, 1993. Includes introduction, glosses, and notes.

Bennett, J. A. W. "The Date of the B-Text of *Piers Plowman*." *Medium Ævum* 12 (1943): 55–64.

Benson, David. "The Function of Lady Meed in *Piers Plowman*." *English Studies* 61 (1980): 193–205.

Biggs, Frederick M. "For God Is after an Hand: *Piers Plowman* B.17.138–205." *YLS* 5 (1991): 17–30.

Blanch, Robert P., ed. *Style and Symbolism in "Piers Plowman": A Modern Critical Anthology*. Knoxville: University of Tennessee Press, 1969. Thirteen valuable essays.

Bloomfield, Morton W. *Piers Plowman as a Fourteenth-Century Apocalypse*. New Brunswick: Rutgers University Press, [1962]. Remains valuable for intellectual and literary milieu; cf. Kerby-Fulton.

Bowers, John M. *The Crisis of Will in "Piers Plowman."* Washington, D.C.: Catholic University of America Press, 1986. Sees Will's sloth as a crucial element in the poem.

Burrow, John. "The Audience of Piers Plowman." *Anglia* 75 (1957): 373–84.

———. "The Action of Langland's Second Vision." *Essays in Criticism* 15 (1965): 247–68. Reprinted in Blanch.

———. *Langland's Fictions.* Oxford: Clarendon, 1993.

Clopper, Lawrence M. "Langland's Trinitarian Analogies as Key to Meaning and Structure." *Medievalia et Humanistica* 9 (1979): 87–110.

Davlin, Mary Clemente. "*Kynde knowyng* as a Middle English Equivalent for 'Wisdom' in *Piers Plowman*." *Medium Ævum* 50 (1981): 5–17.

———. *A Game of Heuene: Word Play and the Meaning of "Piers Plowman" B.* Cambridge: Brewer, 1989.

Donaldson, E. Talbot. *Piers Plowman: The C-Text and Its Poet.* Yale Studies in English 113. New Haven, Conn.: Yale University Press, 1949. Classic comparison of B and C versions that reveals much about Langland.

Dunning, T. P. "Langland and the Salvation of the Heathen." *Medium Ævum* 12 (1943): 45–54.

———. "The Structure of the B-Text of *Piers Plowman*." *Review of English Studies,* n.s., 7 (1956): 225–37. Reprinted in Blanch.

———. *Piers Plowman: An Interpretation of the A Text.* 2d ed. Revised and edited by T. P. Dolan. Oxford: Clarendon, 1980. A useful introduction to much of poem's conceptual world.

Emmerson, Richard K. *Antichrist in the Middle Ages.* Seattle: University of Washington Press, 1981.

Fletcher, Alan J. "The Social Trinity of *Piers Plowman*." *Review of English Studies* 44 (1993): 343–61.

Frank, Robert Worth, Jr. "The Art of Reading Medieval Personification-Allegory." *ELH* 20 (1953): 237–50.

Galloway, Andrew. "The Rhetoric of Riddling in Late-Medieval England: The "Oxford" Riddles, the *Secretum philosophorum*, and the Riddles in *Piers Plowman*." *Speculum* 70 (1995): 68–105.

Godden, Malcolm. "Plowmen and Hermits in Langland's *Piers Plowman*." *Review of English Studies,* n.s., 35 (1984): 138–41.

Goldsmith, Margaret E. *The Figure of Piers Plowman: The Image on the Coin.* Cambridge: Brewer, 1981.

Hanna, Ralph, III. *William Langland.* Authors of the Middle Ages 3: English Writers of the Late Middle Ages. Aldershot, Hants, and Brookfield, Vt.: Variorum, 1993.

Harwood, Britton J. "Imaginative in *Piers Plowman*." *Medium Ævum* 44 (1975): 249–63.

———. *Piers Plowman and the Problem of Belief.* Toronto: University of Toronto Press, 1992. The poem as Langland's personal quest for faith.

Hill, Thomas D. "Davidic Typology and the Characterization of Christ: *Piers Plowman* B. XIX.95–103." *Notes and Queries* 20 (1976): 291–94.

———. "Universal Salvation and Its Literary Context in *Piers Plowman* B.18." *YLS* 5 (1991): 65–76.

Hudson, Anne. "*Piers Plowman* and the Peasants' Revolt: A Problem Revisited." *YLS* 8 (1994): 85–106.

Hussey, S. S. "Langland, Hilton and the Three Lives." *Review of English Studies,* n.s., 7 (1956): 132–50.

Kane, George. *Piers Plowman: The Evidence for Authorship*. London: Athlone, 1965.

———. *The Autobiographical Fallacy in Chaucer and Langland Studies*. The Chambers Memorial Lecture. London: University College, 1965.

———. "The Perplexities of William Langland." In *The Wisdom of Poetry: Essays in Early English Literature in Honor of Morton W. Bloomfield*, edited by Larry D. Benson and Siegfried Wenzel. Kalamazoo, Mich.: Medieval Institute Publications, 1982.

———. "The Text." In Alford, *Companion*.

Kaske, R. E. "The Speech of 'Book' in *Piers Plowman*." *Anglia* 77 (1959): 117–44.

———. " 'Ex vi transitionis' and Its Passage in *Piers Plowman*." *Journal of English and Germanic Philology* 62 (1963): 32–60. Reprinted in Blanch.

———. "Holy Church's Speech and the Structure of *Piers Plowman*." In *Chaucer and Middle English Studies in Honor of Rossell Hope Robbins,* edited by Beryl Rowland. London: Allen and Unwin, 1974.

Kean, P. M. "Langland on the Incarnation." *Review of English Studies,* n.s., 16 (1965): 349–63.

Kellogg, Alfred L. "Langland and Two Scriptural Texts." *Traditio* 14 (1958): 385–98.

Kerby-Fulton, Kathryn. *Reformist Apocalpyticism and "Piers Plowman."* Cambridge: Cambridge University Press, 1990. Reevaluation of poem's relationship to prophetic and apocalyptic tradition; cf. Bloomfield.

Kirk, Elizabeth. *The Dream Thought of Piers Plowman*. New Haven, Conn.: Yale University Press, 1972. Examines the concerns and tensions of the B version in relation to A and C.

Maguire, Stella. "The Significance of Haukyn, *Activa Vita*, in *Piers Plowman*." *Review of English Studies* 25 (1949): 97–109. Reprinted in Blanch.

Middleton, Anne. "Two Infinites: Grammatical Metaphor in *Piers Plowman*." *ELH* 39 (1972): 169–88.

———. "The Audience and Public of 'Piers Plowman.' " In *Middle English Alliterative Poetry and Its Literary Background: Seven Essays*, edited by David Lawton. Cambridge: Brewer, 1982.

Minnis, Alastair J. "Langland's Ymaginatif and Late-Medieval Theories of Imagination." *Comparative Criticism* 3 (1981): 71–103.

Overstreet, Samuel A. "Langland's Elusive Plowman." *Traditio* 45 (1989–1990): 257–341.

Pearsall, Derek. "Poverty and Poor People in *Piers Plowman*." In *Medieval English Studies Presented to George Kane*, edited by Edward D. Kennedy, Ronald Waldron, and Joseph S. Wittig. Woodbridge, Suffolk: Boydell and Brewer, 1988.

Rudd, Gillian. *Managing Language in "Piers Plowman."* Cambridge: Brewer, 1994. The interplay between knowledge and wisdom in passus 8–14 of the B version.

Scase, Wendy. *Piers Plowman and the New Anticlericalism*. Cambridge: Cambridge University Press, 1989. The poem deepens antimendicant criticism into more radical anticlericalism.

Schmidt, A. V. C. *The Clerkly Maker: Langland's Poetic Art*. Woodbridge, Suffolk: Boydell and Brewer, 1987.

Schweitzer, Edward C. " 'Half a Laumpe Lyne in Latyne' and Patience's Riddle in *Piers Plowman*." *Journal of English and Germanic Philology* 73 (1974): 313–27.

Simpson, James. "Spirituality and Economics in Passus 1–7 of the B Text." *YLS* 1 (1987): 83–103.

St-Jacques, Raymond. "The Liturgical Associations of Langland's Samaritan." *Traditio* 25 (1969): 217–230.

———. "Conscience's Final Pilgrimage in *Piers Plowman* and the Cyclical Structure of the Liturgy." *Revue de l'Université d'Ottawa* 40 (1970): 210–23.

Szittya, Penn R. *The Antifraternal Tradition in Medieval Literature*. Princeton, N.J.: Princeton University Press, 1986.

Tavormina, M. Teresa. "Gendre of a Generacion": *Piers Plowman* B.16.222." *English Language Notes* 27 (1989): 1–9

———. *Kindly Similitude: Marriage and Family in Piers Plowman*. Cambridge: Brewer, 1995.

Wenzel, Siegfried. *The Sin of Sloth: Acedia in Medieval Thought and Literature*. Chapel Hill: University of North Carolina Press, 1967.

———. "Medieval Sermons." In Alford, *Companion*.

Wittig, Joseph S. "Piers Plowman B, Passus IX–XII: Elements in the Design of the Inward Journey." *Traditio* 28 (1972): 211–80.

Yunck, John A. "Satire." In Alford, *Companion*.

Index

Abraham (patriarch), 19, 123, 127; as Faith, 128, 129–30

absolution, 25, 26; abuse by friars, 39; and restitution, 80

active life: vs. contemplative life, 175n. 43, 177n. 8; Haukyn as, 113–18

Adam and Eve: fall of, 23, 64, 94, 126, 135, 169n. 23; gift of grace to, 25; wills of, 177n. 10

Adams, Robert, 176n. 3, 181n. 26

adultery, Scripture on, 99

Aers, David, 70–73

affective faculties, 172n. 1

Alan of Lille, 52

Alford, John A., 161n. 9, 163n. 16, 166n. 20, 175n. 46, 176n. 7

allegory, 165n. 9; etymology of, 165n. 4; models of, 70. See also personification allegory

alliterative verse: Langland's use of, 3–4, 33, 156n. 11; vocabulary of, 4

Ambrose, Saint, 162n. 26

amendment, 26, 29–31, 106, 111, 115–16, 122, 123, 140

Ammonites, 163n. 9

Ancrene Wisse, 164n. 30

angels: function of, 59–60; in Prologue, 44

Anglicus, Bartholomaeus, 156–57n. 19, 157n. 22, 168n. 20

Anima (soul), 19, 122, 170n. 42, 176nn. 52, 53; in castle *caro,* 93, 94; on charity, 119–21, 123–24; in dream, 5, 118–21

Antichrist, 20, 141; following of, 150; friars as agents of, 147, 149, 152; Pride as, 143; siege of Unity Holy Church, 147–49, 153

antimendicant literature, 147, 148, 168n. 8, 181n. 31, 182n. 37

antipopes, 150; election of, 46

anti-Semitism, 178n. 30

apocalypse, imagery of, 147, 148

Apostles' creed, 167n. 3, 178n. 31, 179n. 3

Aristotle, 99, 107

Ascension, 125, 138, 167n. 3

associative logic, 48

Athanasian creed, 87, 167n. 3

Augustine, Saint, 162n. 26; on conscience, 165n. 10; on the Fall, 169n. 23; on forgiveness, 140; on the Holy Spirit, 177n. 16; on Lucifer, 60; on Old and New Law, 108; on the soul, 168n. 13; on Trinity, 61, 66, 169n. 25, 177n. 16; use of triads, 164n. 18, 169n. 25; on Wisdom, 32

Avarice, in siege of Unity Holy Church, 148, 150. See also covetousness

Avignon Captivity, 43, 161n. 17

baptism, 158n. 11, 159n. 20; and Christ's treasury of merit, 27; of desire, 107; and Original Sin, 28; sacramental, 172n. 8

barn, Piers's: attack on, 147; meaning of, 180n. 18. See also Unity Holy Church

Bartholomaeus Anglicus. See Anglicus, Bartholomaeus

beadsmen, 161n. 10

beggars, 75; false, 167n. 1; pardon for, 87; professional, 161n. 11; in Prologue, 37, 38

bellatores, 35; hierarchy of, 43; use of truth, 59. See also estates

benefices, 171n. 55

Bennett, J. A. W., 157n. 28, 162n. 24, 163n. 9, 175n. 41

bishops: justness of, 92; in Prologue, 40, 41; at Reason's sermon, 83

Bloomfield, Morton W., 157n. 22

Boethius, *Consolation of Philosophy,* 52, 170n. 45, 172n. 57

Book (Scripture), 135, 179nn. 33, 34

Bowers, John M., 179n. 4

Bromyard, John, 161n. 9

191

pilgrimages: abuse of, 38, 161n. 11; as
penance, 29, 85; in Reason's sermon, 84
pilgrims, in Prologue, 37, 38
poetry: *Piers Plowman* as, 33; and versified
information, 8, 156n. 18
poverty, 22; and patience, 170n. 38;
Patience on, 117; Trajan on, 102–3
Pricke of Conscience, The, 155n. 8, 156n. 18
pride, 36; as Antichrist, 143; attack on
church, 145, 147; as cause of the Fall,
169n. 28; confession of, 79, 80;
hatred of poverty, 117
priest, and Piers's pardon, 86–88, 90
procreation, after the Fall, 103, 172n. 58
producers, 37, 38, 48
prudence, 145, 158n. 6
Psalms, penitential, 83, 167n. 27
punishment, temporal, 28–29
puns, Langland's use of, 65, 165n. 33
Purgatory, 27–29, 136, 159n. 28

quadrivium, 169n. 31

rats, council of, 45–46, 47
reason, 17; confrontation with commons,
83–85; and Conscience, 83; creation's
consistency with, 103, 171n. 56; and
Lady Meed, 68, 69, 73; on natural
disasters, 181n. 28; relationship with
Truth, 73; in *Roman de la Rose,* 163n. 4

The Author

A professor of English Literature at the University of North Carolina at Chapel Hill, Joseph S. Wittig received his Ph.D. from Cornell University in 1969. He has held research fellowships from the American Council of Learned Societies, research leaves supported by the William Neal Reynolds and W. R. Kenan funds, and a grant from the American Philosophical Society. In addition to studies of *Piers Plowman,* his publications include "The Aeneas-Dido Allusion in Chrétien's *Eric et Enide,*" "Figural Narrative in Cynewulf's *Juliana,*" "King Alfred's Boethius and Its Latin Sources," *Medieval English Studies Presented to George Kane* (which he coedited), and contributions to *Sources of Anglo-Saxon Literary Culture.* He serves on the Medieval Studies Committee of the University of North Carolina at Chapel Hill and has been its chair. Formerly associate editor of *Studies in Philology,* he is currently on the editorial board of that journal and of *The Society for Early English and Norse Electronic Texts.* He is now preparing the three versions of *Piers Plowman* for addition to the Database of Late Middle English and is finishing a fully lemmatized concordance to these texts for print publication.

The Editor

George D. Economou has published numerous and translations of medieval English and European literature. He has recently published a verse translation of the sea version of William Langland's *Piers Plowman* (University of Pennsylvania, 1996). He is professor of English at the University of Oklahoma at Norman.